READING RIO DE JANEIRO

READING
RIO DE JANEIRO

Literature and Society

in the Nineteenth Century

ZEPHYR L. FRANK

STANFORD UNIVERSITY PRESS
STANFORD, CALIFORNIA

Stanford University Press
Stanford, California

This book has been published with the assistance of The John Wirth Fund.

Printed in the United States of America on acid-free, archival-quality paper

ISBN 9781503632929

First paperback printing, 2022

The Library of Congress has cataloged the hardcover edition as follows:

Frank, Zephyr L., 1970- author.

  Reading Rio de Janeiro : literature and society in the nineteenth century / Zephyr Frank.

    pages cm
  Includes bibliographical references and index.
  ISBN 978-0-8047-5744-7 (cloth : alk. paper) — ISBN 978-0-8047-9730-6 (ebook)
  1. Brazilian fiction—Brazil—Rio de Janeiro—19th century—History and criticism.
2. Literature and society—Brazil—Rio de Janeiro—History—19th century. 3. Rio de Janeiro (Brazil)—Social conditions—19th century. I. Title.
  PQ9601.F67 2015
  869.3'30998153—dc23
                    2015029815

Typeset by Bruce Lundquist in 10/14 Minion Pro

For Gabriela

TABLE OF CONTENTS

ACKNOWLEDGMENTS

This experiment was a long time coming. Over the past decade, I accumulated many intellectual debts in conceptualizing and writing this book. I am grateful to my colleagues at Stanford University who took time to read sections and listen to my ideas about the study of society through literature. David Como, J. P. Daughton, Sean Hanretta, Franco Moretti, Paula Moya, Richard Roberts, Paul Robinson, and Peter Stansky were especially generous with their time and insights. Many Stanford students contributed directly to the project. The list is long: Taylor Clark, Ryan Delaney, Michael Dinerstein, Fred Freitas, Hanah Gilula, Alexis Guadarrama, Maya Krishman, Lucas Manfield, Veriene Melo, David Sabetti, Kevin Scott, Robert Torres, Noemi Walzebuck, and Andre Zollinger all worked directly on the project in its various manifestations over the years as research assistants. Both Van Tran and Annalise Lockhart read an early version and helped improve the prose throughout the manuscript. Former students, now colleagues, Marcelo Bucheli, Aldo Musaccio, Ian Read, Heather Roller, Lise Sedrez, and Kari Zimmerman read sections, offered suggestions and leads, and otherwise encouraged me. The lab staff in the Spatial History Project contributed to the collection of spatial data and its visualization. I am grateful, in this regard, to Whitney Berry, Jake Coolidge, Mithu Datta, Kathy Harris, Toral Patel, and Erik Steiner. Ryan Heuser and Mark Algee-Hewitt of the Literary Lab helped with textual analysis and conceptualizing the study of Brazilian plays. Finally, I wish to thank Gabriel Wolfenstein and Mark Braude, colleagues and friends, for reading the entire manuscript and for turning me on to Carl Schorske.

The list beyond Stanford is also long. Colleagues around the country have given time and advice to this project. Thanks to Vince Brown, Amy Chazkel, Mariana Dantas, James Green, Lyman Johnson, Linda Lewin, Jeffrey Needell, Daniel O'Neil, and especially my teacher and mentor, Joseph Love. In Brazil, I have had the luck to count on the intellectual support of Afonso de Alencastro

Graça Filho, Claudio Batalha, Tarcísio Botelho, Sidney Chalhoub, Regina Coeli, Luís Ferla, Iris Kantor, Silvia Lara, Douglas Libby, Flávio Saliba Cunha, and Robert Slenes. Sandra Vasconcelos, while visiting Stanford, gave me an after-noon of incisive ideas regarding *Sonhos d'Ouro*. Finally, the whole project would have been impossible while raising two kids and teaching more or less nonstop the past decade without the dedicated research assistance of Tereza Cristina Alves in Rio de Janeiro. Tereza Cristina, I am forever grateful for your work, which went far beyond the mere collection of data. You are a historian.

Finally, as ever, I am grateful to my friends and family. Without Steve and Rosalyn Tran, there never would have been time in the day for all of this. With-out Tram-Anh, Paulo, and Gabriela, there would not have been motivation to keep going.

Thanks to all. I share with you whatever success this book finds. The errors and omissions are all on my account.

PREFACE

I have written a dozen versions of this preface over the years, as this project has grown and changed direction more than once. Started as a largely empirical study of inequality in nineteenth-century Rio de Janeiro, the research gradually shifted to the plane of culture and everyday practices. Dissatisfied with the blank face of data, I started to think of literature as a source of illustration that could liven up the dreary tables I generated. After several years of struggle, I reached an impasse. No longer satisfied with the tables, I was equally unhappy with the treatment of literary sources as illustrations. Naturally, I tried mixing the two together, with inconclusive results. During this period, I presented some of these ideas at conferences and seminars and found that my audience was as perplexed as I was. Literature did not help make sense of the tables and figures; data did not improve the interpretation of literary material. It was time to make a clean break.

So I started to read more literary history, particularly from the Marxist perspective, and less traditional history. I followed an idiosyncratic path into social theory. Franco Moretti led me to Georg Lukács and Georg Simmel; Erving Goffman to George Santayana and William James; and Roberto Schwarz to Antonio Candido and Augusto Meyer. Above all, I read and reread Brazilian literature. What did I learn?

From the Brazilian literary critics, I learned to emphasize an internal reading of the novels rather than try to match what I read in literature directly to what I read in traditional historical sources. My readings focused on the problems the author placed in front of his characters and the possible solutions hinted at or demonstrated through the unraveling of the plot. This new understanding of the social problems described in literature allowed me to make connections to the broader empirical base of historical material I had collected over the years regarding the social structures of Rio de Janeiro. The key was maintaining the relative autonomy of the two kinds of analysis. In effect, I discovered that to write this book, I would have to write drafts of two books, which is what I have done. The final step is placing the two manuscripts side by side and discovering the points of contact and reinforcement. This is how I have read Rio de Janeiro and then written about it.

What were the problems literature set out to delineate and perhaps solve? The answer is relatively simple, although the exploration required to come to it was intricate and ranged well beyond the borders of Brazil. A major focus of the canonical novels written in Brazil during the second half of the nineteenth century is the entry and incorporation of the individual in society. In a word: the bildungsroman—novels of education, finding a path to a career, and marriage. Weighty problems indeed: work and love, the crafting of an identity, and the reproduction of foundational social relationships. Many of the concerns in my parallel manuscript, the quantitative and empirical study of social structures, dealt with work and marriage, incomes and inheritances—points of contact.

Finally, the novels create a sense of the city itself as a protagonist in history. Men and women arrive from the provinces and attempt to read the social topography of the metropolis in many classic versions of the bildungsroman. They project their desires onto the city and discover new desires and new disappointments as they make their way into the urban world. Ideas about the city inform both strategy and tactics. Individuals struggle to comprehend the vastness of the city. They navigate through it. It changes and its spaces are contested and redefined.

There is nothing wrong with declarations of love in prefaces. I have loved Brazilian literature for a long time. Braudel confessed his love of the Mediterranean in a preface. I have no Braudelian aspirations in this book, but love makes a difference: It made me want to write this book, and it encouraged me to share my love of these authors with my readers.

One last note on historiography before we begin: My intention is neither to perform literary analysis per se nor to write the social history of literature. I want to do something else, something without an established name and methodology—something that combines close readings of literary texts, distant readings of corpora, sociological theories of the city and of human interaction, and economic and social history grounded in quantitative empirical evidence. The rhetoric of academic publishing can give the impression that scholarship comes from a neutral place, that it is the natural outgrowth of an engagement with a cumulative enterprise—hence the literature review at the beginning of nearly every history book, the space given over to historiography, the tendency to privilege recent works over "superseded" old ones, the belief in the cumulative that emphasizes the new. Well and good. Why not try something different?

Maps

The maps presented in *Reading Rio de Janeiro* were created using ESRI's ArcMap suite of software. They reflect the physical layout of the city circa 1866, based on Gotto's detailed map of that same year. The use of a digitized version of the Gotto map was made possible by generous colleagues in the Cecult Center, University of Campinas, São Paulo. Cartographic design, wherever it is present, is attributable to the able hands of Erik Steiner, of the Spatial History Project, Stanford University.

Images

There are two kinds of pictures presented to the reader in this book. The first kind is images drawn from contemporary newspapers. They reflect the style and attitudes of the era and illustrate some of the social relations and concepts discussed in the text. The other kind of picture includes two original drypoint intaglio etchings commissioned for the purpose of illustrating this book with particular scenes from the novels and plays that make up the bulk of its source material. These etchings were made by Steve Baird in 2012–2013 based on photos and textual descriptions of the style of clothes worn and the physical locations of the scenes during the era in question.

Money

In Brazil during the nineteenth century, the primary unit of currency was the mil-réis. One thousand mil-réis made up 1 conto, which was the highest unit and would be written as 1:000$ (1 conto and 0 mil-réis). During most of the period contemplated in this book (1840s–1880s), the mil-réis was worth about 50 cents. Thus a rich estate of 300 contos, like that of Quincas Borba, would have been worth approximately $150,000. This conversion rate for mil-réis to dollars comes from archival documents and from Holloway, *Policing Rio de Janeiro*.

Corpora

The primary texts for this study are the novels and plays written and set in nineteenth-century Rio de Janeiro. In all cases the base texts were derived from the definitive collected works of the authors. For the novels, I used the volumes published by Editora Aguilar. The plays of Alencar, Macedo, and França are found in the volumes published by Serviço Nacional de Teatro. Martins Pena's collected comedies are found in the three volumes published by Martins Fontes. PDF versions of all the texts were also obtained online for network and content analysis. Where possible, citations to the texts include both the page number in the definitive editions and the chapter or scene number in order to facilitate identification of passages in other editions.

∾

Unless otherwise noted, all translations, whether of fictional or scholarly works, are my own.

Santiago, 2014

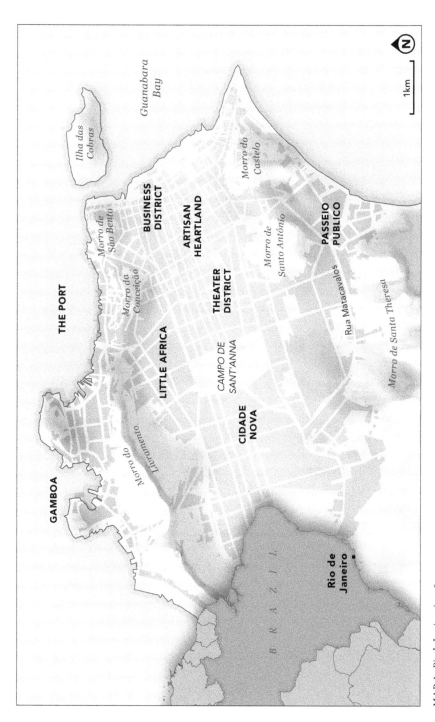

MAP 1. Rio de Janeiro, circa 1870.

SOURCE: Terrain of History Project, Stanford University; cartography by Erik Steiner.

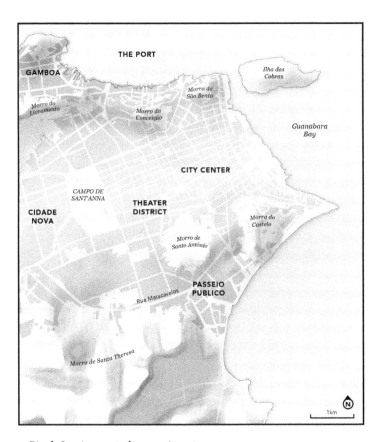

THE PORT

GAMBOA

Morro do Livramento

Morro da Conceição

Morro da São Bento

Ilha das Cobras

Guanabara Bay

CITY CENTER

CAMPO DE SANT'ANNA

THEATER DISTRICT

CIDADE NOVA

Morro do Castelo

Morro de Santo Antônio

PASSEIO PÚBLICO

Rua Matacavalos

Morro de Santa Theresa

1km N

MAP 2. Rio de Janeiro, central areas, circa 1870.

SOURCE: Terrain of History Project, Stanford University; cartography by Erik Steiner.

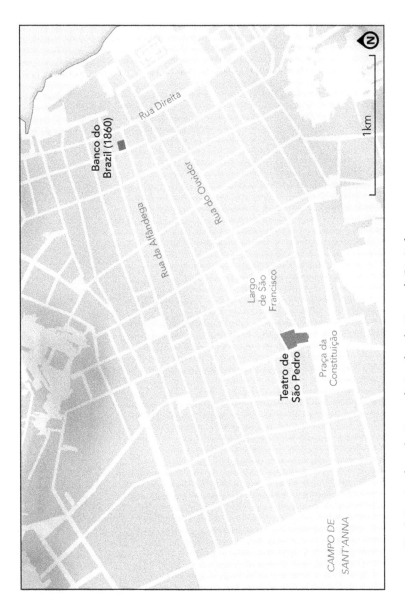

MAP 3. Rio de Janeiro, from the Banco do Brasil to the Teatro de São Pedro.

SOURCE: Terrain of History Project, Stanford University; cartography by Erik Steiner.

INTRODUCTION

The Brazilian Bildungsroman

THE BRAZILIAN BILDUNGSROMAN evoked the cultural experience of an emerging capitalist modernity in the country during the second half of the nineteenth century. This version of modernity was as incomplete and fragmented as the characters in these novels, and it drew its force from financial capital and bourgeois values while sharing space and power with older forms of commerce and older systems of social and cultural mores.[1] The master themes of the genre—youth, education, self-determination, and socialization—are at the center of cultural formation.[2] Transposed to the plane of social and cultural history, the bildungsroman provides vital evidence regarding two poles of historical experience that are notoriously difficult to connect: individual, everyday, ad hoc, tactical, idiosyncratic choices; and the structural, social forces that buffet and shape individual and collective trajectories. Choices and forces: micro and macro. Choices and forces seen, predominantly to be sure, from the point of view of members of or aspirants to the middle or upper reaches of society. In this kind of novel, as E. M. Forster observes wryly in *Howards End*, the very poor are "unthinkable" as protagonists.[3] A limited view and a partial history, then. Not fit for every taste.

Even so, the genre leaves the historian a lot to work with. As Franco Moretti points out, the nineteenth-century bildungsroman held the individual and the collective in a delicate balance.[4] For this brief period, the middle and upper classes could see themselves reflected in the bildungsroman as neither masters nor the mastered. Individuality and socialization were knitted together in a complex give-and-take; the dominance of institutions and the nation-state still loomed over the edge of the horizon, although the world was already saturated in capitalist relations of production and consumption. If the purpose of the bildungsroman is to reconcile the individual to the world, what were the terms of this reconciliation in Rio de Janeiro, Brazil's imperial capital? Asking this question opens up an ample field of research: What are the primary signposts associated with growth, maturity, and socialization? What trajectories do the men and women depicted in the novels follow? What aspects of the world, spatial and material, provide the opportunities and constraints facing these characters? In what ways does the dance between the individual and society go catastrophically wrong? These are fundamental questions, to which we can turn to literature for answers.

Literature and History

Everything in the relationship between literature and history hinges on the questions we ask. Literature speaks to history directly and eloquently when we ask questions regarding the relationship of the individual to society—questions of a biographical nature. What was it like to live as a certain kind of person in a particular time and place? More important, what was it like to live a life over time in a past place? Historians ask many other questions, which the literature of *Bildung* answers only by illustration and texture. These questions touch on the development and activity of the police, the ebb and flow of politics, the discourse and practice of public health, and thousands more topics hinted at in Forster's bald assertion that the poor are unthinkable as protagonists in forming independent social identities—the subject matter of *Howards End*. These kinds of historical processes are not questions posed directly by novels of *Bildung*, although they certainly appear as part of the general context of life, the backdrop for the choices and forces relating to the protagonist. In this way we perceive the distance between social and political history, as it is usually practiced, and imaginative literature, as it is normally read.

Yet literary history and the archive of imaginative prose are not restricted to the domain of culture. The question of the individual and society touches politics and the economy at every point in these novels. Indeed, it is the holistic depiction of human experience and the connection between individual agency and fate and historical structure and process that marks out the realistic novel as the preeminent source for answers to abiding historical questions. The key is to start with the right questions, to start with the problems and answers posed in novels read historically. Character, plot, and language come first; history follows. Accordingly, in this book I seek to reverse the terms of analysis normally associated with historical writing. Rather than begin with conventional historical problems, I begin with literary problems. The novels set the terms, and the historian interprets and accommodates them. History, then, is treated as a source for literature rather than the other way around.

With this shift in perspective, literature regains its autonomous force. It is not an imaginative mirror of the historical past to be fact-checked against a conventional archive. Instead, literature poses and attempts to answer problems of deep historical interest, but it does so for its own coherent purposes, not as ersatz history. Specifically, it does this in the nineteenth-century novel, as Bakhtin suggests, through "the assimilation of real historical time and the assimilation of historical man that takes place in time." Not all novels, to be sure, but particularly novels of emergence through experience—"man in the process of becoming."[5]

If we read the right novels, we follow the development or, more often than not in the late nineteenth century, the underdevelopment of the protagonist in a rich and complex dance with time, with history. Following the lead provided by literary historians, it is possible to read novels as answers to conundrums of historical structure and change, viewed through human-scale hermeneutics of plot and language. How to live and how to fit in? Imperatives posed as questions. Thus, as the literary historian Joshua Esty argues, the bildungsroman in societies undergoing change takes on a particular cast. It becomes the vehicle for exploring failed development, the impossibility of fitting in.[6] Or, to extend Roberto Schwarz's metaphor: misplaced lives in addition to misplaced ideas.[7] Misplaced but belonging, incoherently coherent in historical time—the oxymoron of capitalist modernity.

This experiment in literary-historical analysis begins by focusing on novels written by three of Brazil's canonical authors. Each writer poses a similar set of questions yet provides very different answers to the possibility of integration of the individual in a changing society, because this relationship was particularly unstable between the 1840s and 1880s, when these novels are primarily set. Brazil posed particular challenges to the integration of the protagonist through growth and experience. It underwent a profound capitalist transition and at the same time occupied a peripheral position in an emerging global economy. It was home to the only lasting monarchy in the Americas, yet it was also ruled by a constitution inflected with the currents of liberalism and the Enlightenment.

It was a nation filled with a recently coined aristocracy invented out of whole cloth (sometimes titles were simply purchased) and often involved in commerce (bourgeois aristocrats?) yet without the roots of heredity for sustenance. It was a slave society gradually losing all its slaves. The fractures in national historical time ramified inside and out, disrupting the possibility for narratives that reconcile individuals to a coherent chronotope of idealized progressive national time. Space and time were out of joint, and the protagonists could not fit in.

Following Bakhtin, one can conceive of the Brazilian bildungsroman of this period as grappling with a fractured national chronotope, where the protagonist "emerges along with the world and reflects the historical emergence of the world itself . . . no longer within an epoch, but on the border between two epochs, at the transition point from one to another. . . . This transition is accomplished in him and through him."[8] Such a transition, if it is distorted or blocked, reflects the nature of that historical discontinuity between epochs. It describes an incomplete process of transition in a peripheral capitalist society.

Growth and transformation are always problematic, even in a classic bildungsroman, such as Goethe's *Wilhelm Meister*. In Brazil, during the latter part of the nineteenth century, our authors suggest that for many individuals, cutting across gender and class lines, these problems of growth and integration were nearly insurmountable. Thus, the novels in question are filled with failed promises, delayed reckonings, unconsummated relationships, and incomplete socialization, all of which calls to mind Esty's category of unseasonable youth, found in novels of failed *Bildung*. For Esty, the coherent container of national time is disrupted by capitalist transformations that take place on a global scale. Individuals cannot be reconciled to a national time that has burst its bounds, whether internally, as he deduces in his reading of George Eliot's *Mill on the Floss*, or externally, as at the fringes of empire in Joseph Conrad's *Lord Jim*.[9]

The approach I take in this volume is comparative and holistic. Rather than isolate a particular author or book, I focus on a genre and an overarching problem: the growth of the individual and his or her integration into society. A particular kind of society existed in Rio de Janeiro in the latter half of the nineteenth century—one in which both capitalism and bourgeois norms were ascendant—but it was also a slave society shot through with the residue of colonialism, the ancien régime. In this, I adopt a position suggested by the Brazilian critic Roberto Schwarz and consider the degree to which the Brazilian bildungsroman addresses or is otherwise marked by these contradictions.[10] Following Antonio Candido, the Brazilian master of literary sociology or the sociology of literature,

I ask not only how these novels correspond to an underlying social reality (an important question, no doubt) but also how the social is manifest as an internal dimension of the novel.[11] The social reality, however necessary and useful for historical purposes, is largely limited by its empiricism to registering correspondence and furnishing illustration and color to history. The internal social dimension is inherently interpretive. It engages with questions of power, structure, and agency, as expressed in the logic of character and plot, and it allows for the field of analysis to embrace the individual and the social in an integrated fashion. In this sense, rather than hold a mirror up to an external world, I argue that by internalizing critical elements of the social field, the novel brings society inside.

My subjects are the novels of José de Alencar, Joaquim Maria Machado de Assis, and Aluísio Azevedo—the three A's. Without question, Machado is the "great" novelist in the trio. Stylistically inventive, ironic, and sarcastic, Machado's books can still surprise in the twenty-first century. Because of this fertility, there is an ever-lengthening shelf of books and articles that focus on him: Machado the sociologist,[12] Machado the economist,[13] Machado the historian.[14] The Stanford library lists 335 books with Machado de Assis in the subject field. If, in this study, I can manage to say anything new about Machado de Assis, this alone will have made the effort (of writing; I leave the rest of the judgment to the reader) worthwhile.

Of the other two writers, Alencar is best known for his historical novels, such as *O Guarani* and *As Minas de Prata* (in which he attempts in the vein of Walter Scott to write the origins of the Brazilian nation), and for his mythmaking *indigenista* novels, such as *Iracema*.[15] He is also generally credited, along with his contemporary Joaquim Manuel de Macedo, with introducing the genre of the novel in Brazil. Less well-known, though by no means obscure, are his urban novels, which genuflect to Balzac, not Scott, and offer a rich depiction of life in Rio de Janeiro in the 1850s–1870s.

Last among this trio, Azevedo's fiction is marked by a strong commitment to Naturalism. If Balzac was Alencar's model, Zola is the master in Azevedo's universe. Azevedo is known best for his novel *O Cortiço*, sometimes translated as "the slum," though this is hardly an adequate word to capture the gist of Azevedo's subject. *O Cortiço* is a staple on reading lists in Brazil, but it is an earlier work, *O Coruja*, to which I turn to find Azevedo's version of the bildungsroman.

At the risk of oversimplification in the service of intelligibility, our Brazilian novelists' temperaments follow a sequence, which is, after all, historical: Balzac, Flaubert, Zola.[16] Alencar sought to capture his society in all its variety.

He wrote urban novels and rural novels: an attempt at an abbreviated Brazilian *Comédie humaine*, though Alencar clearly lacked what Henry James referred to as Balzac's "appetite of an ogre for all kinds of facts."[17] It is not so much a lack of detailed descriptions of dress and interiors, particularly in the urban novels. What is missing is the obstinate desire to see through things and describe how they work in great detail. In Alencar's novels, the world of work, of manufacture, of retail, of construction, is largely absent. Given Alencar's manifest project of narrating the reconciliation of traditional (provincial) virtue and capitalist (metropolitan) modernity, this absence is telling. A critical term is missing from the equation, and this forces Alencar to place greater emphasis on the role of individual character and to underplay the actual workings of the world that the individual must conquer to be redeemed.[18] The contrast with Azevedo's Naturalism is stark in this respect, and it is the struggle for meaningful work and the social mobility that it entails that distinguish *O Cortiço* and *O Coruja* from the field.

Machado was more tightly wound and much more stylistically creative than the other two authors contemplated here. His mature novels are cynical and elliptical eviscerations of human frailty and social stupidity. They possess a bit of the spirit of Flaubert's *Bouvard et Pécuchet* and the *Dictionary of Received Ideas*. Lukács, in characterizing Flaubert's *L'Education Sentimentale*, might as well be describing the title character and structure of Machado's *Memórias Póstumas de Brás Cubas*.

> No attempt is made here to counteract the disintegration of outside reality into heterogeneous, brittle and fragmentary parts by some process of unification or to replace absent connections or valences of meaning by lyrical mood imagery: the separate fragments of reality lie before us in all their hardness, brokenness and isolation. The central figure is not made significant by means of limiting the number of characters, by the rigorous convergence of the composition on the centre, or by any emphasis upon the central character's outstanding personality: the hero's inner life is as fragmentary as the outside world, his interiority possesses no lyrical power of scorn or pathos that might set it against the pettiness of reality.[19]

Yet Machado goes further. By shuffling the sequence of time and adopting a first-person narrative style, he further underscores the brittle, fragmentary consciousness of Brás in the face of the "unique and unrepeatable stream of life." Just as in Frédéric Moreau's Paris of the 1840s, the Rio de Janeiro of a similar period narrated in *Memórias Póstumas* is crosscut with economic, social, and political currents, which fragment the world and disrupt any possibility of easy integration into homogeneous national time. The fractured narration of the defunct protagonist serves to emphasize the way the pieces of the puzzle can fit, but only badly.

The difference between the novelistic worlds of Alencar and Machado mirrors, in profound ways, the difference between Balzac and Flaubert. In Alencar, as Vargas Llosa has noted in his reading of Balzac, "The imagination of humanity is still capable of making its dreams come true and of renewing life." In contrast, for both Machado and Flaubert, "Imagination is a crime that reality punishes by breaking those who try to live their dreams." In this regard, Vargas Llosa suggests "Balzac finds life logical while Flaubert finds it absurd."[20] As we will see in Chapters 1 and 2, both positions have merit in the context of nineteenth-century Rio de Janeiro.

Finally, in yet a third register, Azevedo's fiction evinces the values and limitations of Naturalism. Characters come to represent types, the individual fades into the background, and the social dominates. In this, Azevedo follows the path set out by Zola: "We must work with the characters, the emotions, the human and social facts, as the chemist and the physicist work with matter, as the physiologist works with living bodies. Determinism dominates everything."[21]

Azevedo's debt to Zola was such that he was at times accused of plagiarizing the master's plots. Some critics find in *O Cortiço* a virtual copy of the basic elements of *L'Assommoir*.[22] I leave the literary detective work to the experts. In any case, my quarry is different. It would not be too much of an exaggeration to say that I really do not care a whit whether most of these novels are copies. In fact, I would be disappointed if they were not. What Azevedo's fiction allows us to perceive is a third argument posed by literature with respect to the problematic individual and his or her integration into society. If in Alencar, choices are tragic, and in Machado, capricious or absurd, then in Azevedo, they are largely determined.

This volume is divided into two parts. First, I analyze three novels in detail: Alencar's *Sonhos d'Ouro*, Machado's *Memórias Póstumas de Brás Cubas*, and Azevedo's *O Coruja*. These novels were published first in newspapers, in 1872, 1880–1881, and 1885–1887, respectively, and then in book form. Of the three, *Sonhos d'Ouro* and *O Coruja* are unquestionably novels in the tradition of the bildungsroman.[23] *Memórias Póstumas* is notoriously hard to pin down, but it shares enough elements of the genre—namely, the story of a central character's youth, education, and insertion into society—to warrant inclusion for my purposes. In this compressed period of the 1870s and 1880s the bildungsroman registers a profound engagement with the structure of Brazilian society. If, as Doris Sommer argues, the middle years of the nineteenth century were the time of national novels—those romances of consolidation and sexual-political reconciliation— then the last three decades of the century were the time of *Bildung*, narrating the integration of the individual into this problematic new national society.[24]

Of the three novels selected, only *Memórias Póstumas* is truly well-known and widely read; it is considered the single most important work of fiction in the Brazilian canon.[25] Each novel is given an extensive gloss in conjunction with the analysis, providing, it is hoped, sufficient material for readers to orient themselves to the plots, characters, and basic structural properties of each book. Although two of the three books are little known and more seldom read, it is my hope that by describing them in detail and by analyzing their distinctive answers to the problem of social integration, readers will be inspired to pick them up and learn from them as I have. I have chosen to analyze three novels by three canonical authors precisely to allow for triangulation among different points of view and distinct aesthetic commitments.

In the second and concluding part of the volume, Chapters 4 through 6, I broaden the scope to include the whole novelistic oeuvre of each author, with additional references to other novelists, Brazilian and otherwise, and I attempt to show the full range of possible trajectories, material conditions, and successful (or unsuccessful) processes of reconciliation between individuals and their changing society. In this respect, I seek to show how reading certain Brazilian novels alongside major European works can throw light on the aesthetic choices and antecedents discernible in the Brazilian works.

But there is more to the comparison than this. Through these parallel readings, we also see depictions, mutatis mutandis, of universal struggles to imagine the integration of youth into society under the changing and unsettling conditions of nineteenth-century capitalism. In this sense the Brazilian novels are far more than mere copies of European novels transposed uncomfortably to the tropics; rather, they are aesthetic and historical contributions to world literature worth reading alongside such books as Balzac's *Lost Illusions* or Eliot's *Middlemarch*. The corollary: In order to read Brazilian novels in their full artistic *and historical* context, we need to read *L'Education Sentimentale*, *Tristram Shandy*, and their ilk. There is a further advantage to be gained in this procedure: familiarity. Even if one has not read *Sonhos d'Ouro*, one has probably read Balzac and, taken together, the analysis of the one and the familiarity with the other will, it is hoped, make the arguments in this book both meaningful and accessible.

Historical Framework

The cardinal points in the social structure framing the tension to be resolved in the selected novels are slavery, capitalism, immigration and internal migration, and Europeanization. Each point is unstable, and its valence depends on internal factors in transformation and on simultaneous relationships with the other points. Slavery, in the era during which the novels analyzed here were published, was a dying institution. It cast a long shadow, but it would be a mistake to place it alone at the center of analysis. Capitalism is a moving target. In the period after 1850, particularly in Rio de Janeiro, it took an increasingly financial and speculative shape. The curves of slaveholding and financial capitalism cross in this era, with the rapid growth of capitalism and the decline of slaveholding. The population of Rio de Janeiro roughly doubled between 1821 and 1849 and then doubled again by 1890. Slaves, Portuguese immigrant *caixeiros* (retail countermen), and provincial parvenus poured into the Corte, as Rio de Janeiro city and immediate environs were known during the period of the empire (1822–1889), mixing with the native population and providing an impetus, a sense of dynamism, and heightening levels of competition and social complexity. In the realm of ideas and cultural norms, European imports, especially from France but also from England, Italy, and Germany, influenced patterns of consumption and contributed to the formation of elite consciousness, which diffused or found emulation in the middling and even poorer classes living in the capital over time.

Slavery

Slavery and capitalism went hand in hand in the nineteenth-century Atlantic world. This close association should be understood as being both vestigial and symbiotic. It is vestigial because the origins of slavery in the Americas can be traced back to the earliest years of European settlement, when the world economy was quite different from that of the 1800s. In this regard, a deep social and cultural crust had formed over Brazil, creating what Ira Berlin has called a slave society in contrast to a society with slaves.[26] The institution permeated all facets of life. Slaves were ubiquitous in both rural and urban settings. The association between slavery and capitalism is symbiotic in the sense that the rise of industrial and financial capitalism in Brazil was associated with fortunes made in part through the illegal slave trade and was in a significant sense underwritten by the labor of slaves, native and imported, particularly in the booming coffee plantations located in the economic core region of Rio de Janeiro, São Paulo, and Minas Gerais. To reiterate, slaves provided both capital (indirectly) and labor to fuel the growth of the Brazilian economy in the first two-thirds of the nineteenth century. Slaves and slavery were central to the whole social structure.

Yet this centrality was already eroding by the 1850s. This is why one can characterize slavery as a dying institution—indeed, an institution in certain areas and among certain segments of Brazilian society that was undergoing a shift from the realm of the slave society to the society with slaves, from a central place to the periphery of social life. Slavery was also dying because its social legitimacy declined at roughly the same time as the illegal importation of new slaves from Africa was definitively suppressed around 1850.[27] The death of slavery was notoriously slow in Brazil. Half-measures and gradualist abolition schemes were the order of the day right down to 1888 and the so-called Golden Law of emancipation.[28] This slow death meant that for a prolonged period, from the 1830s through the 1880s, the topic of slavery was discussed as a problem and, in literary circles, the institution came in for sustained, if never intense, criticism. The fact of the matter is that after the suppression of the Atlantic trade, one of the chief objects of criticism was ameliorated. Literary texts abound with harsh characterizations of the infamous *negreiros* (slave traders), and characters with fortunes rooted in the not too distant illegal slave-trading past continued to be portrayed as villains even after they were no longer active in the trade.[29] After the Atlantic trade ended, other significant measures followed, including most importantly the so-called Law of the Free Womb in 1871. This law guaranteed that all children born to slave mothers would henceforth be considered free, consigning slavery to a gradual end by means of attrition.[30]

Despite the importance of these laws and the political debates swirling around different emancipation schemes, slavery and slaves appear as themes or characters only rarely in the fiction and drama of the 1860s through 1880s. Why the strange absence? Two major reasons. First, as slavery lost social legitimacy, it ceased to figure in the imagined social lives of fictional characters. To give a prosaic example, in a sample of novels by the three authors under consideration, the word *piano* occurs twice as often as words for *slave* in all its permutations. Nonetheless, when slaves or slaveholding appear in the imaginative

literature of the era, we have good reason to sit up and pay close attention—
rarity should not be confused with insignificance. Second, slavery really was
in terminal decline by the 1870s. The proportion of slaves in the city of Rio de
Janeiro declined from 46% in 1821 to 38% in 1849 and then more precipitously
to 16% in 1872.[31] By the time the books analyzed in this study were written, slavery was well on its way out.[32] In making these observations, it is not my wish
to excuse the neglect of the theme in so much literature of the era, though it is
easy with moral hindsight to cast stones. Surely human beings and their suf-
fering are more important than pianos! Rather, my intention is to explain why
for many writers and even more for their readers, the subject of slaves could
be left on the margin. It is always there, but other institutions and social forces
hold center stage because the central problematic of the novel is the integration
of the free, white, usually male individual into what has become, in the most
advanced segments of Rio de Janeiro, a society with slaves on the wane.

Capitalism

The economic order we call capitalism is the pivot on which the whole of my
analysis turns. This is not the place to enter into the long and never resolved
debate concerning the origins and foundational characteristics of capitalism.
That would be another book. Having said this, some working concepts are in
order, both in general terms of definition and in specific reference to the Brazilian case.

Let me begin with what capitalism is not. It is not an ahistorical "economic
system" untethered to historical specificity. The ahistorical version of capitalism tends to focus on markets and trade rather than on relations of production
or institutions.[33] Where there are markets, there is capitalism. This is, I hold,
quite mistaken. In taking this position, I follow Robert Brenner, who famously
argued against what he called neo-Smithian Marxism—a vision of capitalism
in which exchange and markets dominate.[34] Capitalism, then, has two faces,
and they cannot be separated. There are markets and there are relations of production (pace Douglass North, governed by formal and informal institutions),
which, according to Marx, must necessarily involve the accumulation and cir-
culation of capital in a context where labor is free but cut off from the owner-
ship of the means of production. Where these two aspects intersect in specific
ways, we have capitalism. This does not imply that all relations of production
in an economy are necessarily based on free labor. Nor does it imply that all
the modern institutions of capital—banking, finance, stock market—are fully

formed and predominant. Rather, because capitalism is historical, it emerges and evolves discontinuously against a backdrop of other social formations. Because this emergence is utterly transformative of social relations, politics, and culture, it is violent (in the broadest sense) and disruptive. In its birth and adolescence, it makes social integration especially problematic. If the old ways no longer will do, the new ways are contested and socially disorienting.

Capitalism in *urban* Brazil, and this distinction is critical, grew in strength and sophistication and took up an increasingly important place in the imaginative literature of the era. In particular, the speculative financial capitalism of the second half of the nineteenth century posed special problems for narrating individual lives in historical time. Banking, joint-stock companies, and the stock market became favorite targets for literary depiction and critique just as they grew to dominate the economic scene in Brazil's capital city.[35] With these institutions came new forms of social mobility, new questions about the provenance of wealth, and new elites with complex ideologies shot through with the warp of capitalism and bourgeois values and the weft of the paternalism of the ancien régime. Emilia Viotti da Costa captures this process well, suggesting ways in which the old and the new coexisted throughout the first half of the nineteenth century, building up tensions that were released with the qualitative and quantitative transformations of capitalism after 1850. She identifies the emergence of a bureaucratic and professional group, which, rather than forming a new class, was "integrated into the clientele of the agrarian elite, to whom they were often tied by links of family and patronage, and whose world view they shared."[36] This accommodation was increasingly strained by the rise of financial capitalism and the growing incorporation of Brazil into the world economy. In 1850 the slave trade was definitively suppressed. In 1854 a new land law expanded markets and codified property rights in keeping with capitalist norms. Viotti da Costa goes on to suggest that after midcentury, the growth of the economy "created opportunities for the emergence of new groups that made a critique of the social and political order, in the name of liberal ideals and bourgeois notions."[37] These critiques were not limited to the economic and political spheres. They were at the heart of Brazilian literature in the 1870s and 1880s.

Sometimes, a graph is worth a thousand words. Evidence I collected from a large sampling of estate inventories from the city of Rio de Janeiro tells the tale of emergent financial capitalism against the backdrop of slavery's waning as the lynchpin of economic relations (see Figure 1).[38] The curves cross and a new, unsettled world appears.[39]

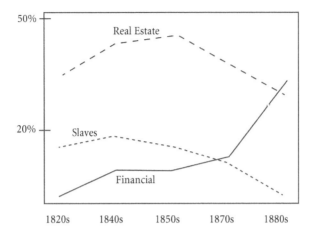

FIGURE 1. Shifting composition of wealth: Estate inventories in Rio de Janeiro, 1810–1880s. Lines show percentage of net inventoried wealth by category over time.

SOURCE: "Inventários," Arquivo Nacional, Rio de Janeiro.

What is particularly noteworthy in Figure 1 is the *velocity* of economic change. Financial wealth measured in credit, stocks, bonds, and cash explodes, whereas wealth measured in slaves dives toward zero. Processes that took shape in gradual movements during the 1840s and 1850s accelerated.

Perhaps even more socially disruptive was the rise and changing composition of inequality. The forms of wealth changed, but so too did the distribution. By using a subset of 705 estate inventories with the most complete and detailed information available concerning the internal distribution of assets within each estate, it is possible to trace out the evolution of wealth inequality in the city over time. Table 1 decomposes inequality into its constituent parts. The radical change in the last decades of the nineteenth century, already demonstrated in Figure 1, now takes on even greater social significance. Inequality was rising along with capitalist competition and financial wealth—taken together, this is what is meant by the concept of an emerging capitalist modernity.

Last, along these lines, evidence from the records of business partnerships registered with the Junta Comercial in 1870 and 1888 shows how entrepreneurs in the world of trade and finance came to occupy the top rungs of the economic elite. Businessmen, especially traders in commodities such as coffee, formed the most highly capitalized partnerships. In 1870, 40 out of 344 firms were clearly designated as belonging to this category of economic activity. The average paid-in capital of these partnerships was 94 contos, whereas the average for

TABLE 1. Decomposition of Inequality (Nonhuman Wealth)

	Contribution to Inequality (%)		
	Before 1850	1850s	After 1880
Form of wealth			
Urban houses	36.5	31.0	24.4
Furnishings	0.4	1.0	0.4
Credit	13.1	7.3	13.0
Cash and bank deposits	9.5	11.0	9.4
Stocks and bonds	4.7	6.1	22.1
Business	1.2	9.3	10.0
General statistics			
Gini coefficient	0.71	0.69	0.79
Number of observations	185	233	287

SOURCE: Inventários, Arquivo Nacional, Rio de Janeiro.

all other firms was 42 contos. By 1888 the gap had widened, with the broker and commission firms capitalized at 126 contos (47 firms) and the rest (261 firms) capitalized at just 38 contos on average.[40] Taken together, the evidence shows a generalized shift toward financial capital, an increase in inequality driven in large part by this shift, and the growing economic power of businessmen and investors engaged in partnerships that rely on and contribute to these changes.

I hesitate to pile on more statistics, because the point of this study is to interpret history through literature rather than write an economic history of the last third of the nineteenth century. Still, it may be worth including a few lines about incomes as opposed to wealth holding. Inequality in income tends to be significantly less pronounced than inequality in wealth. The lower the levels of inequality in both dimensions, the greater the degree of social mobility. Because income data are extremely hard to come by in sufficient quantity and coherence to allow for measurements of inequality, we are forced to use the best available resource: voter qualification rolls. These lists are obviously problematic on several accounts. First, they pertain only to Brazilian citizens qualified to vote, and there was an income requirement, albeit a low bar, to getting listed in the first place. Second, the values given in the rolls are self-reported in round figures. They are nothing like a true value one might find in a tax return today.

With these caveats in mind, the analysis of voter rolls provides two useful pieces of information. First, among voters, the self-reported income figures yield a Gini coefficient of 0.48, which we can interpret as moderate to high income inequality.[41] The second useful clue is found in the spread between incomes by occupation. The highest income group, capitalists and property owners, reported earning just over 8 contos (presumably from capital), whereas artisans reported incomes of just over 1 conto (mainly from labor). Taken together, the wealth and income inequality measures and the spread between the two suggest a society in which a modicum of social mobility coexisted with rising levels of wealth inequality, driven by the constant forces of inheritance and the variable winds of marriage and financial speculation.

A new social order first emerges and then becomes hegemonic over the course of two generations. The Brazilian bildungsroman confronts this transformation and offers diagnosis and orientation, in different measure, with respect to the place of individuals in a rapidly changing urban social world: a new world with new people in it and new problems to resolve. The character of the capitalist strides confidently toward center stage, embodied in historical figures such as the Baron of Mauá or, more negatively, in bankrupts such as A. J. A. Souto.[42] Money, particularly financial wealth, and material possessions increasingly rival the older marks of distinction in ancestry and education. Money, abundant but unstable, feeds back into these older forms of status and transforms their meaning, shoring up the winners and undermining the losers.

Perhaps the best illustration of this process is found in the sale of nonhereditary titles of nobility, often to successful capitalists, during the latter decades of Pedro II's reign. Titles had been granted, even sold, before the 1850s, but usually in small numbers. After the emergence and consolidation of the financial elite, the pace of title creation and sale quickened; social distinction, like everything else, was for sale to men on the make, something of which our novelists were keenly aware.[43] Of course, every age probably thinks that money plays an outsized and distorting role in status and social structure. The point here is that, particularly the 1850s–1880s, some of the fundamental characteristics of the economy had shifted, and with this shift came new structures of feeling and new artistic attempts at understanding the consequences of these changes.

Immigration and Internal Migration

Immigrants from Portugal and elsewhere in Western Europe provided much of the motive force behind the rise of industrial and financial capitalism in Rio de Janeiro. They were to be found in every position in the economic hierarchy, from banker down to retail clerk. More than half of all partners in

TABLE 2. Rio de Janeiro, 1872: Population, Immigration, and Internal Migration[a]

Population Group	Area of Birth							
	Rio de Janeiro	São Paulo	Minas Gerais	Ceará	Maranhão	Bahia	Rio Grande do Sul	Sample Total Less Rio[b]
White male								
Single	30,184	669	782	226	237	546	559	3,019
Married	5,646	150	244	68	76	258	210	1,006
White female								
Single	27,251	265	258	69	60	250	225	1,127
Married	8,968	171	179	23	40	135	190	738
Slaves								
Pardo								
Single	4,493	65	91	64	51	150	60	481
Married	31	3	8	0	0	3	0	14
Preto								
Single	10,858	122	246	85	185	496	86	1,220
Married	81	2	4	0	0	4	0	10
Parda								
Single	4,818	96	120	87	71	176	70	620
Married	27	4	1	0	1	2	1	9
Preta								
Single	11,957	174	247	61	184	601	114	1,381
Married	112	7	11	2	2	3	0	25

a. The table contains only a selection of the categories listed in the census schedule. The point is to highlight the two poles of society and relative access to marriage.
b. Sampled internal migrants.
SOURCE: "População em relação á nacionalidade brasileira," Recenseamento (1872), 11.

registered partnerships in the city of Rio were Portuguese by birth.[44] According to the census of 1872, 30.6% of the population of Brazil's capital city was of foreign birth, with men making up nearly three-fourths of the immigrant total.[45] Despite the growing importance of the immigrant population over the course of the nineteenth century, the presence of the foreign-born is distinctly muted in the novels under consideration in this study. This absence stands in sharp contrast to the frequent appearance of foreigners in dramatic works throughout the century—a subject about which I write at length in a planned companion volume on nineteenth-century plays. Once again, as with that other underrepresented population, slaves, the underlying characteristics of the bildungsroman make immigrants from Europe peripheral to stories of education and social integration into the world of the bourgeois, the capitalist, and metropolitan society. A Portuguese immigrant could play a central part in a Naturalist exposé of tenement life, as in the case of Jerônimo in Azevedo's *O Cortiço*; in the *Bildung* of Teobaldo and André, the protagonists of *O Coruja*, no such character is called for.

More important for the story I am going to tell are the many migrants to the city of Rio de Janeiro from Brazil's far-flung provinces. To give the reader a sense of the scale of internal migration and its basic demographic profile, in Table 2 I present information from Brazil's first modern census. Note that this is a sampling of provinces and categories and not a complete rendering of the census data. As the data suggest, most of the population in the city was native to the province of Rio (and, we can infer, in most cases, the city itself). What is particularly important for the purpose of the present study is the significant presence of "white" men from the provinces in the Corte, because these figures make up an important social category in Brazilian literature of the time—indeed, two of the three authors on whom this study focuses belong to this group. These are the strivers, the parvenus, and the country bumpkins who will play important parts in the novels discussed in this volume.

The figures in Table 2 also suggest two other salient facts. First, far more unmarried provincial men were wandering about Rio de Janeiro than unmarried provincial women. When we add to this the fact that there were far more foreign men of European origin in the Corte at the same time than there were foreign women of the same extraction, we are immediately made aware of one of the determining factors in the competitive marriage market. Finally, in contrast, the experience of slaves could not be more different. Marriage was virtually unknown among this group, even though the demographic balance between women and men was much more favorable. These facts are not new. Still, it is well to be reminded in cold numbers of the reality that marriage had a color and a class in nineteenth-century Rio de Janeiro. Again, for the purpose of the present volume, the key thing to remember is the surplus of single provincial men fighting over scarce brides, their dowries, and jobs and social positions in the growing city.

The Novel and European Cultural Influences

Brazil is the child of European settler colonialism—conquest, expropriation, native removal—yoked to the labor of millions of enslaved Africans. There is no question then of the authenticity of European cultural artifacts and practices in Brazil. They are authentic but at times strangely out of place. This is Schwarz's great insight: Certain ideas, in specific conjunctures, expressed in literary form, do not fit easily with Brazil's fractured history and hybrid society. Nineteenth-century novels in the realist tradition, with their European (bourgeois) concerns, are thus akin, in Brazil, to the wearing of black wool suits from Paris in the summer heat of Rio de Janeiro. This must not be seen to say that European ideas are always out of place owing to geography or the unique essence of nationhood in Brazil. Indeed, in the West during the nineteenth century, with few exceptions, *there are no ideas other than European ideas*, just as there are no suits other than black wool ones.

It must be remembered that the importation of European ideas and attendant material culture was a discontinuous and heterogeneous process. Old regime concepts and practices persisted. These too came from Europe and were sometimes "modernizing," as in the case of Pombaline administrative reform and urban style. Older European forms steeped in Brazilian realities overlapped with the liberal, modernizing spirit of nineteenth-century Europe, which itself was riven by conflicts between the forces of liberalism and conservatism, the old and the new. Thus, the Europeanization of Brazil during the 1800s must be seen both as something taking place in a specific, unique cultural and social environment (e.g., the city of Rio de Janeiro) and as a global process in which the novel, in its quintessential European form, is constituted by and inserted into these struggles over the meaning of the nation and the interpretation of individual destinies that are woven into a changing social fabric shot through with past, present, and visions of the future. In this, the novel is hardly alone. The realms of architecture and urban design, fine art, politics, law, finance, and everyday consumer society all participated in the same broad process.[46] Classical architecture on a monumental scale patterned on European models, commercial codes governing the issue of stocks and bonds, and ladies' fashion in hats and gloves seen at the theater where traveling opera companies presented the latest European compositions—all provided signs for novels to use and interpret, just as they read the signs of the slaves working in the streets selling sweets or of the muleteer from Minas Gerais with his cargo of bacon and cheese.

Together the factors described in the previous sections—slavery, capitalism, immigration, and European culture—framed the conditions under which individuals could be imagined as educated and integrated into society. With these points in mind, let us delve into the novels themselves.

SONHOS D'OURO

JOSÉ DE ALENCAR rededicated himself to his writing after seeing his political star eclipsed—losing a ministerial post and being passed over by the emperor Dom Pedro II for senator despite receiving the most votes in his native Ceará— although he also stayed involved in politics as a member of the lower Chamber of Deputies.[1] In 1871 the so-called Law of the Free Womb was passed on September 28. Although the law meant that henceforth no child would be born a slave in Brazil, ensuring the *eventual* extinction of the institution, the mothers remained slaves and their children remained wards of their mother's owners for up to twenty-one more years.[2] This gradual emancipation scheme nonetheless drew Alencar's ire. Although no friend of slavery, Alencar was a classic conservative concerned with the protection of private property rights and the maintenance of social order.[3] He did not hold the citizenship capacity of slaves in high esteem and believed that slaves were genuinely better off with their paternalistic masters than cut loose and left to their own devices.[4] Alencar's novel *Sonhos d'Ouro* does not address the issue of slavery or property rights head on, but it can be read as an attempt to offer a solution to the problem of modernity in a prospectively post-slavery urban metropolis. The rub: Reining in the excess of the new capitalist wealth required joining the new rich to the traditional values (if not the slaveholding) of the interior.

It is against this backdrop, while Alencar was living in the hills of Tijuca, which became one of the central settings of the novel, that *Sonhos d'Ouro* was written. Perhaps Alencar chose Tijuca, on the mountainous rural fringe of Rio de Janeiro, as his refuge after his stinging political defeats because it reminded him of happier days; he had met and courted his wife, Georgiana Cochrane, the daughter of a wealthy Englishman, in that same rural neighborhood.[5] Certainly, life and fiction entwined.

Published in 1872, on the heels of a series of devastating personal and professional setbacks, *Sonhos d'Ouro* deserves to be considered among the finest novels of Alencar's career. The book recounts the story of Ricardo Nunes, a young lawyer from São Paulo, and Guida Soares, the daughter of a wealthy Rio de Janeiro businessman. Ricardo represents the virtuous but poor man marked by talent but lacking connections; Guida is the capricious and spoiled rich girl with a good heart. Bringing these two characters together, Alencar writes as an alchemist: Virtue and wealth together transmute into a golden dream.

From the start, the theme of virtue in relation to wealth is sounded out. Ricardo's first internal monologue begins:

> Gold . . . gold . . . You reign over the world, absolute monarch, autocratic ruler of all the world's riches! You, yes, you reign and govern, without law, without opinion, without Parliament. . . . Law? What law have you save for the caprice with which you toy with men?

> Ouro! . . . ouro! . . . És o rei do mundo, rei absoluto, autocrata de todas as grandezas da terra! Tu, sim, tu reinas e governas, sem lei, sem opinião, sem parlamento. . . . Lei. . . . Que lei é a tua, senão o capricho com que escarneces dos homens?[6]

These thoughts pour out of Ricardo as he rests on the side of a trail in the bucolic woods of Tijuca, drawing the outline of a golden wildflower in his sketchbook. He has come to Rio de Janeiro seeking his fortune; or perhaps it is better to say that he has come seeking to close the chapter of his youth and, upon earning the 20 contos he needs to establish a household of his own, return to São Paulo to marry and raise a family. His needs are not great. But Ricardo has no money and no connections. Amassing such a sum seems nearly impossible to him as he reclines in the grass and reflects on life. Twenty contos, he thinks, when "millionaires have paid much more than that just to have the right to a five letter name." *Barão* (baron). *Conde* (count). Four contos per letter.[7] His needs seem small in comparison. How might one get such a quantity of money quickly? Winning the lottery, in a card game, through an unexpected inheritance.[8] As Ricardo ponders these possibilities, he becomes aware that he is being watched. Looking up, he sees a beautiful young woman astride an

Arabian horse. She stares down at him. Without thinking, he kisses the golden flower he has been holding while sketching. The girl laughs. Although Ricardo senses that there is some malice in the girl's demeanor, he returns laughter with laughter. Thus Ricardo and Guida meet for the first time: poor virtue meets golden caprice.[9] Later, Ricardo will draw Guida's beautiful figure in his sketchbook alongside the flower and discover that she is the daughter of one of the richest men in Rio de Janeiro. Critically, for Alencar's purposes, her father will be rich but scrupulously honest and humble, the antithesis of those men who paid "four contos per letter" for a flimsy title of nobility.[10]

In Illustration 1, which was commissioned for this volume and etched in drypoint intaglio by Stephen Baird, the critical first meeting between Ricardo and Guida is presented for the reader. Guida has taken advantage of her fast horse to lose her chaperone, the prim Mrs. Trowshy. Ricardo is absorbed in a typical bourgeois pastime: taking the air in the forest and sketching a flower. Thus they meet for the first time, alone, in the poses of youth seeking experience.

In Alencar's version of the Brazilian bildungsroman, the twin paths of Ricardo and Guida represent the ways in which youthful pride and voluble caprice interact and complicate courtship and social integration. Ricardo is too proud at first to admit his love for Guida, fearing that he will appear as nothing more than another treasure hunter chasing the girl's rich dowry; Guida, unthinking, allows herself to take advantage of her situation, her power, in abusive games and pranks. Ricardo explains to his friend Fábio:

> In a millionaire's house, in the midst of people accustomed to luxury and status, what kind of figure would we cut? I believe it would best be said to lie at the balance between parasite and servant; we'd be the links in the chain betwixt the two.

> Em casa de um milionário, no meio de uma sociedade habituada ao luxo e às grandezas, qual seria nossa posição? Creio que a classifico bem dizendo que faríamos o ponto de transição entre o parasita e o criado; formaríamos o elo desses dois anéis da cadeia.[11]

To which Fábio responds, "Indeed, such modesty slips into pride" ("Com efeito! Modéstia tão requintada degenera em orgulho"). Pride, then, his friend suggests, is the barrier to social progress, not to mention pretty and rich young girls. Ricardo willfully misses Fábio's point, replying, "I have my dignity, not pride" ("Não tenho orgulho, mas dignidade").[12]

ILLUSTRATION 1. Guida and Ricardo meet for the first time in the hills of Tijuca.
Original artwork in drypoint intaglio by Stephen Baird.

In the meantime, in contrast to the identification of Ricardo with the sin of pride, Alencar refers to Guida with the term *caprice* no less than twenty-five times over the course of the novel. Guida, a free spirit by upbringing and character, admits her capricious nature openly. She has been brought up to do and say as she pleases. At the midpoint of the novel, Ricardo and Guida have a long conversation while riding on horseback through the forest paths of Tijuca. Ricardo has been trying to avoid Guida but to no avail. The girl is persistent. She calls herself rash. Ricardo adds capricious and naughty (see Illustration 2). Guida replies, "What do you want from me? I am of the habit of being pleased" ("Que quer? Estou habituada a me fazerem todas as vontades!").[13] Ricardo, ever the serious one, responds with a sermon on the dangers of following one's whims.

Although Alencar doubtless has in mind a moral to his story—one in which it is Guida who ultimately submits to the discipline of virtue—the novel itself contains a distinct reading in which Ricardo can be seen playing an inverse role as the chaste partner in the marriage dance. This inversion springs from his need to retain his "dignity" and to make his own way in the world without the helping hand of Guida, the vile Visconde de Aljuba (a character introduced

ILLUSTRATION 2. "Barometer of Love: Variable Woman." This image, showing woman as young and capricious, appeared along with seven other images as a jocular "barometer of love." The other two images, in which women hold the center ground, represent "stormy" and "cold."

SOURCE: *Semana Illustrada*, 43 (1861): 340.

midway through the text to tempt Ricardo with easy but illicit gain), or anyone else for that matter. The central contradiction is the preservation of the spirit and one's dignity when faced with the need for money. Antonio Candido says:

> The young man of talent, who in [Alencar's] books is always seeking love and social consideration, has in his path the problem of ascending in the capitalist world without breaking faith with his honor.

> O moço de talento, que nos seus livros parte sempre a busca do amor e da consideração social, tem pela frente o problema de ascender a esfera do capitalista sem quebra da vocação.[14]

Candido goes on to dismiss Alencar's solution, "marrying him off to the daughter of a rich man" ("casando-o com a filha do ricaço"), in *Sonhos d'Ouro* and in many other novels.[15] This claim, given the tenuous nature of the postscript of the novel, is at best half-true. Ricardo's choice is more complex. He is caught in a double bind with commitments to his mother and his cousin Isabela that cannot be reduced to this formula. Guida adds a third dimension. Less central to the plot is the Luisinha-Fábio engagement, involving Ricardo's sister and best friend, which adds a fourth dimension.

It is not even quite true that Ricardo seeks social ascent or a place in the world of capital. His aim, the equivalent of $10,000 at the time, is a sum far below the minimum level of wealth required to enter society, whether in its economic sphere or that of the salon. Not an insignificant sum, to be sure, but far from constituting a fortune circa 1870.[16] Alencar is, I argue, making a profound and subtle point more in keeping with Roberto Schwarz's observation regarding the impossibility of making an honest living in Rio de Janeiro at this time. The point is that a man of great talent, "top of his class," cannot, without "protection," earn a living commensurate with his abilities or, for that matter, commensurate with the incomes of mediocre businessmen or second-rate public employees.[17] The distance from 0 to 20 contos is practically unbridgeable without sacrificing his values. Through Ricardo, Alencar asks, What kind of society *is* this?

The novel presents Ricardo with a series of trials. He states early on in a conversation with Fábio the dangers of succumbing to the temptation of easy money.

> Gold is the touchstone of conscience; the plumb line that sounds the depths. I believe I am an honest man, but I'm not certain, because I have yet to see proof, choosing between the scruples of probity and the certain profits of a less worthy act.

O ouro é a pedra de toque da consciência; o prumo que lhe sonda a profundidade. Creio que sou um homem honesto; mas não tenho a certeza disso, porque ainda não me vi à prova, entre os escrúpulos da probidade e os lucros certos de uma ação menos digna.[18]

Throughout the novel Alencar has Ricardo give little sermons on virtue and the value of independence in the face of these trials. Ricardo's chastity is doubled, as it reflects outward and condemns easy money gained through questionable means or marriages of convenience. The idea that easy money and corrupted marriage join to form the worst possible combination recurs in Alencar's works. In *Senhora* it is practically the entire plot—a man sells himself for 100 contos to a vengeful bride.[19]

The difference between *Sonhos d'Ouro* and the better-known novel *Senhora* is worth considering here in more detail. Roberto Schwarz, in his study of the works of Alencar and Machado, dissects *Senhora* with skill and perception. Although he mentions other so-called urban novels from Alencar's pen, he does not cite *Sonhos d'Ouro*. This is an odd omission, because the novel is discussed at some length in Antonio Candido's foundational study of Brazilian literature.[20] The fact is, *Sonhos d'Ouro* does not fit easily in Alencar's oeuvre, nor does it quite fit the model that Schwarz erects around his reading of *Senhora*.[21] In any event, throughout *Sonhos d'Ouro* Ricardo holds out against all temptation, although in the end Alencar arranges a romantic solution that allows the happy ending—the wished-for marriage between Ricardo and Guida—to take place in a none-too-convincing postscript. Here we see Alencar's imagination struggling to conjure an alternative social order. The fact that the imagined world where virtue and wealth can wed is tacked on in the postscript should tell us something. Throughout the novel itself this "third" point in the triangle of desire is kept at a great distance.[22] It is not presented as within the grasp of the characters, and it is out of reach not because society is too strong but because duty and virtue will not permit it.

Setting aside the postscript, *Sonhos d'Ouro* offers no easy solutions to the thorny problem of marriage between poor virtue and capricious wealth: The girl pursues the boy; virtue is tested and wins out; no immediate resolution is offered; the very boundaries of virtue, where dignity ends and pride begins, are open to question. In his interactions with Guida, Ricardo acts like a poor Mr. Darcy: He chastises her for her willfulness, shows himself master of the situation, and withdraws behind a mask of dignity. Guida, full of life, has the spark if not reminiscent of Elizabeth, then perhaps of Emma. Alencar is no Jane

Austen, and *Sonhos d'Ouro* is no *Pride and Prejudice*. Alencar's chaste hero and capricious heroine lack charm and depth. Ricardo is stiff and earnest; Guida, although livelier, particularly when her exploits are recounted thirdhand, strikes the same two contrasting chords: caprice and generosity.[23]

Even so, the fact remains that Alencar manages to evoke the intractable barrier between Ricardo and Guida in such a way that he remains true to the social realities that underpin the context of the story. Leaving aside the problematic postscript, the effect generates a genuine sense of longing in the elliptical circuits of affection closed first in the hills above Rio and then held together intermittently and realistically for the remainder of the body of the novel. Space. Longing. Impasse. These terms have to be added to the shopworn themes of provincial virtue and metropolitan vice. Money does provide the touchstone of conscience, but it neither triumphs nor fails. This is interesting in its own right, and for this reason alone *Sonhos d'Ouro* deserves to be considered among the highest achievements in Alencar's oeuvre.

Sonhos d'Ouro is rich in atmosphere and detailed descriptions of people and places. Alencar describes with loving care the bucolic setting of Tijuca, where Ricardo and Guida have no less than seven chance meetings. In doing so, he maps an important terrain of elite courtship: a space defined by rustic beauty and opportunities to "get lost," to escape the patriarchal gaze of fathers and their dependents. Although Alencar does not indicate this directly, it can be inferred from the construction of the novel that Tijuca is a privileged, perhaps really the only, place for a meeting, usually on horseback, between the worlds of Guida and Ricardo. The young man eventually succumbs to Guida's insistence and visits her in her father's house, but this occurs only after the seven chance meetings on the trails of the forested hillsides of Tijuca. It is there in the setting of steep trails and shady nooks that Ricardo first sees Guida and returns laughter with laughter; it is on a steep and dangerous stretch of trail that Guida's dog is knocked off a cliff after nearly causing Ricardo's horse, Galgo, to tumble down with its rider; it is in the woods of Tijuca that Ricardo shows his bravery and horsemanship in an episode in which Guida rashly attempts to descend a steep slope to pluck a golden wildflower, a *sonho d'ouro*.

All these chance meetings, Ricardo reflects, culminate in an effect much more powerful than any planned courtship could have obtained.[24] By virtue of their spontaneity and their marked equality (in these occasions both characters are usually mounted on horseback) these encounters offer a space of equality, predicated on the space of the forest and the social practices of passing weekend days riding the trails, necessary for Ricardo and Guida's initial meetings and incipient courtship. To a significant degree, the combination of open space and horses cancels out the inequality in positions. This exception to the rule drawn by Candido with regard to Alencar's male protagonists' social inferiority highlights the way that different kinds of opportunities and encounters were encoded in the space of the city and its environs.[25]

The contrast between the relatively open and egalitarian space of the forested slopes of Tijuca and the claustrophobic environment of Comendador Soares's mansion in Larangeiras is drawn out in clear lines by Alencar's description of the presence of Guida's suitors at a luncheon shortly after Guida has seen Ricardo again on the trails of Tijuca and learned from one of her suitors, the dilettantish Guimarães, that Ricardo is a poor lawyer without social connections.[26] Out on the trail, Ricardo has his dignity and his fine Brazilian horse. In the house of Guida's father, he would be seen as a parasite or a pretender to Guida's dowry. The luncheon serves to introduce Guida's three principal suitors: the lawyer who does not practice law and lives off loans taken against his eventual inheritance, Guimarães; the lawyer who seeks political fame, Nogueira; and the wealthy stockbroker Bastos.[27] Despite her immaturity and volubility, Guida has for her part, as Ricardo puts it, "a scruple of conscience, I'd even say, a reservoir of goodness" ("escrúpulo de consciência, direi mesmo, um fundo de bondade").[28]

With this bit of conscience, Guida can hardly be expected to find any of her "official" suitors appetizing. Guimarães is a cad, the antithesis of the dignified and hardworking Ricardo. Nogueira is a self-absorbed climber who thinks he is more eloquent and expert than he really is. Bastos is just a man who happens to have a bit of money and therefore orbits in the gravitational pull of Comendador Soares's millions. Ricardo surpasses all his rivals but lacks money, the fundamental source of independence and social position. Without money he cannot be at ease in Comendador Soares's house; without 20 contos, he cannot fulfill his life plan and return to marry his cousin in São Paulo. Thus the dilemma confronting Ricardo at the outset—whether or not he will bend his scruples to ease his path to those 20 contos (or much more in the case of Guida's dowry)—is enacted spatially. On the paths of Tijuca, he is independent and in control; entering Guida's private world, he is uncomfortable, tempted, no longer in control of the situation.

Inside the house people and objects fall into other spatial arrangements and configurations. The space is filled with rich furnishings, huge dining tables, salons for gathering and listening to music played on the piano. Characters interact in this space and make tactical moves that take advantage of the material at hand. For instance, in a crucial scene with Ricardo where the conversation reaches an impasse, Guida gets up and walks over to the piano; this concludes the conversation and initiates a different kind of encounter, a different "definition of the situation," as Goffman would put it.[29] Once again, we see the utility of this instrument in Guida's everyday life. Staying seated would mean continuing a conversation that is going nowhere. Getting up and leaving the room would send a strong negative signal. Picking up a book would seem antisocial. The piano is there as a prop. When she needs something to do that frees her from conversation but is entirely neutral with respect to the others in the room, the piano is there for her. Seen in this light, a piano is more than merely a symbol of elite culture or an instrument for the refinement of young women. These immanent characteristics emerge in literary sources, not in the traditional documents of history.

Protection

The tension produced in the passage from the open space of Tijuca to the closed space of Comendador Soares's mansion hinges on Ricardo's desperate need for money. Ricardo begins the book with a soliloquy on the caprice of money and its ubiquitous social power. He laments his inability to obtain the 20 contos he needs through licit means. At the same time, he imagines how such a sum might be obtained: lottery tickets, card games, unexpected inheritances, the protection of a millionaire.[30] It is noteworthy that all these imaginings involve obtaining the money through chance or happenstance, or at the very least by the grace of God.

As Roberto Schwarz notes regarding the economic realities of the time, "An honest, independent life does not lie within the reach of a poor person," and for the large population of free but poor residents of the city, this results in a situation of dependency.[31] This situation, the asymmetric but reciprocal relationship between a person of wealth and power and a dependent, Schwarz insists, is founded on the practice of favor. It will do no violence to Schwarz's argument to add the word *protection* as a category of favor. The concept of protection has the added advantage of linking the Brazilian bildungsroman more tightly to its European model—both literary *and* social. In doing so, it does cut against the implicit exceptionalism of Schwarz's arguments about favor.

With his law degree but without "protection" on the part of well-connected individuals, there is no legitimate pathway for Ricardo to earn enough money to fulfill his plans. *Protection* is a word that recurs in the novel and conjures up the pervasive power of paternalism, of client-patron relationships, in Rio at the time. When Ricardo expresses his distaste for Guida and his disinclination to attempt to pursue the connection, Fábio reminds him, "We must make relations, acquire friends; otherwise we'll get nowhere" ("É preciso fazermos relações, adquirir amigos, do contrário nada alcançaremos").[32] Later on, when Guimarães reveals Ricardo's identity and social position to Guida, the following exchange takes place:

> Guida: What's he doing now?
> Guimarães: I don't know. Lawyering I guess; but wasting his time; he's not getting anywhere.
> Guida: Why not? Has he no talent?
> Guimarães: Sure, but what use is talent if no one's heard of him? He'd be better off with half the talent and the other half protection.
> Guida: Protection?
> Guimarães: See here: Businessmen to give him good cases and recommend him to their friends.
>
> Guida: Que faz ele agora?
> Guimarães: Não sei. Creio que está aqui advogando; mas perde o seu tempo; não faz nada.
> Guida: Por quê? Não tem talento?
> Guimarães: Mas de que lhe serve se ninguém o conhece? Servia-lhe mais ficar com metade do talento que tem, e a outra metade de proteção.
> Guida: Como proteção?
> Guimarães: Ora: negociantes que lhe dêem boas causas e o recomendem a seus amigos.[33]

Care should be taken before assigning a particularly Brazilian interpretation to this concept of protection. Yes, we are dealing with a society still very much based on personal connections and client-patron relations.[34] But consider Madame d'Espard's comment to Madame de Bargeton on the subject of Lucien, whom Madame de Bargeton is trying to sponsor and thereby introduce into society: "He looks good, but he appears to be a fool and he can't stand properly or speak; all in all, he's a poor study. Why ever do you protect him?" ("Sa figure est belle, mais il me parait fort sot, il ne sait ni se tenir ni parler; enfin il n'est pas eleve, par quel hazard le protegez-vous?").[35]

It would probably also be a mistake to take these cases of Ricardo and Lucien and ascribe a unique importance to protection for the provincial arriving in the metropolis, though this is implied by both Alencar and Balzac. As Raymundo Faoro points out in his rambling and always fertile study of Machado de Assis, the theme of introductions and stamps of approval appears throughout Machado's works and does not depend on a city-country distinction.[36] Clearly we are dealing with a range of situations, where the provincial might indeed be said to need protection during the entry period into society in a way that differs from the city dweller with his or her larger social network. On the other hand, the provincial interloper does not necessarily draw the worst cards in the game. The possibility of creating a new persona with the help of a protector is greater for those without too many local entanglements. Choosing the right protector, then, is of the utmost importance. The problem, in terms of *Bildung*, is that protectors tend to choose the protected as much or more so than the other way around.

Marriage

Read superficially, the plot of *Sonhos d'Ouro* conforms in many respects to the rules of the classic marriage plot, particularly if the postscript is taken into account. Two people, destined one day to marry, meet and undergo a series of trials and overcome a number of seemingly insurmountable obstacles. A classic ingredient present in the novel is the discrepancy between the social positions of the protagonists, although we have seen that this can be partly effaced in certain settings and circumstances. Guida is unimaginably rich; Ricardo has practically no money. Missing, however, is a second typical ingredient: parental opposition. Comendador Soares gives Guida full freedom to choose a husband. The element of parental opposition, which is present in nearly every marriage plot and which certainly reflects truths about social relations and the manner in which marriage was perceived as a kind of transaction between families, is replaced in *Sonhos d'Ouro* by a different obstacle: prior commitment.

For all his talk of independence and dignity, Ricardo has already sold himself to his uncle through his promise to marry his cousin Isabela. The connection to Isabela, to be sure, is not one based on money; neither he nor she has any to speak of. Rather, it is based on "childhood affection," which we can take as common enough between cousins. Ricardo's promise to Isabela to make something of himself and thereby allow a marriage, in combination with debts owed to his uncle for assistance during his legal studies, creates a great obstacle for him.[37] He cannot marry Isabela without first getting his hands on some money, as Isabela's father will not consent without first seeing Ricardo established. His pride, in any case, would not allow for it. On the other hand, Ricardo cannot withdraw his commitment to his cousin, because love and scruples prevent him from abandoning his betrothed. Moreover, he is constrained by the significant debts his father left his mother from a mortgage on her house and property that, with interest, had ballooned to 20 contos.[38] As the son on whom his family has put all its hopes, Ricardo shoulders the responsibility of repaying his mother's debts and thereby allowing her to live out her life in poor but dignified fashion. Finally, to further complicate matters, Ricardo needs to repay his mother's debts so that his sister Luisa can marry his best friend, Fábio.

For her part, Isabela faces the difficulty of waiting for Ricardo to make his 20 contos and fending off her father's demands that she marry another man with a ready fortune. Luisa likewise waits for Ricardo to clear the path for her to marry Fábio. Finally, upon turning 18, Guida begins to feel pressure from her father to make up her mind and choose a husband. Thus the power of patriarchy in *Sonhos d'Ouro* regarding marriage is expressed through the relationship of fathers to daughters, not in opposing marriage but in demanding it.

The tangled knot of commitments created by Alencar for his protagonists underscores several critical issues regarding marriage in Rio circa 1870. First is the obvious issue of money. Young men and women of a certain class did not marry without it. Here, the question is both quantitative and cultural. It is quantitative because the threshold of wealth (or income) associated with the ability to marry can be measured with a degree of precision. This threshold underscores Alencar's realism, his Balzacian command of the facts of his time.[39] It is also clearly a question of culture because the threshold was determined not by objective conditions but by social expectations.

What were these expectations?

First, to paraphrase Jane Austen, it was a truth universally acknowledged that a sole heiress would be in want of a husband.[40] She would find herself besieged by suitors, hence the traditional roles of the father as final arbiter and the mother as coach in these proceedings. In Guida's case there is only the father, her mother having died some years before. Suitors, then. The shady and tranquil grounds of Comendador Soares's estate and its enormous dining room with a table to seat thirty provide a critical space of courtship. There, in a choreographed sequence of small talk, food, drink, music, and cigars, the suitors, among the invited guests, maneuver. Gaining entry, this is the first step a suitor must take. As Ricardo makes clear in his debate with Fábio about whether to accept Guida's invitation, there is no way for a single man of any talent and ambition to appear as anything other than a suitor in the presence of the rich and available young woman. Marriage ceremonies take place on a single day; as a central concern in life it is always present, coloring the everyday routines of fathers and daughters, suitors and stand-ins alike.

From the roster of suitors present together at multiple points in the novel, the following facts emerge. All the pretenders to Guida's hand are either rich or holders of law degrees. As for age, this ranges from men in their 40s down to Ricardo and Guimarães, who are in their late 20s. Guida is just 18. The dominant cultural expectation, at least among the wealthier and more educated, was thus for marriage to involve a young bride, still in her teens, and an older man, already established with social status vouchsafed by education, pedigree, and money, preferably plenty of it.

This leads to an important conclusion: The period of a girl's *Bildung*, her education and growth and creation of an individual personality, was extremely compressed by these cultural expectations. After marriage, of course, she would

Ha no Botafogo um pai com quatro filhas ; tem uma mania o bom do homem : quer casar todas as filhas ao mesmo tempo. A dificul-dade está em achar os quatro noivos....

ILLUSTRATION 3. "Marriage Markets and Patriarchy Lampooned." This illustration, which appeared in the November 24, 1861, issue of *Semana Illustrada*, captures the essence of bourgeois anxiety relating to marriageable daughters. The text at the bottom translates to "In Botafogo there lives a father with four daughters. The gentleman has a mania: he wants to marry off all his daughters at one time. The difficulty is in finding the four bridegrooms . . ." The fat, top-hatted bourgeois father has the girls on a leash, but can he hold on?

SOURCE: *Semana Illustrada* 50 (1861): 396.

engage in a continued process of growth, but the cultural expectation was that this would be entirely subordinated to the career and needs of her husband and later her children. Growth as a wife meant learning to carry out wifely duties with elegance and, most fundamentally, to become a mother, to reproduce.

Taking this compression of identity formation into account casts a different, more nuanced light on Alencar's depiction of Guida's youthful follies. As a moralist, Alencar doubtlessly condemns Guida's caprice, in keeping with the mores of his time; but in his Balzacian mode as amanuensis of urban society in Rio, he cannot help but reveal something else: the foreshortened and intense struggle to create a personality, which, in the case of a rich heiress like Guida, takes a particular form.[41] Guida's pranks can be read as rehearsals for the use of the power of money. She is learning to manipulate when she summons the most famous doctor in Rio to her father's estate to treat Sophie, her dog.[42] She tests boundaries while out riding her Arabian horse in the hills of Tijuca. Her playful exchanges with Mrs. Trowshy, her English tutor and companion, underscore her irreverent and independent nature. Taken together, these episodes and descriptions reveal an independent and willful personality.

Guida's youthful caprice is not just a phase she will grow out of, ending in maturity and marriage. It is a strategy for prolonging her youth and holding her suitors at bay; it is the promise of an individuality and independence that will transcend the cultural expectations of marriage. Guida's unwillingness to marry early and her volubility point the way to an alternative path, one in which her *Bildung* creates an excess of personality that ensures that her eventual marriage, her eventual integration into the mature world of adulthood, will not obliterate her former self.

In this sense, *Sonhos d'Ouro* is especially interesting from a historical perspective, because it forces the reader to reconsider the relation between everyday practices, youth, and the formation of personality, *particularly with respect to women*. It calls forth the image of a shortened but highly significant period of *Bildung* for young women of wealth, and it traces out the means by which an individual personality emerges through everyday practices. In the case of Guida, these are given a particular charge, or valence, in the direction of independence and agency: horses and pianos, trails and salons, elements drawn together in settings—and choices, positionings, the emergence of an individual personality. Guida takes the givens, the mundane everyday she is structurally condemned to live, and makes a personalized version of that world. Moretti, following Baudrillard, points out that "if everyday life is a system of interpretation, the same holds true for personality: both are ways of reshaping the world."[43] Thus, to ride recklessly is to create space—or, better yet, distance—from the clichéd plodding of the idle rich in the forests of Tijuca, an opportunity to "wander and get lost."[44] To tease and play pranks is to create space, elbow room in which to move in the claustrophobic social space of the mansion, the salon, and the manicured garden. A reputation for caprice allows Guida to flirt without needing to fear the consequences.

A key passage in the heart of *Sonhos d'Ouro* demonstrates this manifold operation of personality in creating space.

> Guida: Have you heard the news?
> Ricardo: What?
> Guida: You still haven't been congratulated?
> Ricardo: For what?
> . . .
> Guida: Very well, I ought to tell you. You are set to marry me.
> Ricardo: I don't understand!
> . . .
> Guida: . . . Don't worry, I was uncomfortable with these impertinences at first too; now I'm used to them; and I'm even thankful, in this case, they haven't given me a crazy or useless fiancée, as so often in the past.[45]

> Guida: Sabe a novidade?
> Ricardo: Qual?
> Guida: Ainda não lhe deram os parabéns?
> Ricardo: Por que motivo?
> . . .
> Guida: Pois então, deve-me as alvíssaras. O senhor está para casar comigo.
> Ricardo: Não entendo!
> . . .
> Guida: . . . Não se importe! A princípio também me incomodavam essas impertinências; agora estou habituada; e ainda agredeço quando não me dão por noivo algum bobo ou algum traste, como já tem sucedido.

In this exchange Guida shows her command of the situation, both in conveying the thinly veiled provocation—you do want to marry me, don't you—and in showing how she has turned the incessant siege of suitors and the rumors in their regard to her advantage, shielding her from having to take any one of them seriously. Still, she concludes, thoughtfully: "Be patient; tomorrow they'll invent a new fiancée for me; and you can rest easy. I'm the one, unfortunately, who hasn't anyone who can get me out of the limelight" ("Tenha paciência; amanhã me inventarão outro noivo; e o senhor ficará descansado. Eu é que infelizmente não tenho quem me tire da berlinda").[46]

A reputation for caprice allows Guida to keep her suitors at a distance. It does not, as she says, get her out of the limelight. Until she marries, there will be men circling; the subtext of every event and every conversation will be marriage. In the end, this is tiresome. One suspects that a fair number of wealthy young women simply wore down under the constant pressure and chose whoever was close at hand. Guida's father, meanwhile, has not abdicated all authority. With respect to the rules of courtship and Guida's eventual choice, he clarifies matters with Nogueira, one of Guida's long-standing admirers: "On the subject of marriage, my dear doctor, I am the crown and Guida is the Parliament. She has the right to legislate the project and I limit myself to the right to veto" ("Nesta matéria de casamento, meu caro doutor, eu sou a coroa, a Guida é o parlamento. Ela tem o direito de votar o projeto; eu limito-me à sanção do veto").[47]

As for his daughter, Comendador Soares made a bargain on her sixteenth birthday. Rather than pressure Guida into an immediate marriage, he would allow her to remain unattached until she is 18, whereupon she would choose a mate subject to his veto and be settled. In the event that there was disagreement regarding the choice, there would be a one-year observation period during which the father might be persuaded to change his mind. As it happens, 18 comes and goes, and Guida insists that the bargain was only that she marry during her eighteenth year. Her father's concern to see her well married is, along with conforming to social norms, a sign of his care for her future. Because he is rich and experienced, he considers himself uniquely able to evaluate the true qualities of Guida's suitors. Should he die before her marriage, he assumes that she would be exposed to speculators and men of poor character without his steady hand to guide her decision: "Eighteen is the flower of a woman's youth, and fifty-five the old age of a man. Tomorrow might be too late for both of us" ("Dezoito anos é a mocidade da mulher, como os cinqüenta e cinco que já estão cá, são a velhice do homem. Amanhã pode ser tarde para nós ambos").[48]

In addition, Guida's father worries:

> What good is this great wealth, for which I am envied, to me, if it compromises rather than secures the future happiness of my daughter? If only with a million, two million, everything I possess, I could create a man worthy of you.

> Essa imensa riqueza, que me invejam, de que me serve, pois em vez de garantir,
> compromete o futuro de minha filha? Se com um milhão, dois, tudo quanto
> possuo, pudesse criar um homem digno de ti.[49]

Romantic overstatement aside, Soares's words suggest that having too much money is dangerous because it might prevent Guida from ever finding a genuine mate. Men with no scruples and a thirst for money swarm about while men with scruples, like Ricardo, are more likely to stay away, not from aversion to Guida but from a desire to avoid falling into the undignified camp of speculators and dowry chasers.

Money is required for marriage, but in the process, it cancels the possibility of affection free of the taint of calculation, as Illustration 4 mockingly suggests. This state of affairs calls to mind Raymond Williams's comments regarding the cynicism surrounding marriage as a property transaction in Restoration comedies.

> For the point about the cynicism of these weary and greedy intrigues—the
> coarse having and getting which reduces its players to a mutuality of objects—is
> that it is only the scum on a deeper cynicism, which as a matter of settlement, of
> ordered society, has reduced men and women to physical, bargainable carriers
> of estates and incomes . . . . When marriage is like that, it is not properly avail-
> able as a moral contrast to the intrigues of the whores and the fortune-hunters
> in residence. (This point is reinforced when Alencar depicts Ricardo translating
> Balzac's *Eugénie Grandet*, a novel filled with marriage problems generated by
> money and greed.[50])

The key theme of *Sonhos d'Ouro*, then, is, Can honest, dignified love transcend the corrupting power of great wealth? The *Bildung* of Guida and Ricardo must resolve this dilemma. If we take the central dilemma of modern urban society to be the drive to self-determination in opposition to the necessity for socialization, then the question of Guida's marriage captures the impossibility of complete resolution.[51] On meeting Ricardo, Guida is ready to choose, and in so doing she keeps true to herself and at the same time submits to the social norm. Ricardo, encumbered with prior commitments and a prideful dignity, cannot respond in kind. Lacking resolution of this dilemma, the novel ends in an impasse.

Roberto Schwarz, writing with regard to *Senhora*, captures nicely the double-sidedness of Alencar's position on money and marriage: "Explicit subject: money represses natural feelings; latent subject: money, contempt, and refusal form an eroticized triangle" ("Assunto explicito: o dinheiro recalca os sentimentos naturais; assunto latente: dinheiro, desprezo e recusa formam um conjunto erotizado").[52] This is at the heart of the matter, where we see that, in language similar to that used by Williams regarding an older tradition of cynicism regarding marriage, "the formal duality we have been studying . . . places in the center of the novel the bourgeois objectification of social relations" ("a dualidade formal que viemos estudando: coloca no centro do romance a coisificação burguesa das relações sociais").[53]

Marido.—Todos dizem, que minha mulher é horrenda; mas eu a acho divina, quando me lembro que ella me trouxe cincoenta contos.
Muther.—Todos gabão a gentileza de meu marido : mas não sa-em que elle me custou cincoenta contos!

ILLUSTRATION 4. "Dandies and Dowry-Chasers." In this image a man comments on how everyone says his wife is ugly, but he finds her divine when he remembers that she brought along a dowry of 50 contos. The woman says that although everyone lauds her husband's style, they do not realize he cost her 50 contos.

SOURCE: *Semana Illustrada* 111 (1863): 883.

As Guida's father worries, money threatens to spoil every true connection. Guida's dowry has the dehumanizing effect of making her appear to her suitors as a walking gold mine.[54] Only the postscript brings tidings of a wedding, and this feels tacked on and out of step with the novel itself.

᭒

On this aspect of Alencar's better novels, Antonio Candido remarks:

> We see that his best books are those marked by maximum conflict; those which can only have a "happy-end" thanks to expedients tacked on against the coherence of the narrative . . . and which thereby leave a mark of melancholy in the spirit of the reader.

> Veremos que os seus melhores livros são aqueles em que o conflito é máximo; nos quais só pode haver happy-end graças a um expediente imposto à coerência da narrativa . . . e que deixam um sulco de melancolia no espírito do leitor.[55]

Yes, but then Alencar is attempting to tackle a difficult problem. The shift from an emphasis on social patterns that contain individuals who can adjust (through growth) to the novel of the distanced, separated individual was in its infancy when Alencar published *Sonhos d'Ouro*. As a romantic, Alencar still had to believe that his creations could reconcile happiness and money, virtue and social integration, provided that certain structural facts could be finessed or swept under the rug. He was not destined to apprehend the world of the resigned individual and a fictional method to represent it along the lines sketched out by George Eliot, Flaubert, or, in Brazil, by his contemporary Machado de Assis in his breakthrough novel of 1880–1881, *Memórias Póstumas de Brás Cubas*.

Raymond Williams, contrasting Trollope with Eliot, also sheds light on the awkwardness we find in Alencar's golden dreams.

> To read *Doctor Thorne* beside *Felix Holt* is not only to find ease in Trollope where there is disturbance in George Eliot; to find a level of interest corresponding with the plot instead of struggling to break free of a dutifully sustained external complication; to find the conventional happy ending where property and happiness can coexist and be celebrated instead of an awkward, stubborn, unappeased resignation. It is also, quite evidently, to see the source of these differences in a real social history.[56]

Yet, save for the epilogue, Alencar delivers nothing if not a sense of an awkward, stubborn, unappeased resignation. Ricardo is true to himself, and to life, even if, in the end, Alencar is not. Particularly in his depiction of Guida, wittingly or not, Alencar reveals the process of formation, the medium in everyday life, and the results of a certain kind of personality. The novel poses the question of social integration in a realistic register, even if the main characters are hardly typical people. A world of young girls forced to become women and wives as teenagers appears before our eyes. Guida's and Ricardo's difficulties in resolving the tensions latent in a society dominated by things, by money, suggests Alencar's own misgivings about the emerging capitalist economy centered in Rio de Janeiro. The internal, personal world appears together with the external social pattern. Seen from different perspectives, the two cannot quite be brought into alignment. In this regard, Alencar's failure to "solve" the problem of *Bildung* for Guida and Ricardo in convincing fashion ought to be seen as a triumph of his artistic talent and capacity for social observation and characterization.

2 MEMÓRIAS PÓSTUMAS DE BRÁS CUBAS

This book and my style are like a pair of drunks: they stagger to the right and to the left, they start and they stop, they mutter, they roar, they guffaw, they threaten the sky, they slip and fall.

Este livro e o meu estilo são como os ébrios, guinam à direita e à esquerda, andam e param, resmungam, urram, gargalham, ameaçam o céu, escorregam e caem.

Brás Cubas[1]

JOAQUIM MARIA MACHADO DE ASSIS is one of the marvels of world literature, the author of four unquestionable masterpiece novels.[2] His origins are as unusual as his path toward a life in letters is conventional by the standards of the time: unusual because he was the sporadically educated son of a *pardo* house painter and a white, immigrant mother from the Portuguese Atlantic island of São Miguel; and conventional, because he passed through the common stages of poetry, journalism, and theater writing on his way to becoming a master novelist. That is, Machado apprenticed in the hothouse of the literary world of Rio de Janeiro in much the same way as other leading writers of his time. When he made his breakthrough, he was already a noted writer and established member of the literary and social scene in the Corte.

The future "wizard of Cosme Velho" was born in 1839 on the slopes of the Morro do Livramento, a hill at the northern edge of the city center. His mother, Maria Leopoldina Machado da Câmara, worked in domestic service in the household of a wealthy family. Her status was that of an *agregado*—something more than a servant and less than a full member of the family. His father, Francisco José de Assis, painted and worked in the neighborhood. The couple was married in 1838 with socially prominent men standing as witnesses. Their first child was born just under a year later, again with socially connected godparents listed in the baptismal register. If the family was poor and unorthodox (marriage between a white woman and a free man of color was uncommon), it was nonetheless connected to "good society." The birth of a sister followed in 1841.[3]

Machado's childhood was marked by two tragic deaths: his sister from a *sarampo* (measles) epidemic in 1845 and his mother from tuberculosis in 1849. These losses hit the sensitive youth hard. His mother was a frequent subject in subsequent writings, and one can catch a glimpse of the sense of randomness of death from the frequent epidemics that wracked the city in the death of young Eulália in *Memórias Póstumas*.

Notwithstanding his inauspicious educational and social background, Machado was a precocious writer, publishing his first poem at the age of 15 in the aptly titled *Periódico dos Pobres*.[4] In the following years he developed a reputation as a writer in venues such as Paula Britto's *Marmota Fluminense*, the *Correio Mercantil*, and the *Jornal das Famílias*. He wrote poetry, theatrical pieces, short stories, occasional journalism, and four rather conventional novels in the years preceding the publication of his groundbreaking novel, *Memórias Póstumas de Brás Cubas*. Along the way, he moved from the unstable employment offered by literary work to the stable and ample life of a salaried member of the imperial bureaucracy, rising in time to chief of section in the Ministry of Agriculture.[5] This move toward financial independence coincided with a good marriage to Carolina Augusta Xavier de Novais, a woman of culture and intellect who collaborated in his later works, going so far as to take dictation of stretches of *Memórias Póstumas* when Machado's failing eyesight made writing impossible for a time.[6] Despite this health scare, Machado wrote his masterpiece from a position of social and personal security. He was at the peak of his powers in 1879 when he began work on the book that would transform Brazilian literary history forever.

Turning to the novel itself, in *Memórias Póstumas* we are shown an entirely different path through life from that traced out in Alencar's *Sonhos d'Ouro*— different in beginnings as much as in endings. The story of Brás Cubas is one of defeat without consequences, of experience without growth. It is the anti-bildungsroman featuring a hero without qualities and a life without resolution. In this regard Machado is akin to the "prophet without wrath" that Carl Schorske found in Arthur Schnitzler, the Viennese chronicler of fin de siècle bourgeois malaise. Machado's hero, Brás Cubas, has no real tragic stature, although, in the end, the effect Machado accomplishes is less one of "sadness" than of ironic bemusement.[7] He dismisses an impossible society with the equivalent of a shrug of the shoulders.

The fact that the book centers—and by centers I mean in the most complete and egocentric way—on the life of a wealthy, educated, and socially connected man is all the more telling. It is Brás's wealth, education, and social position that open up his path through life and allow him the means of self-indulgence, volubility, and caprice.[8] Defeat holds no consequence that money and position cannot obliterate—and the sense of impunity is heightened only by the fact that the novel is narrated by a defunct version of Brás. All things are possible and thus nothing is particularly meaningful, which calls to mind Sergio Buarque de Holanda's insights regarding the *homem cordial* as a social type.

> The private life of a Brazilian is neither cohesive or disciplined enough to evolve and control his whole personality, integrating it, as a sentient part, of the social order. He is free, thus, to abandon himself to the whole range of ideas, gestures and forms that he encounters on his way, assimilating everything without great difficulty.

> A vida íntima do brasileiro nem é bastante coesa, nem bastante disciplinada, para evolver e dominar toda a sua personalidade, integrando-a, como peça consciente, no conjunto social. Ele é livre, pois, para se abandonar a todo o repertório de ideias, gestos, e formas que encontre em seu caminho, assimilando-os frequentemente sem maiores dificuldades.[9]

Early on, Brás identifies the origins of his attitude toward life.

> The important thing is the general complexion of the domestic environment, and this the reader has doubtless already derived: vulgarity of character, love of loudness and ostentation, weakness of will, domination by whim and caprice and the like. Of such land, fertilized by such manure, this flower drew its substance.

> O que importa é a expressão geral do meio doméstico, e essa aí fica indicada,— vulgaridade de caracteres, amor das aparências rutilantes, do arruído, frouxidão da vontade, domínio do capricho, e o mais. Dessa terra e desse estrume é que nasceu esta flor.[10]

We begin then with the child, first viewed through the eyes of his family. In the first days of life, a path is being traced out for him. His uncle João, a military man, sees traces of Napoleon in Brás's face. Uncle Ildefonso "scented a future canon in me." Then, tellingly, his father responds that Brás will be "what God desired." That is, anything he wants. As for his social position more broadly, Brás traces this out with maximum economy with the following lines regarding his godparents:

> My godfather? He is the Most Excellent Senhor Colonel Paulo Vaz Lobo Cesar de Andrade e Souza Rodrigues de Mattos. My godmother is the Most Excellent Senhora Dona Maria Luiza de Macedo Rezende e Souza Rodrigues de Mattos.

> Meu padrinho? É o Execelentíssimo Senhor Colonel Paulo Vaz Lobo Cesar de Andrade e Souza Rodrigues de Mattos; minha madrinha é a Excelentíssima Senhora Dona Maria Luiza de Macedo Rezende e Souza Rodrigues de Mattos.[11]

The joke here, the proliferation of titles and names, is at the same time absolutely serious. Godparents with many surnames, if fanciful here in number, were a sure sign of a deep and solid connection to the core of traditional elite society.

As for Brás's upbringing and its subsequent influence on his life path, Machado leaves no doubt in the title to Chapter 11: "The Child Is the Father to the Man." In this chapter we see Brás described as riding on the back of his house slave, Prudêncio, with a rope between his teeth as a rein and bit: I "would beat him, and he would turn this way and that, and he would obey." His treatment of houseguests was not much better, as he would hide their hats, pin tails to their trousers, and pull their hair. All of this his father allowed, assuming implicitly that such willfulness would transmute in time into the makings of a strong and confident man.[12] This kind of upbringing was, to a lesser degree, depicted in the case of Guida Soares, as we have seen in the discussion of Alencar's *Sonhos d'Ouro* (Chapter 1). It will also appear in the depiction of Teobaldo's childhood and his relation with his father in *O Coruja* (Chapter 3).

In one of the longest chapters in a book filled with short chapters (Chapter 13), Brás narrates a dinner party held at his father's mansion in 1814. Napoleon has fallen, and news of this great event has arrived in Rio. Brás's family is celebrating the event with a dinner party so ostentatious that word of it might be expected to reach the ears of the emperor, then residing in Brazil on account of Napoleon's invasion of Portugal. Dinner parties can be weapons in social combat. During the meal, Brás overhears a guest bragging about a shipment of slaves about to arrive in Rio. The commerce in people that undergirded the wealth of Brás's family and other elite families in Brazil at that time is mentioned, in passing, by a guest who is immediately shushed into silence. Brás recounts this episode but does not comment on it. This underscores how commonplace the slave trade was at the time and how willfully the rich repressed this fact. Still, as dinner is winding down, Brás's father "ordered a slave to serve dessert" to him. Surrounded by evidence of the trade, served by its victims, the men and women seated at the table refuse to contemplate its ongoing and constant operation.[13]

In this same chapter, after the dinner has ended and Aunt Emerenciana has deprived Brás of his dessert, Brás witnesses Dr. Villaça kissing Dona Eusébia in the garden. Villaça is a married man and Dona Eusébia is not his wife. And it was Vallaça's long speech that cut off the discussion of the slave trade and, in Brás's mind, deprived him of dessert. So Brás seeks revenge by announcing to one and all what he has seen.

These two episodes, presented together and linked through the person of Dr. Villaça, show the hypocrisy of elite society. Villaça is described as "a dignified man . . . poised and deliberate, forty-seven years old, married and a father." That is, he has all the qualities expected of an upstanding member of the social elite. Yet he shushes a guest who breaks decorum by mentioning the slave trade and then proceeds to steal kisses from Sergeant-Major Domingues's sister, "a robust, middle-aged lady, who, if not exactly pretty, was certainly not ugly."[14]

In tandem, these two chapters reveal the internal and external coordinates of Brás's social world during his childhood. The remaining chapters regarding his youth conform to this pattern. He is capricious and self-regarding; his social milieu is superficial and hypocritical. What is revealing from the point of view of *Bildung* is the sequence of steps Brás takes along his path to adulthood. First school, a *colégio* in Rio de Janeiro, where he meets Quincas Borba, a friend who will exercise some influence over Brás in the years to come; then

Do not weep, my Love, lest the redness of the dawn be reflected in your eyes.

ILLUSTRATION 5. Brás in the garden. Original artwork in drypoint intaglio by Stephen Baird.

the first kiss and affair, with Marcela, the "Spanish beauty"; culminating, finally, in Brás's being sent away to university in Coimbra, Portugal, by his father, in no small part to break the connection between Brás and his lover. An utterly conventional trajectory.

Brás's *Bildung*

Consider the kinds of behavior depicted in these episodes. At school, Quincas Borba torments Ludgero Barata (colloquial name for cockroach) by placing dead roaches in his pockets. "A real flower, this Quincas Borba," the boy, like Brás, comes from money, "his mother, a widow with considerable property . . . gave him everything he wanted."[15] With Marcela, Brás learns that with a little money, a lover can be bought. Marcela, in her turn, uses this as leverage when disappointed by Brás's blandishments. When he fails to buy her a necklace she wants, she observes that "she had only been joking, that our love needed no such vulgar stimulus." Later, she tells Brás about a gold necklace given to her by Duarte, a previous *amante*. With the embers of jealously kindled, the next day Brás buys the necklace she wanted all along.[16] Going to Coimbra, he discovers two things: the ultimate power of his father, who breaks up the affair with Marcela by force; and the sweet-sour sensation of aimless ambition. He is willing to contemplate "any profession, provided that it entailed preeminence, reputation, a status of superiority."[17] After Coimbra, it is on to a version of the Grand Tour, with a stop in a Venice "still redolent with Byron's verses," where Brás receives the sad news of his mother's terminal illness. Upon returning to Rio, Brás retires to the countryside, taking up residence in a house in Tijuca owned by his family. His idyll is marked by a Wertherian "voluptuousness of misery," during which time he hunts, sleeps, and reads. After a period of mourning for his dead mother, he is roused from his rural torpor by his father, who brings him "two projects, a seat in the Chamber of Deputies and a marriage." His father has arranged things such that a marriage to Virgília will grease the tracks to a seat in the Chamber of Deputies, as Virgília's father, Conselheiro Dutra, has considerable political pull. As Bento Cubas puts it, "She is his daughter, and I have no doubt that, if you marry her, you will become a deputy much sooner."[18]

At this point, Brás is on the verge of completing his apprenticeship for life as a member of the social, economic, and political elite. He has sown his wild oats; he has tasted ambition. It is significant that neither the idea of a political career nor one of marriage springs from Bras's own volition. They are taken as givens by his father; they are given by Brás's upbringing and social position.

> I went down from Tijuca the next morning, partly embittered and partly pleased. I kept telling myself that it was right to obey my father, that it was desirable to embrace a political career . . . that the constitution . . . that my bride to be . . . that my horse . . .[19]

He is not elected and does not marry; it does not matter. This is the core of the book. Eventually, however, he *is* elected, and if he does not marry, he carries on an affair with Virgília. He is defeated; he is victorious. It does not matter.

What went wrong? Brás stayed too long in Tijuca, vacillating between love and repulsion for the pretty but lame Eugênia. Then, in the heat of battle for the hand of Virgília, he takes a fateful detour in the Rua do Ourives, where he reencounters Marcela. She has been utterly transformed from the courtesan of old into an ugly, pockmarked hag. Beauty is fleeting. She asks Brás whether he has married; he responds, not yet. Marcela, down but not out, is still using her charms on a neighbor, a watchmaker with a wife and daughter. This episode throws Brás off kilter. There is something acrid in this encounter, a reminder of how love is bought and sold.[20] This happens just as Brás is on his way to see his betrothed. He arrives late. "We expected you earlier," says Virgília in greeting. For a moment, underscoring the sense of unease engendered by his chance meeting with Marcela, Brás hallucinates. He sees Marcela's pockmarked face superimposed on Virgília's "fresh, youthful, flowering" visage.[21]

Machado interrupts the narrative at this juncture, roughly at the midway point of the novel, to expound, in Brás's posthumous voice, the following mock-scientific explanation for the fatal interconnectedness, with all its unforeseeable turnings, of life. Using the classic language of physics, Brás observes:

> Start a ball rolling; it rolls along, comes in contact with another ball, transmits its motion to the other, and the second ball rolls along. Let us call the first ball Marcela; the second, Brás Cubas; and a third, Virgília. Let us assume that Marcela, having received a fillip from the past . . . came in contact with Brás Cubas, which, in turn, yielding to the force transmitted to it, began to roll, until it bumped into Virgília, which had been wholly alien to the first ball; and thus, by the simple transmission of force, opposite extremes of society come into relationship with each other, and there is established something that we may call the Unity of Human Misery.

> Dá-se movimento a uma bola, por exemplo; rola esta, encontra outra bola, transmite-lhe o impulso, e eis a segunda boa a rolar como a primeira rolou. Suponhamos que a primeira bola se chama . . . Marcela,—é uma simples suposição; a segunda, Brás Cubas; a terceira, Virgília. Temos que Marcela, recebendo um piparote do passado rolou até tocar em Brás Cubas, o qual, cedendo à força impulsiva, entrou a rolar também até esbarrar em Virgília, que não tinha nada com a primeira bola; e eis aí como, pela simples transmissão de uma força, se tocam os extremos sociais, e se estabelece uma cousa que poderemos chamar solidariedade do aborrecimento humano.[22]

Fatalism. In retrospect, Brás sees himself carried along by events and forces outside his control. He absolves himself of responsibility. It is true that every step along the way he acts and makes choices. But no series of actions, no particular concatenation of planned steps, could bear out over and against the general capriciousness of society—again, paradoxically, capricious and shifting on a constant, unchanging base. To further underscore the importance of this turning point, Brás admits that "from that point on, I was lost."[23] His father, heartbroken by his son's failure, dies soon thereafter and intones on his deathbed in disbelief, "A Cubas!"

In the first half of the book, Brás looks at the world through the eyes of a rich young man; and, though dominated in his attitudes and desires by his class and social position, he sees the world as an open field for his ambitions and for the fulfillment of his desires. In the second part of the book, he no longer has illusions. He has delusions and dissolutions.

Social Blindness

It is a commonplace to juxtapose Machado de Assis's irony and cynicism with the romanticism of Alencar or the earnestness of Aluísio Azevedo's Naturalism. But the passage about the colliding balls is no less blatant in its environmental determinism than the descriptions of the denizens of Azevedo's *Cortiço*. The difference, perhaps, is the degree to which Machado grants this determinism an interiority and hence an autonomy from the environment. From such land, and such manure, Brás emerges, but the land and the manure are inside Brás, not around him. It is his substance, not his surroundings that determine his attitude. He is shaped from the inside out and therefore concomitantly blind and all seeing. For this reason, he tends to betray a monstrous disregard for the interiority of others. His self-awareness, transposed, sees through the people in his life. Irony, wit, disinterested analysis—with these tools, sharpened with much practice on himself, Brás pins people's masks to the wall as he under-scores their flaws and reveals their hypocrisy. But he does not see the person; he can afford not to.

Augusto Meyer, an astute reader of Machado, observes in this connection that "the sickness starts with his consciousness . . . because excess lucidity de-stroys life's indispensable illusions" ("O mal começa com a consciência . . . pois o excesso de lucidez mata as ilusões indispensáveis à subsistência da vida").[24] This combination of insight and blindness manifests itself repeatedly in the novel. Perhaps the most troubling example occurs when Brás is confronted with Dona Plácida's pathetic life story. The woman, poor and vulnerable, has been co-opted by Brás and Virgília as a cover for their little house in Gambôa, their secret love nest. Her purpose, from Brás's perspective, is limited to playing a role, as "in some respects the real lady of the house." He describes his method of corrupting the poor woman.

> I wanted to win her over; I treated her with kindness and respect . . . with con-siderable effort, I won first her good will, then her confidence. When I knew I had her confidence, I trumped up a pathetic story of the great love between Virgília and me before she married, her father's obduracy, her husband's cruelty, and I do not remember what other novelette clichés. Dona Plácida accepted every page of the novelette. . . .
>
> [Then, twisting the knife] I was not unappreciative: I established a fund of five contos.

> Eu queria angariá-la, e não me dava por ofendido, tratava-a com carinho e res-peito; forcejava por obter-lhe a benevolência, depois a confiança. Quando obtive a confiança, imaginei uma história patética dos meus amores com Virgília, um caso anterior ao casamento, a resistência do pai, a dureza do marido, e não sei que outros toques de novela. D. Plácida não rejeitou uma só página da novela; aceitou-as todas. Era uma necessidade da consciência. Ao cabo de seis meses, quem nos visse juntos diria que D. Plácida era minha sogra.
>
> Não fui ingrato; fiz-lhe um pecúlio de cinco contos.[25]

There, then, at the end of his description of Dona Plácida, the true nature of the arrangement, the true measure of the balance of power, is revealed. Yet even in this, when the power of money screams, there is room to see the tactical maneuverings of a crafty subaltern woman. Did she believe every page of the novelette? Hardly likely for a woman of her age and experience. Like any good dependent in nineteenth-century Rio de Janeiro, she knew how to nod her head and appear to acquiesce in empty-headed awe of her superiors. Brás takes her at face value. But he also gives her 5 contos, which, by the way, he happened upon by chance—even his seeming acts of charity are corroded with hypocrisy.

Who "wins" this round of masters and servants? A good case can be made for Dona Plácida. We can leave aside the question of her honor and its putative value. Brás's planned activities in his little love nest have already discounted the value of honor below par. Money, on the other hand, is extremely valuable to the poor widow. Brás gives her money he has found in the street—money that has practically no "value" to him—and in doing so, provides her with a small fortune. Five contos is much more than a poor domestic servant could ever hope to possess in a lifetime of toil. The scene takes place around 1844. At the prevailing wage for domestic servants, it would have taken Dona Plácida thirty-four years to earn the same amount of money she obtained for sacrificing her honor in the name of Brás and Virgília's love affair.[26] Brás grossly overpays for this sacrifice.

Having won over Dona Plácida's confidence (probably more with money than tall tales), Brás is subjected to hearing her life story. With false enthusiasm ("Never repent your acts of generosity") he half-listens to her tale of woe, only to end the chapter, silent, staring at the cap of his shoe.[27] In the next chapter he ruminates on the plight of Dona Plácida. He imagines her asking at birth why she has been summoned into existence. The answer:

> We summoned you so that you would burn your fingers on pots and your eyes in sewing; so that you would eat little or nothing, rush around, become sick and then get well so that you might become sick again . . . until you wind up in the gutter or in a hospital. That is why we summoned you, in a moment of love.

> Chamamos-te para queimar os dedos nos tachos, os olhos na costura, comer mal, ou não comer andar de um lado para outro, na faina, adoecendo e sarando, com o fim de tornar a adoecer e sarar outra vez, triste agora, logo desesperada, amanhã resignada, mas sempre com as mãos no tacho e os olhos na costura, até acabar um dia na lama ou no hospital; foi para isso que te chamamos, num momento de simpatia.[28]

Her existence is nullified and flattened out into a series of clichés of poverty. Love itself is shown up as absurd and self-defeating. At least, that is how our blasé dead narrator sees things.

These chapters are as telling as a dozen thick tomes on the subject of relations between the rich and the poor in Rio de Janeiro during the nineteenth century. Brás concludes this section of the book, in some respects the heart of the story, by observing that without his "illicit love, probably Dona Plácida would have faced the same miserable old age as so many other human creatures." Cleansing his conscience, he offers the maxim, "Vice is often the fertilizing manure of virtue."[29] All true enough. It is Brás's strategic position, his wealth, that makes the arrangement possible. The river of life flows down from on high. But it is Dona Plácida's tactical decision to accept his offer that nets her 5 contos—and one can say that without Brás's blasé attitude and his general disregard for money, she would have come out much worse, regardless of the narrator's illicit love.

This ironic attitude emerges again in Brás's treatment of his brother-in-law, Cotrim.

> They used to call him avaricious, and perhaps they were right; but avarice is only an exaggerated form of a virtue, and with virtues as with budgets it is better to have an excess than a deficit. As his manner was very sharp, he had enemies, who accused him of barbarity. The only fact alleged to support this charge was that he frequently committed slaves to dungeon and that they were always dripping blood when released.

> Argüíam-no de avareza, e cuide que tinham razão; mas a avareza é apenas a exageração de uma virtude e as virtudes devem ser como os orçamentos: melhor é o saldo que o déficit. Como era muito seco de maneiras tinha inimigos, que chegavam a acusá-lo de bárbaro. O único fato alegado neste particular era o de mandar com freqüência escravos ao calabouço donde eles desciam a escorrer sangue.[30]

Following from Brás's original position regarding the particular soil and manure from which an individual grows, he absolves Cotrim of barbarity on account of the fact that "as he had long been engaged in smuggling slaves into the country, he had become accustomed to long-established methods of treatment that were somewhat harsher than those practiced in the regular slave trade." Brás concludes that Cotrim is blameless, because "one cannot honestly attribute to a man's basic character something that is obviously the result of a social pattern."[31]

Rather than read these passages simply as examples of Machadean irony, it is well to also read them directly, as depictions of consciousness in a particular social context, under the influence of a particular field of forces, at a particular moment in the trajectory of the lives in question. Any schoolchild can identify the irony in the passages regarding Cotrim's "virtue" and "blamelessness." It is more of a challenge to apprehend the truth, from a certain point of view, that gives the irony its bitter cutting edge. Here, we readers have wandered or been led into a box canyon. Society is built up with lies and clichés, but these are no less real; and the rules of the game, despite the appearance of chance and caprice, have worn deep ruts into the paths of men and women.

Excess lucidity destroys life's indispensable illusions.

Seeing too much, losing the capacity to go along with the fiction of the social order, Brás, defunct, has this "advantage." Certainly, in his life as he tells it, his decisions and perspectives are perfectly in tune in a literal sense with his appraisal of Cotrim. Brás, despite his volubility and caprice, is nothing if not conventional. He absolves himself in the same manner. Here, too, Augusto Meyer is particularly revealing; he observed as early as 1935 that the superficial play of caprice and irony covers over but does not obliterate a deeper consistency: "In Machado, the appearance of movement, the twists and jocularity are masks that hide a profound gravity—that is to say, a terrible stability. All the whirling movement ends marking time" ("Em Machado, a aparência de movimento, a pirueta e o malabarismo são disfarces que mal conseguem dissimular uma profunda gravidade—devia dizer: uma terrível estabilidade. Toda a sua trepidação acaba marcando passo").[32]

Meyer, here, refers to Machado and his oeuvre, but I argue he might just as well be referring to the social order underpinning this world of surface movement and interior stasis. This profound observation must be put in dialog with the equally perspicacious Antonio Candido, who points out that Machado is intensely attentive to the movement of society and the play of social forces: "Throughout his works there is a profound sense, much more than just documentary, of status, of the duel of salons, the movement of social groups, the power of money" ("Pela sua obra toda há um senso profundo, nada documentário, do status, do duelo dos salões, do movimento das camadas, da potência do dinheiro").[33]

An apparent paradox: A society that moves without changing, and volubility—a changeable and inconsistent character expressed in a talkative and chatty manner in which act and obligation are lost in a torrent of words—are layered on fundamentally stable structures. A caricature published in the *Bazar Volante*, one of Rio's many cultural periodicals of the era, captures the essence of this spinning movement without any change of position in the metaphor of the wind vane (Illustration 6). Here politics spins on an axis characterized by three politicians and their representative values.

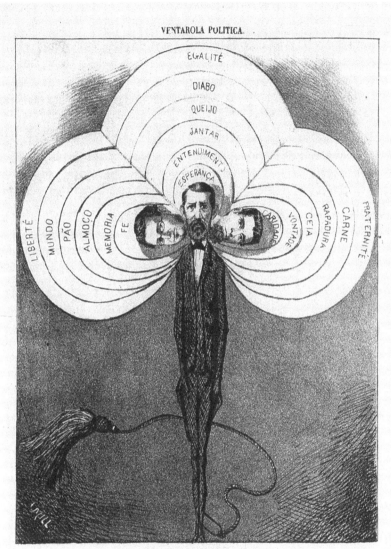

VENTAROLA POLITICA.

POR CAUSA DO INTENSO CALOR.

ILLUSTRATION 6. "Politics Blows with the Wind." Three imperial-era politicians, represented as a weather vane, spin according to empty ideas and inconsistent priorities.
SOURCE: *Bazar Volante* (1864).

The chief difference, among people confronted with this reality, is that the rich, like Brás, are playing heads I win, tails you lose; the poor, like Dona Plácida, are just losers. Money and social position ensure that nothing will change in Brás's life, regardless of his twists and turns, his serial defeats in love and politics. A terrible stability to be sure. The poor feel the blows more directly with burnt fingers and bent backs; their position is always vulnerable, susceptible to reversals and new hardships, the gutter and the hospital. This too, reveals a terrible stability in the shape of inevitability.

Machado drives home the point toward the end of the novel, as Dona Plácida's sickness and death are recounted. Brás and Quincas Borba have just returned to Brás's house, only to find a letter waiting from Virgília. Brás is surprised to read that Dona Plácida, sick and at death's door, wishes to be admitted to the Misericordia (public) hospital. He overcomes his initial reluctance to act and seeks out the poor woman, describing her as "a heap of bones covered with rags and stretched out on an old, nauseatingly dirty cot." A week later, she dies in the hospital. Reflecting on this, Brás references a previous chapter (Chapter 75), in which he pantomimed Dona Plácida, asking her progenitors why they had summoned her into existence. In his supreme egotism, Brás thinks:

> If it had not been for Dona Plácida, perhaps my affair with Virgília would have been interrupted or even terminated just as it was getting under way. . . . This, perhaps, was the purpose of Dona Plácida's life. A limited, relative purpose, I agree; but what the devil is absolute in this world?

> Se não fosse D. Plácida, talvez os meus amores com Virgília tivessem sido interrompidos, ou imediatamente quebrados, em plena efervescência; tal foi, portanto, a utilidade da vida de D. Plácida. Utilidade relativa, convenho; mas que diacho há absoluto nesse mundo?[34]

Role Distance

If Brás's volubility is taken as constituting the signature of a social class in a specific conjuncture following Schwarz's analysis, then what of his irony? Why the incessant drip of self-deprecation and the throwaway lines that undercut his position? Here, the concept of role distance, as elaborated by Erving Goffman, provides a useful frame of reference. According to Goffman, role distance is characterized by "actions which effectively convey some disdainful detachment of the performer from a role he is performing."[35] For example, adolescents riding a carousel will display role distance, showing that they know they are "too big" for such games, whereas young children will abandon themselves to the role of little horseback riders. Like many of Goffman's concepts, role distance is deceptively simple. It calls attention to something that we knew was there all along but failed to notice, to put a name to.

Brás studies "with profound mediocrity" while in Coimbra. He recounts how he did learn a few things at university: three lines from Virgil and two from Horace—the "shell, the ornamentation" of knowledge.[36] His pose is self-protective; he does not commit wholeheartedly to the role of student. The tendency appears throughout the novel and is indeed predicated on his pose as a defunct narrator. A dead man has the greatest possible role distance imaginable—his status as narrator reinscribes his detachment.

The role distance introduced by Machado in *Memórias Póstumas* appears to have both a stylistic and a structural dimension. Stylistically, following Eugenio Gomes's lead, it is possible to think of role distance in relation to what Gomes termed microrealism.[37] On the surface, this might sound like a contradiction: little details of big significance versus calculated attitudes of disinterest. As is typical in Machado, things are not quite what they seem. The microrealist insistence on the detailed and idiosyncratic generates a fragmented narrative. Things happen; they are what they are. The individual is subtly distanced from "things that happen" precisely by the microrealistic detail and the inevitable sense of narrative fragmentation created by such scenes. On a structural level, this process has already been well described by Schwarz. I would only add, from the more narrow perspective of this chapter and the theme of the bildungsroman, that the effect of role distance at both the microrealistic level and the structural level is to vitiate any chance of growth and integration. This is significant both with respect to the big picture, if we take the novel to be a metanarrative of Brazilian history and society, and to the story of Brás Cubas, if we take the novel to be a realistic depiction of a fictional character's experience and consciousness.

The Power of Money

Gold, that balm for disappointments and salve for the defeated, is something Brás has in abundance. After the death of his father, we learn that the size of his estate is large enough to ensure Brás a comfortable life without any necessity to work or to economize. In this sense, Brás occupies an unassailable position of privilege. He can continue to play to his whims and to treat others with contempt.

The settlement of the estate is made complicated by a feud between Brás and his brother-in-law, Cotrim. Brás argues that his father's house is worth at least 58 contos; Cotrim thinks it is worth at most 30. Their difference of opinion itself stems from their attitudes toward money and its relation to the value of things. Brás appeals to the fact that the house cost 58 contos. Cotrim argues that, with the real estate market down, it could not be sold for much more than 30. Given the precision with which Machado lards the text with these figures, it is well worth putting such sums in a broader historical context, because Machado's writing is never casual in *Memórias Póstumas* and because the figures in context help better place the characters in their social milieu. Whether the true value of the house is the higher figure preferred by Brás or the lower one proffered by Cotrim, this is an extremely expensive property, almost to the point of caricature. A graph of property transactions from around the time this scene in the novel is set illustrates the distribution of values (Figure 2).

From Figure 2 we see that only one house in the whole transaction sample approaches the value Brás cites.[38] The sum of 58 contos was, in 1849, equivalent to the market value of approximately 135 adult slaves or 300 years' worth of pay for an unskilled laborer.[39] With this kind of money, it is easier to see how Brás ends up so out of touch with the reality surrounding him.

Returning to the novel, we see that Brás takes the naïve view of the idle rich, thinking things are worth just what they cost. Cotrim, the crafty businessman and slave trader, sees a market and opportunities to bargain. The quarrel ex-

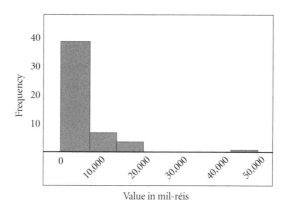

FIGURE 2. Distribution of housing sales by value: Rio de Janeiro, 1849.

SOURCE: "Recebedoria das sizas dos bens de raiz do ano financeiro de 1849/50," Arquivo Nacional, Rio de Janeiro, livro 19.

tends to the division of slaves and personal property. Cotrim wants to keep just one slave, Bento Cubas's coachman. Brás, keeping the coach, wants the coachman as well. Cotrim yields and says he is willing to take Paulo and Prudêncio. But Prudêncio has been freed. Cotrim shows his callousness in the next lines, where he thrusts sarcastically, "How about the silver? I don't suppose your father liberated the silver." Brás wants the silver, as someday he "may get married." Sabina asks, "What for?" Cotrim parries with an offer of Paulo and the other slave for the silver. The argument ends at an impasse.[40]

Further examples of the corrosive power of money abound in the novel. There is, of course, the famous line about Marcela loving him for 11 contos. Money buys sex. Then there is the digression, reminiscent of a scene in *Sense and Sensibility*, where Brás is saved by a muleteer and goes through the winding thought process of determining the right amount of money to give the man as a reward: a gold coin? silver? would copper do? He gives silver and then regrets being so generous.[41] Money calls forth this kind of casuistic calculation in everything it touches.

The Space of the City

Machado, like Alencar in his urban novels, uses the space of Rio de Janeiro as a principal component in the plot of *Memórias Póstumas*. Locations here are less thoroughly described. There is a shorthand to the space of the city. Botafogo, Tijuca, Gambôa, the Rua do Ouvidor—each space conjures up a complex amalgam of physical attributes, relationships to other spaces, and cultural significations. If one were to map the city of Rio de Janeiro in light of *Memórias Póstumas*, one would discover a set of coordinates in three dimensions: public-private, rich-poor, and open-closed. Chance encounters take place in open public spaces, such as the theater, public parks, and streets. Brás chances upon his old slave, Prudêncio, in the street. Prudêncio, since freed, is now the owner of a slave of his own. As Brás watches Prudêncio whip his slave, he reflects without any hint of criticism on how his former slave came to understand the ways of the master through his own sufferings at Brás's hands.[42] While carrying on his affair with Virgília, Brás bumps into Lobo Neves, the cuckold in the theater, where "we were ill at ease and cool to each other" at first.[43] Walking in the park, he encounters his old school friend Quincas Borba, now reduced to rags.

The urban milieu, then, is a space of chance encounters, any of which may turn out to be decisive. Brás runs into Marcela, pocked and ugly, and this encounter throws him off track in his courtship of Virgília. The other extreme is closed private space, the little love nest lost in the back streets of Gambôa. There, Brás feels he has found a refuge, a small paradise where, with Virgília, he could start "a new phase in our love, an appearance of exclusive possession, of absolute dominion." The advantages of getting lost in the urban milieu are manifold: "Now I could avoid the frequent dinners, the tea every evening. . . . The house would set me free from it all; the ordinary world would end at the door. Inside, would be the infinite, an eternal, higher world, with no laws, no institutions."[44] The Brazilian social historian Sidney Chalhoub pointed out to me the deep irony in this last statement of Brás's regarding the little house in Gambôa: the love nest "with no laws" is located in precisely the same neighborhood as was the focal point of the clandestine slave trade.[45]

Between these opposed spatial regions, best thought of as permeable and unstable, lie the many semipublic and semiprivate spaces of the urban milieu. Among these, one could highlight the dinner party, the dance, and the box at the theater. Brás witnesses the illicit kiss between Villaça and Dona Eusébia in the garden after a dinner party. The shadows of the garden *might* be a place for a little private scene, underwritten by the semipublic shell surrounding the event.[46] Brás rekindles, or better discovers in definitive fashion, his love for Virgília by waltzing with her at a dance.

Finally, it bears noting that the space of Tijuca, which represents an alternative world far from the hubbub of the city, appears in Brás's story just as it did in Ricardo's. In Tijuca, Brás withdraws to mourn his mother's death. He engages in a bout of "voluptuous" solitude. While in Tijuca, he is removed from the game, from the competition in the city down below. It is here too that he glimpses his first chance at true love—the difference, of course, being that Eugênia, the girl he meets and considers briefly as a potential love interest, is poor, lame, and a "natural" child tarred in Brás's memory by her connection "to the thicket, to Villaça." Thus Brás excuses himself by dumping shopworn social prejudice on the lame girl, doubting that she could be "false to your blood, to your origin . . ."[47] The ellipsis evinces a thought trailing off, underlining the lazy prejudice, the cliché, in Brás's thinking.

Brás Cubas and Ricardo Nunes Compared

The lucidity and self-awareness of the narrator in Brás Cubas derives, on one level, from his status as a deceased narrator—that is, retrospective lucidity. As he recounts his life story, he knows how things will end. Yet, at the same time, Brás reveals to us his state of mind, his consciousness, at each specific point of time in the narrative. Although he knows how the story will end, he does not generally allow himself to interpose posterior knowledge or outcomes on the telling of the story itself. This is not to say that the interpretation of Brás's consciousness is in any way unproblematic. Rather, the value of the book is to be found in the odd combination of a terribly lucid narrator who nonetheless hides from himself the retrospective meaning of events as they unfold. As Brás himself puts it in a posthumous soliloquy directed to Virgília:

> It is this very capacity (to reconstruct the truth *as of that time*) that makes us masters of the earth, this capacity to restore the past and thus to prove the instability of our impressions and the vanity of our affections. Let Pascal say that man is a thinking reed. He is wrong; man is a thinking erratum. Each period in life is a new edition that corrects the preceding one.

> Mas é isso mesmo que nos faz senhores da Terra, é esse poder de restaurar o passado, para tocar a instabilidade das nossas impressões e a vaidade dos nossos afetos. Deixa lá dizer Pascal que o homem é um caniço pensante. Não, é uma errata pensante, isso sim.[48]

This mode of narration and this depiction of consciousness, of a certain man of a particular class, bears comparison with the depiction of the state of mind of Ricardo Nunes in *Sonhos d'Ouro*. Both Brás and Ricardo are highly self-aware; in both novels the protagonist sets out on the path of *Bildung*. The difference in class and consciousness, and therefore in approach to building a life, is not only marked by the stylistic choices of Alencar and Machado but also deeply stamped in the trajectories of the two men. Here, we are confronted with the difference that great wealth made in the lives of sensitive (Ricardo) and self-aware (Brás) young men in Rio de Janeiro during the nineteenth century.

Expectations

Ricardo, as the son of a poor family in São Paulo, represents the provincial man striving for education, career, and ultimately marriage in the competitive world of Rio de Janeiro. Having obtained his law degree, he moves with his friend Fábio from law school, to the Corte to seek his fortune. His choices are highly constrained. First, as a poor young man in São Paulo, the law school is his best and indeed his only option with respect to obtaining a respectable education. As a student, he lives on the limited funds that his uncle is able to provide and the limited resources of his own family. His education is a collective effort, entailing sacrifices on the part of his mother and sister. For Ricardo, the first steps along the path of the bildungsroman are laden with the weight of obligations incurred, debts to be repaid, and promises made in the light of a long time horizon. Although Antonio Candido is probably right in observing that Alencar's characters lack the sense of drama found in the struggle in Balzac's young men of similar coinage, in Ricardo we find elements of the carefully wrought life plan, with all the baggage such plans bring. Although it is true that Ricardo ends up being helped up the ladder secretly by Guida, this does not detract from the value of the depiction of Ricardo's life plan and its attendant representation of *Bildung* for a particular class of provincial men.[49]

Recall that Ricardo's plan was simply this: obtain an education at all costs, move to the Corte to earn 20 contos, and then return to São Paulo to marry. Complications, however, made the plan all the more urgent and binding. Ricardo needed this money to repay debts and provide for the marriages of both his sister, betrothed to his friend Fábio, and himself, betrothed to his cousin in exchange for her uncle's assistance with student bills. Many lives, not just his own, were hanging in the balance. How many families must have made similar desperate wagers on the hopes of a bright young man? Thus with this weight on his shoulders, Ricardo sets out into the competitive world of Rio de Janeiro. And there is one further crucial complication: He is sensitive, proud, and conscientious to a fault. With these characteristics, Alencar asks in the voice of Ricardo's opening soliloquy, Is there any hope for success?

For Brás Cubas, a similar life plan is traced out. Although Brás's great wealth ensures that his position in society is guaranteed and that there will be no need for struggle, a common chord is struck in the degree to which his life path is laid out for him by his family and his social position. Education, in this case overseas in Coimbra, is expected, not so much to guarantee a career as to mark with the proper distinction a young man of his social background. He will never actually need to use his education to obtain an occupation. This is for the best, because he admits that at Coimbra he studied "with profound mediocrity." Yet his degree is "a letter of enfranchisement," and his university experience has given him, as he puts it, "an impulse, a curiosity, a desire to elbow other people out of the way, to exert influence, to enjoy, to live—to prolong my college days throughout my life."[50] Brás is indifferent to the content of his education because his wealth ensures that it does not matter what he learns or whether he learns it well.

Ricardo studies hard and is one of the most brilliant students in his cohort at the law school in São Paulo. His counterpart, Guimarães, is by way of contrast, a character similar to Brás Cubas. Guimarães is sent to law school by his rich father not so that the son might pursue a career in the law but as a sign of status. The young man shows no inclination to work, instead living off loans on his future inheritance.[51] As for his expectations, these are limited to living and marrying well: virtually ensured outcomes on account of his wealth.

3 O CORUJA

IF *SONHOS D'OURO* involved the problem of not having enough money and *Memórias Póstumas* was about having too much, then *O Coruja* is about having and then losing a fortune. Aluísio Azevedo (1857–1913), most famous for his naturalistic novel *O Cortiço*, is the author of a dozen novels and several plays and a range of shorter pieces and journalism. Born in the province of Maranhão, he studied in mediocre local schools until the age of 13 and then was apprenticed to a commercial firm on the wishes of his father. Bookish and uninterested in business, Azevedo left São Luís at 17 to follow in his older brother Arthur's footsteps and seek his career in Rio de Janeiro.

Aluísio Azevedo was the natural son of David Azevedo, a Portuguese merchant resident in Maranhão since the 1820s. There is nothing unusual in being a natural child. As seen in the discussion of José de Alencar, children born out of wedlock made up nearly half of all births in urban Brazil. What was unusual was the fact that Aluísio was listed in the parish register as the natural son of David Azevedo rather than his mother, who was not named. In practically every other case, the roles would be reversed. The explanation is simple: Aluísio's mother, Emília Amália Pinto de Magalhães, was married to another man at the time of Aluísio's birth. Such a child, technically speaking, would be considered adulterine and spurious rather than natural. Naming the mother would have therefore made a natural designation impossible. Once the erstwhile husband of Emília died in 1864, David Azevedo immediately recognized his sons again, conferring rights to them as though they had been born legitimate.

The significance of Azevedo's unusual family background to his art can be traced in at least two main directions. First, as Jean-Yves Mérian's biography takes pains to show, Azevedo's parents provided an example of freely given love in a situation outside conventional marriage. The experience of his mother, if he was privy to it, would also have made him sensitive to the ills of arranged marriages and the brutality of husbands toward their wives in many such situations.[1] These unconventional parents also provided a nurturing and bookish environment for their sons. David was a founder of the Gabinete Português de Leitura in São Luís, where Aluísio and Arthur could peruse the latest edition of the *Revue des Deux Mondes* or a French or Portuguese novel at their leisure.[2] This home setting, typified by love and books, was doubly important, because from all accounts Azevedo's school experience was more likely to quash than inspire intellectual growth. He generally disliked his teachers, and it seems they returned the sentiment; learning was shallow and rote.[3] This too would become material for the young writer's fiction.

Second, the fact that Aluísio's father failed in business and was not, therefore, able to place his sons in the typical institutions of elite education—the law schools in Recife or São Paulo or the medical schools in Rio or Salvador—meant that the boys' education was truncated and that they were apprenticed to Portuguese merchant houses as teenagers. Both Aluísio and Arthur chafed against the reins of workaday commerce; each left to seek his literary fortune in Rio de Janeiro before turning 20. Yet this experience in the world of work and commerce stood them in good stead during their writing careers. Aluísio mined his days of commercial apprenticeship when writing the detailed descriptions of the business scene in books such as *Filomena Borges, Casa de Pensão*, and *O Cortiço*. The failure of his father's business, though it occurred before he was born, probably also colored his sense of the drama of commercial life and the tenuousness of fortune.[4]

Such were the early years of Aluísio Azevedo's life: a mixture of intellect and boredom, of fine sentiment and temporary resignation to the rather poor hand life had dealt him in his family's relatively penurious financial standing and provincial location. The location problem could be solved relatively easily by moving to the Corte. The financial end of things would prove a more substantial struggle and require a return trip to Maranhão to help care for his mother in the aftermath of his father's death in 1878. It was back in the provinces that Azevedo wrote his first novel, *O Mulato*, which has been credited with helping introduce the Naturalist novel to Brazil.[5]

In the month immediately preceding the first appearance of *O Coruja* in
O País, Azevedo began to publish a satire of student life with the title "Ruy
Vaz, cenas da boêmia fluminense" in the magazine *A Semana*.[6] Mérian suggests
that more than a little bit of autobiographical material crept into this never
completed fragment of a book.[7] One cannot help but read "Ruy Vaz" and think
of the experience Azevedo must have had arriving in the great city roughly
a decade earlier. In an early scene the protagonist is depicted on the deck of
a steamship bound for Rio de Janeiro. A conversation with a more seasoned
traveler transpires as the city approaches.

> Traveler: What are your plans in Rio de Janeiro?
> Ruy: Who knows! To work, study, make a man of myself, earn a living.
> . . .
> Traveler: And you still don't have your eye on a particular career?
> Ruy: Lots of them. . . .
> Traveler: That's bad.
> Ruy: Yes, but that's how it is.
> Traveler: And which of them tends to grab your fancy?
> Ruy: I still don't know, perhaps painting, maybe literature, or theater or jour-
>   nalism, maybe all of them at once.
>
> Traveler: Quais são os teus projetos no Rio de Janeiro?
> Ruy: Sei lá! Trabalhar, estudar, fazer-me homem, ganhar a vida.
> . . .
> Traveler: E ainda não tens alguma carreira de olho?
> Ruy: Muitas.
> Traveler: Isso é mal.
> Ruy: Será, mas é assim.
> Traveler: E qual d'elas tencionas abraçar de preferência?
> Ruy: Ainda não sei . . . talvez a pintura, talvez a literatura, talvez o teatro, talvez
>   o jornalismo, talvez tudo isso a um tempo.[8]

The last line can serve as Azevedo's curriculum vitae circa 1885: He moved
to Rio with the idea of becoming a painter; he worked as a caricaturist for various newspapers and eventually tried his hand at literature and the theater. It
is in *O Coruja* that he explores most completely the themes of education and
social integration, the heart of the bildungsroman. "Ruy Vaz" can be seen as a
first attempt at such a novel, and perhaps in the end is was too autobiographical for Azevedo's purposes. What is clear is that the author planned to write a

novel in the genre of the bildungsroman and that there is a direct connection between the fragment and the completed novel, both written in the same year and in consecutive months.

In contrast to Azevedo's more famous works, *O Coruja* has fallen almost completely from critical view, perhaps, in part, because it has been rather unjustly classified as one of his light serial fictions (*romance-folhetim*). This is a pity because the book has both literary and historical merit. No less a critic than Oliveira Lima observed a century ago that *O Coruja* is "in some sense the most suggestive and attractive of all his books" ("de algum modo o mais sugestivo e o mais atraente dos seus livros").[9] Indeed, Azevedo's best biographer, Jean-Yves Mérian, while placing *O Coruja* in the *romance-folhetim* category, notes that even though these books are not "romances de tese" in the manner of Zola, they nonetheless are hybrid confections, with social and political critique overlaid on fantastic elements more typical of the form.[10] Here, I would go further: *O Coruja* contains little of the fantastic or fanciful; it is not, by content or structure, a serial novel of the light entertainment type in any way. Consequently, it belongs in the same discussion as *O Cortiço* on the grounds of literary seriousness, if not on the grounds of literary quality.[11]

Careers

In Azevedo's novel, Teobaldo and André are two young men on the threshold of life who offer a study in contrasts. Teobaldo is the son of a baron—rich, suave, and confident. André, a son of a deceased *procurador* (administrator), is orphaned and raised by a priest. He is poor, socially inept, and antipathetic. Together in their adolescent years while students at a small *colégio* in the interior province of Minas Gerais, they become friends through the one thing they have in common: the hatred they inspire in the rest of their schoolmates. Hatred, then, of the rich son of a baron for his airs; hatred of André for the simple fact that he is small and ugly.

O Coruja offers the story of two men as they traverse the ups and downs of life together in Rio de Janeiro during the second half of the nineteenth century. The plot has many of the elements of the classic bildungsroman: young men, finding their way, or getting lost, in the world.[12] First there is the provincial back story, followed by the story of arrival in the big city, with its possibilities and pitfalls, and then the period of education and, for André, work. In parallel, the characters are subject to amorous experiences, again quite distinctive according to their place in society and temperament. The novel reaches a kind of plateau when Teobaldo kidnaps and marries the rich, but in the end not quite rich enough, Branca. The last half of the book shows the unraveling of Teobaldo's life, owing in no small measure to his partial and essentially failed *Bildung*. That is, not having learned or truly evolved into an integrated personality with a stable relationship to society, he disintegrates as the ineluctable result of his own internal failings, which are exacerbated by his milieu.

In this regard *O Coruja* explores the pathways trod by the principal characters, and it attempts to show how those paths are influenced and circumscribed by the broader environment. Ultimately, Azevedo's determinism throws into doubt the degree to which true autonomy and growth were possible in nineteenth-century Rio. The elements of the bildungsroman are present, but the Naturalistic emphasis on heredity and milieu cuts the characters off at the knees. They cannot help but act as they do. Their growth is stunted, blocked, undercut. The great theme of the novel is the failure to grow up, not that the grown-ups in the novel fare better. They too, perhaps as victims of a society that refuses to grow responsible and sober, fail to attain their goals.

Bildung cut short, flustered, stymied. If this is the primary theme, then the secondary theme is love: love denied, stolen, betrayed, lost. The theme of love can be divided into two parts: the carnal and the sacred. Often unthinking, always excessive, carnal love in *O Coruja* ends in bitter tears and recrimination. Chaste and calm, the sacred love of marriage also ends in tears owing to the falsity and hypocrisy that rot away its foundations.

Pursued by lovers from the demimonde, stealing the love of a young girl with a large dowry, losing her love through callous vanity and inconstancy, finding hollow success in literature and politics, Teobaldo, who is incapable of growing up, exemplifies Azevedo's extremely pessimistic vision of Rio de Janeiro's social and cultural life during the second half of the nineteenth century. André, Teobaldo's best (and only) friend from their school days in Minas Gerais, represents the opposite kind of personality: a person who is driven to good deeds and self-abnegation. The results are not all that different. Without Teobaldo's looks, money, and confidence, André cannot hope to rise above the lowly status of a teacher in a *colégio* or, in the days of his highest hopes, the owner of such a school. This is not a society where paths of social mobility open for the virtuous and hardworking. The best case for André is a modicum of success in the strictly delimited space open to him. Teobaldo can work on a broad canvas. He can do anything; therefore in the end he does nothing. André, hardworking and honest, is equally stymied, derailed time and again by his friend.

Taken as a whole, the portrait of society painted in *O Coruja* is one with strong tones of fatalism and futility. Either people are hopelessly flawed and ill-equipped for the slings and arrows of real life and the milieu of the metropolis, or they are doomed to be defeated by the contradictions and caprice of a rotten society that sees "talent" in a vacuous parasite like Teobaldo.

It is instructive to note that the son of a baron (hence, in this period, the son of a slaveholder of major proportions) is expected to study and to take on some kind of liberal profession. Law or medicine, which will it be? Teobaldo, upon arrival in Rio de Janeiro with his friend André, nicknamed "O Coruja" (the owl) in tow, sets about deciding on his future. Arrival. Teobaldo does not merely show up in Rio de Janeiro. Sampaio, a business associate of his father, meets him at the Porto da Estrela station and provides a place to stay while Teobaldo makes living arrangements. He also offers words of advice to the young student.

> Keep clear of the *francesas* [women of easy virtue]! . . . They do nothing but empty the pockets of fools! . . . You came to Rio to study, right? Well then, bury your nose in books and close your eyes to the rest!

> É preciso ter muito cuidado com as francesas! . . . Esses diabos de que vai se enchendo o Rio de Janeiro e que não fazem outra coisa senão esvaziar as algibeiras dos tolos! . . . O senhor veio ao Rio foi para estudar, não é? Pois enterre a cara dentro dos livros e feche os olhos ao mais!

He continues:

> Not that you can't enjoy yourself, go to the theater once in a while . . . avoid bad company, flee from the lazy bums, stay clear of the Rua do Ouvidor, don't enter the cafes . . . (and in a low voice) don't mess around with writing.

> Não digo que não se divirta . . . consinto que vá ao teatro de vez em quando . . . evite as más companhias, fuja dos vadios e dos viciosos; não freqüente a rua do Ouvidor; não entre nos cafés! E, abaixando a voz e chegando-se mais para o moço, disse, com o mistério de quem faz uma revelação terrível:—E, principalmente, meu amigo, não se meta a escrevinhador.[13]

Of course, Teobaldo will violate each of Sampaio's dicta. And the dicta spell out the itinerary of youth in the city: the pathway of experience. Teobaldo's tragic flaw, his vanity and attendant volubility, ensure that, rather than pass through these experiences, he ends up hopelessly lost. Or rather, he passes twice through the itinerary: once as the rich, handsome son of a baron and then as the destitute son of a bankrupt suicide. The second is a fraudulent passage, a thicket of debts and lies to sustain an image and a way of living no longer in reach. It is worth noting that in this story the countryside offers no counterbalance to the city. It is neither a place of virtue nor a reservoir of resources.[14]

Meanwhile, what to do? Teobaldo considers law at first. But this would require him to leave Rio de Janeiro and return once more to the provinces, this time São Paulo, because there was no law school in the capital during the era in question. Besides, the law is boring and seems to require a degree of duplicity—proving the guilty innocent and such—that Teobaldo claims to find revolting. Given what we learn about the man's lack of scruples over the course of the novel, this objection smacks of a cheap excuse rather than a genuine aversion to legal casuistry. Medicine also does not attract him at first, neither for that matter does engineering, because he is terrible at mathematics. Yet as André insists on reminding him, Teobaldo must "choose something."[15] His position and pedigree demand it. For a young man of his talent—that is, with his parentage, looks, and money—there is no question of abandoning study altogether and entering into business, that is, working.[16]

Teobaldo ends up deciding on medicine, not so much out of great love for the subject or desire for a genuine career, but because he can study medicine in Rio and carry on his bohemian student ways in the comforts of the capital with all its nocturnal attractions.[17] The arbitrary nature of his choice is brought out in a brief exchange with André.

> "I've decided on medicine!"
> "But I thought you were going to the military academy . . ."
> "I changed my mind."[18]

The study of medicine, in fact, requires a degree of serious commitment, and Teobaldo is constitutionally incapable of advancing in his studies. He abandons himself to a life of the theater, hotel restaurants, and taverns. Given the subsequent trajectory of his life, it is not possible, however, to conclude that Teobaldo, in abandoning his studies, misses a true opportunity for growth and the chance at a calling and an honest occupation. Whatever the case, whether he completes his studies or not, he belongs to the class of men for whom university degrees are essentially decorative. In literary terms he is in the company of Brás Cubas, Bento Santiago, Carlos Maia, Frédéric Morreau,

Juanito Santa Cruz, and so forth.[19] In historical terms the record provides no direct accounting of doctors who practiced their vocation versus their colleagues who held the title of doctor but otherwise dedicated themselves to other pursuits, such as literature, journalism, politics, and business, or, in cases akin to Teobaldo's, to pure dissipation and parasitic existence on the money of family and friends.

For Azevedo, the emphasis on heredity and environment means that the profile of a character such as Teobaldo, however detailed and realistic, is at its core essentially static. The situation could and did change, but the character stayed the same. Teobaldo, it is important to emphasize, is not static in the sense of being insensitive or incapable of adaptation. Quite the contrary. He is mutable, almost Zelig-like. Yet at root, he is always the self-regarding and capricious son of a baron, with a sense of entitlement and a taste for idle living, pleasure, and praise. His *Bildung* is stunted because he is incapable of inner transformation; he cannot adjust his personality in such a way as to create a healthy integration of his inner life and the social world surrounding him. Instead, he manipulates his friends and lies to himself. Through extremely questionable means, he attains a superficial success, but he remains forever restless and unreconciled with society. His mask, worn so long yet changed so often, has become his face—an unstable and unfulfilled face representing the decadent bourgeois subject in Azevedo's gallery of portraits.

> Thus he became habituated to this false life, which many young men lead: free tickets to the theater, tabs open everywhere; he owed the mercer, the shoemaker, the hotel, but went about always with the same elegance, drinking the same wines.

> E assim se foi habituando a essa fictícia existência, que no Rio de Janeiro levam muitos rapazes: entrada franca nos teatros, contas abertas em toda a parte, devia ao chapeleiro, ao sapateiro, ao hotel, mas andava sempre com a mesma elegância e bebia os mesmos vinhos.[20]

This state of affairs is aggravated by meeting acquaintances from better times. The only way to uphold the image, to sustain the fiction, is to accompany them to the theater or to the restaurant, and to dig ever deeper into debt.

Later, after Teobaldo has ascended to the pinnacle of conventional "success" and spent most of Branca's dowry on frivolities and rich living, he has not changed in any significant way from his first days as a bohemian student in the

Corte or his days of secret poverty and debt. With a cutting sense of irony, his rival, Aguiar, lists his "accomplishments." Azevedo then sums up:

> [He could] with the same ease compose a waltz, write a poem, draw a landscape, makes a speech, write a political article, write editorial criticism, sing a baritone part, sustain conversation in a salon, direct a cotillion, invent a trifle for a ladies' hat, come up with an exquisite dish for dinner, as much as make a list of the best wines in the world as to classify all the philosophical systems known to man. . . . He knew everything and yet nothing at the same time.

> Com a mesma facilidade com que compõe uma valsa, escreve um poema, desenha uma paisagem, faz um discurso, escreve um artigo político, engendra um folhetim de crítica, canta uma parte de barítono, sustenta uma conversação de uma sala, dirige um cotillon, inventa um feito de chapéu para senhora, um prato esquisito para o jantar, e tão pronto está para fazer uma lista dos melhores vinhos do mundo, como para fazer a classificação de todos os sistemas filosóficos até hoje conhecidos. . . . Conhecia tudo e nada conhecia ao mesmo tempo.[21]

And what of André's story? Genuine ability and a serious disposition are not enough to open a path for André in the capital. He tries and fails to obtain positions as a teacher. Despite his ability, he is no doubt passed over by this society, fixated on surface appearances, because of own his appearance and manner. His first job is arranged by means of the tried and true client-patron system. Through a "friend" of Sampaio's, the business associate of Teobaldo's father, a position for André is arranged at a newspaper. His starting salary is 30 mil-réis per month. That is, 360 mil-réis per year. Teobaldo, shocked at the low pay, asks what hours André will work, and his friend responds, from 7 in the morning to 11 at night.[22]

Over the course of the book, André's role is essentially secondary: a foil to Teobaldo and an occasional enabler of his wayward friend's schemes. He is a minor character in every sense, yet his nickname graces the cover of the book. Here, Azevedo reveals another layer of his artistic sensibility. The presence of André, "O Coruja," decenters the narrative just enough to keep it from collapsing into the vortex of Teobaldo's egoism. I address this subject in greater detail in Chapter 4 with respect to the comparison between Teobaldo and Brás Cubas. For now, I focus on the internal dynamics of the novel and the way that André's entry and integration into Rio society is also a failure, caused in no small part by his elegant friend.

André, like Teobaldo, is static at heart. He does not change or grow in the course of the novel. From start to finish, he is earnest and loyal. He is hardworking and unlucky in business and love. His environment changes, and he moves slightly up, then down, then up the social scale. In every instance he maintains the same front. He wears only one mask. If Teobaldo represents the cautionary tale of having and wanting too much, of selfishness cutting off access to a good life, André's is the story of having and wanting too little. Too much self-abnegation prevents the Owl from capitalizing on opportunities and having the life Azevedo implies he deserves—marriage, a decent job, a happy home. This self-effacing character approaches tragic stature precisely because Azevedo provides a believable set of motivations for his worst decisions. He is the childhood friend of Teobaldo, and his friend shows him kindness when he needs it most. Manipulative and selfish friends have been the downfall of loyal and selfless comrades since time immemorial. Only a bit of artistic license need be granted to make André conform to our sense of what constitutes a realistic personality. What is more, his odd codependence with Teobaldo speaks directly to one of the most important themes in the literature of the era: the vexed relationship between the rich and the free poor—the mutual entanglements created by the presence of semi-autonomous dependents in the world of powerful and wealthy men like Teobaldo.

Why does André maintain the connection to his own material and spiritual detriment? Certainly, the answer is not for any pecuniary reason. Teobaldo is a constant drain on André's limited resources. No, the reason is as simple as it is sad: The relationship offers André his only connection to a life of beauty and grace (as hollow as it ultimately proves) and to a friend who is beautiful and graceful. For a poor and ugly man to be recognized, spoken to, even loved in the limited fashion available to a personality like Teobaldo, is to be elevated. The tie is almost feudal in essence, and the bond of loyalty from the poor and ugly to the rich is unbreakable. Plus, everyone knows schoolyard friends are often friends for life, regardless of the twists and turns of individual fates. The relationship offers a subtle inversion of the theme of favor in Brazilian society. It is not always the powerful who bestow favor upon the weak; the powerful are not always strong.

The description of André's poor childhood and his unloved condition as an orphan boy raised by a nasty and cold priest primes the reader to accept his subsequent adulation of Teobaldo. School is depicted as a spiritual and mental desert, populated by bullies in the playground and ignorant teachers at the head of the classroom. Azevedo probably drew on his own rather desultory school experience for some of the realistic coloring of this period in André and Teobaldo's upbringing. André finds an alternative world in the books lining the shelves of the library, where he retreats to escape the insults and pummeling handed out by his uncouth classmates. Again, we know that Azevedo spent many hours reading books from the Gabinete Português de Leitura, a library founded in São Luís by his father. Unfortunately for André, unlike his creator, he is far too poor, ugly, and antipathetic to have any chance of translating what he reads in books into a pathway of life. Rather than immersing himself in novels or plays, the quintessential tools for the imagining of bourgeois personalities and solutions to social integration, André ends up surrounded by arcane history tomes, writing the impossible history of Brazil. André is a valid precursor to the much more famous literary creation of Lima Barreto— Policarpo Quaresma, another man of some considerable talent beating his head against the proverbial wall of Brazilian society and history.

To the extent that André finds himself making choices rather than being buffeted by chance and the powerful waves created by those around him, especially Teobaldo, his choices center on his long and never consummated courtship of the young Inez, daughter of the colorful Dona Margarita. André finds himself courted by the girl's mother, who is desperate to get her daughter married to a decent man, the sooner the better given her little family's marginal social position. At first, he seems like a good catch with his learning and seriousness (and low but respectable income and position).

The problems of getting married for poor people rear up in this case with a vengeance. André in this sense is like a poor and ugly version of Ricardo in *Sonhos d'Ouro*. His sense of scruples and honor prevent him from marrying Inez without first establishing himself financially. The mother also holds out, waiting to see some signs of true success in the suitor's endeavors. A poor man without a profession faced even longer odds than the talented penniless lawyer in Alencar's bildungsroman. In the end, the ebb tide of poverty and social marginalization proves too strong. André's fatal friendship with Teobaldo leads him to make a series of loans to his childhood companion, none of which are repaid.

The last loan is for Teobaldo's ill-fated attempt at currency speculation. All the money is lost in this get-rich-quick scheme, and André is unable to redeem a note of credit with his bank for the original capital from his *colégio*. The bank forces a sale, André is ruined once more, and he loses Inez to the semi-employed drunkard Alferes Picuinha.[23] His reputation in tatters, his wallet empty, and his fiancée lost, André closes himself up in his room and returns to his hopeless project of writing the complete and true history of Brazil. Beneath the layer of burlesque and farce, the undoing of André and his impossible history project sound the depths of an essentially capricious social order, which, making no logical sense, cannot be put back together in a coherent narrative. Instead, his room is filled with notes, extracts, incomplete chapters, and disconnected threads. The more André collects and learns, the more lost he becomes.[24]

Azevedo draws an explicit contrast at this juncture between the falsity of Teobaldo's political maneuverings and André's solitary studies.

> Thus, as one could not descry the sacrifices and miracles invented by Teobaldo in order to maintain his opulent appearance, no one was able to discover that, during these glittering parties, a poor sod was losing sleep there above in the attic, engaged in a war without quarter, to devour books, dive into old tomes, and pass hours paralyzed in front of a page with the vain hope of clarifying some obscure historical fact about his country.
>
> Never in his life was Teobaldo so brilliant and the Owl so obscure, so forgotten and difficult. Now the poor devil needed more than ever to make some money; his resources were in vertiginous decline. Unable to lie, incapable of the least charlatanism, he was his own worst enemy.

> E, assim como não se podia adivinhar os sacrifícios e os milagres inventados por Teobaldo para manter aquela aparência de grandeza, ninguém seria capaz de desconfiar que, durante essas reuniões, um desgraçado perdia as noites lá em cima, no sótão, entregue a um trabalho sem tréguas, a compulsar livros, a mergulhar em alfarrábios, a passar horas e horas estático defronte de uma página, só com a esperança de esclarecer algum ponto mais obscuro da história do seu país.
>
> Ah! se jamais a vida de Teobaldo foi tão brilhante, a de Coruja nunca foi tão obscura, tão despercebida e tão difícil. Agora precisava o pobre diabo empregar todos os esforços para fazer algum dinheiro; o círculo dos seus recursos apertava-se vertiginosamente. Incapaz de mentir, incapaz do menor charlatanismo, ele tinha em si mesmo o seu maior inimigo.[25]

Later, when Teobaldo has succeeded in being named a government minister, he recognizes the scale and value of André's efforts and makes more promises he will never keep, telling his friend that he will have the history published at government expense. The same caprice that warps the timbers of history and makes finishing the work impossible will also ensure that it never sees the light of day.

Lovers

The contrast between Teobaldo and André continues in the story of their love lives. Teobaldo is Don Juan to André's fastidious lifelong bachelor. Teobaldo cannot help himself, so Azevedo lets the reader know repeatedly that he is too beautiful and apparently distinguished to avoid a constant state of siege when it comes to his relations with women. Ernestina and Leonília chase him, not the other way around. The ease Teobaldo experiences with women makes him cynical. When Ernestina throws herself at his feet, saying she is miserable without his love, the young man replies, If loving me hurts, don't love me.[26]

Soon after making this heartless comment, Teobaldo thinks to himself that if he is to have love affairs, these ought to be with women who, "in opening their arms to him, also open the door to a comfortable and guaranteed future" ("A ter de ter amores, que fossem estes com mulheres que, lhe abrindo os braços, abrissem-lhe também as portas de um futuro garantido e cômodo").[27] Clearly, the humble Ernestina will not do.

For a time, it appears to Teobaldo that Leonília might. She displays promising signs: jewels, a rich boudoir, social esteem of a certain kind. The trajectory of Leonília provides an instructive subplot. As with Marcela, the "Spanish beauty" in *Memórias Póstumas*, she is destined to lose her looks, her money, and hence her charms. The courtesan is doomed because, having fallen, she is no longer marriage material. In the best case she can accumulate enough money when her looks and charms are at their peak to see her through the long declining years. Marcela is reputed to have squirreled away a tidy sum in spite of living in relative squalor. Leonília ends up practically destitute. She displays a certain dignity, however, when she refuses Teobaldo's offer of help when he happens upon her by accident in her poor rented rooms.

Leonília's story is also a tale of chance encounters, of the demimonde, rumors, and introductions in the shadows. I pick up this theme in some detail in Chapter 5, where I explore the means by which courtesans take advantage of certain open spaces to pursue their conquests. Meanwhile, the ambiguity of Leonília's private space (as this is also to a certain extent public) is in pointed contrast to the space of a chaste and virtuous woman.

In a critical moment midway through *O Coruja*, Teobaldo, having lost his parents and his fortune, finds himself falling into debt and living beyond his means. This is attributed to his "blood" as well as to the social world he is accustomed to moving in. At this point he is out at a cafe when he runs into his former *amante*, Leonília. Having abandoned her financier in Italy, she has just returned from Europe draped in diamonds and more beautiful than ever. The refining power of the Old World is represented by her newfound gracefulness and fashionable dress.[28] Teobaldo is enchanted, but his vestigial pride and social scruples tell him that, poor as he his, Leonília is no longer for him. They drink a bottle of champagne. She invites him back to her house for a late supper. He resists at first but eventually lets her convince him; she is beautiful and very persistent.[29]

Back at her house, the door is opened by an English servant and Teobaldo finds himself in a small furnished room filled with luxury. There is a sense of closeness, of cloying feminine desire. Teobaldo has his second moment of doubt and thinks of leaving. He starts to write a note while Leonília is in her bedroom changing into something more comfortable. She emerges before the note is ready, and he tries for a second time to take his leave. A powerful dialogue, Socratic in structure, about pure and fallen women follows.

Leonília leads off with the observation that Teobaldo and men in general are inconsistent egoists because they do not want to be beholden to the free affections of a woman: They want to be in the position of power, and they want their affections owed to them. Teobaldo responds by saying that there are some women from whom free affections cannot be accepted. His *amante* counters with the romantic maxim that love can only be repaid by love. In essence, Leonília's position is based on notions of fairness and equality. It is also predicated on a flexible sense of circumstance; love can be disinterested and free under the right circumstances, which must ultimately be determined by the purity of feeling and the autonomous choices of individuals: "Every woman can be honest or lose her virtue, according to the circumstances that determine her life. . . . They are subject to the same physiological laws" ("Toda a mulher é capaz de ser honesta ou deixa de ser, conforme as circunstâncias que determinam a sua vida. . . . Elas estão sujeitas às mesmas leis fisiológicas").[30]

In contrast, Teobaldo's position represents the classic patriarchal and categorical understanding of virtue dictated by society. For this reason, when he is discomfited by some of Leonília's cogent arguments, he responds with, "I didn't make the law" ("Não é uma lei criada por mim"),[31] distancing himself from the social norm but accepting its suzerainty all the same.

The argument ends at an impasse. Neither side can be gainsaid, although it is clear that Leonília is fully aware that her position will always lose the war with society. Upon hearing Teobaldo's harsh statement of the relevant social facts, she laments, "Yesterday innocence and persecution; today shame and disdain; tomorrow misery and perhaps the hospital" ("Ontem a inocência e a per-seguição; hoje a vergonha e o desprezo; amanhã a miséria e talvez o hospital").[32]

Such is the socially sanctioned trajectory of the lost woman. Purity, once lost, can never be regained. Responding to Teobaldo's doubts about the possibility of freely given love from a *grisette*, Leonília contrives to move from her luxurious den of iniquity to a quiet side street in Santa Tereza, a symbol of semirural calm at the edge of the city. Selling her luxurious furnishings and jewels, she installs herself in a modest house in the hills above the Rua Matacavalos. To Teobaldo, she sums up, "It's a veritable love nest for poor lovers. . . . Here, all is as simple as can be: manufactured American furniture, everyday tableware . . . you see? . . . I've even got a sewing machine" ("É um verdadeiro ninho de noivos pobres. . . . Aqui tudo é simples quanto pode ser: mobília americana, louça de família . . . Vês? . . . Tenho até uma máquina de costura").[33]

Dressed simply and surrounded by simple objects, Leonília attempts to transform herself into a woman of virtue—the first and best kind of woman according to Teobaldo in a previous conversation. She has selected functional furnishings without pretense and a sewing machine as a symbol of domesticity, a proof of genuine femininity pacified and ready to serve. Here, we see the role of furnishings as representations of a way of life, a certain kind of person, and again, the desperation behind the facade. Teobaldo responds cynically: In no time, you, like all *pobres filhas do vicio*, will be back to your luxurious furnishings and your dissolute, unchaste ways: "You've changed your clothes and taken off your jewelry, you've put on the disguise of this modest little cotton dress . . . but you have to admit, my dear, that your soul doesn't belong in this poor house without mirrors" ("Mudaste de roupa, tiraste as joias, tomaste para disfarce esse modesto vestidinho de chita . . . [mas] hás de confessar, minha querida, que a tua alma não se prende a esta pobre casinha sem espelhos").[34]

In the end, Leonília will not do any better than Ernestina. Teobaldo shucks her off and, in doing so, unwittingly authors his own ultimate fate.

Marriage

In *O Coruja* marriage is inextricably linked to questions of money and status. It turns out that there is no such thing as pure love or marriage based on simple affinity. No example of a happy marriage is to be found, save, perhaps, that of Teobaldo's parents. Marriage is not just imperfect, it has side effects: jealousy and rumor, unrealistic expectations of perfection, encounters taken the wrong way—the difficulty of keeping love's embers alight. For the poor the difficulty is getting together enough money to marry in the first place. This is epitomized in the case of André and Inez, who face a litany of problems and postponements.

Spaces

Social space is the product of a society at a given time; it is rooted in the relationships of production and reproduction that underpin the social order.[35] Azevedo's novel, along with developing its theses regarding the destiny of characters owing to heredity and milieu, also presents a series of wonderfully rendered set pieces that illuminate the contours of social space and designate the places from which dominant characters conduct strategy and the open spaces, such as theaters and the chambers of courtesans, where the weak use various tactics to try to manipulate or deflect/inflect the trajectories of the powerful.[36] Azevedo is highly sensitive to the importance of context. The spaces where Teobaldo once felt powerful, where his money and suave demeanor made him appear brilliant and desirable, become spaces to be avoided, reminders and plumb lines marking the depth of his fall.

The panorama of society depicted in *O Coruja* extends from the mean rooms of provincial Minas Gerais, to the space of a great *fazenda*, and then to the whole range of life in Rio de Janeiro. According to the Naturalist creed, spaces and their furnishings comment on, reflect, and influence states of mind and ways of life. Azevedo recounts Teobaldo and André's failed *Bildung* in the metropolis in terms of their living quarters, starting with the rented rooms of students with a certain amount of money and taste.

Mata-Cavalos, circa 1860, was a street with a certain chic. It is the same street where Bento Santiago and Capitu share a residence in Machado de Assis's *Dom Casmurro*. Azevedo describes the way Teobaldo furnishes his rooms in the following way:

> Teobaldo, wrapped in a silk dressing gown, stood in the middle of the house, a cigarette between his fingers, directing the placement of the furniture.
>
> "André, put the mirror there. And the desk here on the other side. That's it! Now let's see where the piano ought to go. . . . Ah, there's the place for it, between these two windows here."

> Teobaldo, no meio da casa, envolvido em um robe de chambre de seda azul, um cigarro entre os dedos, dirigia a colocação dos moveis.

"Esse espelho ali, o André! E a secretária deste outro lado. Assim! Agora vejamos onde deve ficar o piano. . . . ah cá está o lugar dele, aqui entre estas duas janelas."[37]

Sampaio, arriving to check in on the young men, is shocked at the luxurious furnishings.

"Then there's still more along with all this stuff?"

"Doubtlessly. It is necessary to brighten up the house with some objects of art. I've got four of five statuettes on the way."

"Statuettes?"

". . . [and] a tasteful clock, two vases for flowers and half a dozen paintings."

"Há então ainda outras coisas além disto?"

"Sem dúvida. É preciso alegrar a casa com alguns objetos d'arte. Chegam-me quatro ou cinco estatuetas."

"Estatuetas?"

". . . uma pêndula de bom gosto, dois jarros para flores e meia dúzia de quadros."[38]

Sampaio, even more shocked than André, asks where Teobaldo has ever seen such a luxuriously furnished house for a student. Teobaldo replies that this is the only way he knows how to live. The taste of the baron's son: an ensemble of objects, a piano, statues, all displaying a certain way of living and status, "refined taste" ("o gosto bem educado").[39] From this rich beginning of life in the city, the fall is vertiginous. The fall begins when André finally gets a job as a teacher in a *colégio* and moves out to live in a room at the school. Teobaldo's dissolute habits turn the well-ordered house into a veritable student dive.[40]

Sabino and Caetano, the dependents from the country, remain attached to the household. At no point does Teobaldo consider dispensing with their services. The prospect of living without a servant is unthinkable.

Azevedo follows Teobaldo along his road to ruin, with a stop in the richly furnished *Hotel de França*.

The bed was very wide, with a thick spring mattress to envelope one's body; the pillows were enormous and figured with lace and ribbons; and above all this immense curtain filled with dust. On the marble of the counter rose a washbasin of giant proportions . . . and in contrast with all this luxury, a miserable chip of

inexpensive soap, furnished by the hotel . . . [and to Teobaldo] all the false com-
fort of a never unoccupied but ownerless room saddened and overwhelmed him.

A cama era muito larga, com um grande colchão de molas, onde o corpo se
abismava; os travesseiros monstruosos e enfeitados de rendas e fitas; e por cima
um imenso cortinado de labirinto, enxovalhado de pó. Sobre o mármore do
lavatório via-se a bacia de gigantesca proporções . . . e em contraste com o resto,
um miserável pedaço de sabão de 200 réis, fornecido pelo hotel . . . todo esse
falso conforto de quarto sem dono e nunca desocupado, tudo isso ainda mais o
entristecia e acabrunhava.[41]

Then, continuing down into closer, darker, more squalid spaces, it is on to
the spare rooms of a *casa de cômodos.* Having left all of his rich furnishings,
his piano, the statues, the painting, the drapes, and the rest of it in the Rua
Mata-Cavalos, the setting in the *casa de comodos* (rooming house) would have
been spare and poor. Inside, the truth; outside, in the street, the same elegance
as before. Rotten insides hidden by appearances outside, in the street, at the
theater. This gambit is repeated by Filomena and her mother in the hopes of
landing a rich husband and by Seixas in Alencar's *Senhora.* The rooms themselves are not described. There is nothing to describe: a bed, perhaps a cheap
wardrobe and a rickety chair, and a chipped mirror.

Azevedo next takes us to the rich gardens and rooms of Teobaldo and
Branca's mansion in Botafogo, formerly the home of Branca's father, deceased
as a direct result of Teobaldo's kidnapping of Branca.

From the gate of the estate one's eyes took in a luxurious scene; paths lined with
myrtle, beds of fresh flowers, nooks, fountains and statues, arbors and little ar-
tificial groves.

Desde o portão da chácara vão os olhos descobrindo em que se regalar; caminhos de murta, canteiros de finas flores, repuxos, cascatas e estatuetas, globos de
mil cores, caramanchões e pequenos bosques artificiais.[42]

Even here, something is rotten. Branca's inheritance, a fortune for an everyday
worker, is far too small to sustain the grand style of life that Teobaldo believes
is expected of them. The rich furnishings and the manner of riding about town
in a sumptuous carriage present a front and the facade of a rich and well-wed
couple. Teobaldo pursues this systematically. To hide from everyone the truth
regarding the actual value of the estate—to better pull the wool over the eyes
of society—Teobaldo takes half of Branca's dowry and dedicates it entirely to

luxury. That is, he spends 50 contos on furnishings and appearances, which is much more money than most residents of Rio de Janeiro could earn in a lifetime. In this act, Azevedo shows the reader just how definitively Teobaldo has failed to progress in his *Bildung*. The same spendthrift ways and the same mania for spending on appearances recur at this point in almost perfect symmetry to the earlier moment when Teobaldo first arrived in the capital and set up his sumptuous rooms. Teobaldo dedicates the other half of the dowry to business; again, as with his studies in that earlier epoch of life, he is compelled to do something, but without genuine commitment, and so, as with his medical studies, he is destined to fail. Instead: "'Appearances are everything!' He thought, still dominated by the ideas of his father. 'If the world thinks I am rich, sooner or later I will be rich in fact.'"[43]

As Teobaldo's fortunes rise and fall and rise again, André follows along like a shadow, his simple way of living drawing a sharp contrast to the excesses of his friend. First, in the rented house, it is André who cleans up and maintains order. Then, in the *casa de comodos*, it is André who arranges the rental and keeps to an orderly schedule of work, by living within his means and saving up for a marriage that never comes about. Eventually, even as Teobaldo reaches the apogee of luxury in the mansion inherited from Branca's father, André is there in the background, literally, living in the spare rooms of the *sotão* at the back of the garden, keeping to himself, working hard, and saving money. There, his taciturn manner and ugly countenance strike a discordant note. Space is divided: There, in front, Teobaldo and Branca live in the midst of their fine furnishings and the society of people of good breeding and taste; there, behind this facade, André, with his piles of notes for an unfinished history of Brazil, lives a threadbare, poor existence: "And always good, hiding from others his privations and disappointments, seeking to occupy the smallest space possible in the world" ("E sempre bom, escondendo de todos as suas privações e os seus desgostos, procurando ocupar no mundo o menor espaço que podia").[44]

Let me finish this discussion of spaces with a reminder and a warning about the theater and the space of social display and competition. The theater and box seats create a sense of the private in the public—spaces of encounters. It is in a box at the theater for a presentation of *The Huguenots* that Aguiar whispers calumnies against Teobaldo to his cousin Branca. There, in the half-light of the theater, he tries to woo her away from his rival. Teobaldo, moving through this space, encounters another woman: the wife of a rich man whom Teobaldo is eager to touch for money to support a political magazine.[45]

Entre a cruz e a caldeirinha.

.... Eu era um bonito rapaz ; mas não sei que diabo levou-me uma vez ao theatro Lyrico e sentou-me entre D. Carlota e D. Eugenia, duas moças encantadoras. Tive de olhar ao mesmo tempo para ambas, afim de não desgostar qualquer dellas ; e tanto torci os olhos que... fiquei vesgo. Ah, mulheres!.....

ILLUSTRATION 7. "At the Theater: The Dandy's Dilemma." As a social event, attending the theater was at least as much about seeing and being seen by other theatergoers as it was about the action on stage. The caption reads, "I was a handsome young man, but I don't know what the hell led me one time to attend the theater and sit between D. Carlota and D. Eugenia, two enchanting girls. I had to look at both of them at the same time, so as not to offend either of them, and I strained my eyes so much that I ended up walleyed. Oh, women! . . ."

SOURCE: *Semana Illustrada* 34 (1861): 268.

In the theater box, Teobaldo woos the wife to get to the man. Lamenting the absence of the *conselheiro*, Teobaldo receives the desired response from the wife: "Then join us Friday. You're invited" ("Pois então aparece-nos sexta-feira. Está convidado").[46] Teobaldo kisses the woman's hand as he takes his leave. Upon seeing this, Branca, her attention drawn to the box by Aguiar, begins to have her doubts. Later on, Aguiar seizes the opportunity to entrap his detested rival. He takes advantage of Teobaldo's credulity and offers his house as a meeting place. Teobaldo, unwitting, meets the woman there, with Aguiar and Branca watching from a hidden place.[47]

The theater, then, is a place of intrigue, where encounters, however dubious, take place in full view of society. As such, a patina of propriety covers these meetings. Private interactions between men and women take place in the theater boxes. But the theater is public and the encounters, in this sense, are licit. Meeting a potential lover in a private home, with no one watching, at least presumably, can be nothing but illicit. Branca turns away at the sight of

Teobaldo embracing the older woman, "a zaftig forty-something" ("uma gor-dachuda quarentona"). Nothing more need be seen or said.

The Ultimate Frustrations of Failed *Bildung*

Teobaldo's career in business and politics is no more successful, in the end, than his marriage. He makes disastrous gambles on exchange rates. He dabbles with journalism. He manages, by a quirk of political horse trading, to be named a minister for a few days. To a certain extent, this appointment is a vindication of the philosophy pursued by Teobaldo throughout the novel: to appear in the best light possible and position himself to be in the right place at the right time—and always, to manipulate the impression made on others and to maintain appearances at all costs (costs not just to him but to others). This attitude leads to the beginning of Branca's loss of respect, when to keep up appearances, Teobaldo denies the connection with his old friend André. To paraphrase his rival: Teobaldo addresses himself not to the listener but to those around watching, concerned not with the other but with the impression he, himself, is making.[48]

᠃

As suggested at the outset, *O Coruja* can be situated in relation to the earlier novels by Alencar and Machado, as discussed in Chapters 1 and 2. In *Sonhos d'Ouro* marriage is made nearly impossible by an excess of scruples. In *O Coruja* it is precisely Teobaldo's lack of scruples that opens the way for his doomed marriage to Branca. In Alencar's vision, refusal to play by the rules of the game in marriage and society leads to ultimate redemption, a redemption that would be every bit as certain without the tacking on of a happy ending. For Azevedo, acceptance of the rules of the game leads to ineluctable dissolution.

Meanwhile, the cynical attitude toward politics connects *Memórias Póstumas* to the machinations of Teobaldo and his associates. It is no accident that Alencar was much less cynical about the prospects of political service. He was, after all, an elected and appointed official for much of his adult life. The journalists-turned-writers, Machado and Azevedo, see politics (and love) through a darker lens. Their protagonists' successes in political life are, like their private lives, actually failures. Having refused to grow up, these men continue to make the mistakes of youth, whether the fault is found in them or in their stars, in the blood or in the warped society that birthed and educated them. The difference is this: Brás's failed *Bildung* is comic; Teobaldo's is pathetic. The other side of comedy is tragedy, and the losses are thus more deeply felt. This is why we still read *Memórias Póstumas* and come away from the experience with a smile of recognition—a wan smile, but a sense of having tasted from the wellspring of life. *O Coruja* leaves a bitter taste. Its lessons read like reports from a hopeless battlefield. In artistic terms there can be no doubt of Machado's superiority. In historical terms Machado and Azevedo have much to teach us.

INTERLUDE

The Problem of the Individual and Society

I HAVE ARGUED, following Moretti and Lukács, that the novel is a problem-solving genre. What does it mean to say that a book solves problems?

The bildungsroman, the object of my analysis in the first three chapters of this book, addresses a particular set of issues that arguably can be seen as arising from the special circumstances of the social and economic transformations of the long nineteenth century—the problem of education, growth, and social integration in a changing world roiled by the rise of capitalism, nationalism, and the emergence of new social actors on the stage of history. In Europe, where the genre originated, new actors included the rising bourgeoisie and their antagonists: organized workers and their allies as well as the old vestiges of the aristocracy and the clergy.[1] Flaubert's *Education Sentimentale*, perhaps the greatest continental bildungsroman, is set against precisely this backdrop, with the heady days of 1848 occupying a central place in the narrative, providing fodder for idealists and opportunists alike to imagine their place in this changing world. Flaubert's pitch-dark pessimism gave no quarter, and no successful integration of individual and society transpires in the book. Still, the problematic individual is there, dissected in relation to a problematic social order.[2]

Novels, at least in the form the genre took as it rose to prominence in the eighteenth and nineteenth centuries, set about narrating the lives of ordinary people. Plots came to center on everyday experiences and the choices and dilemmas facing men and women in contemporary society. Low subjects were broached: material ambition, lust and adultery, hypocrisy and self-delusion.

Losers and lost causes emerged as proper subjects for literature in a way distinct from the victims of fate in tragedy and epic literature. Not new subjects to be sure, but a new subjectivity—the "realistic" and "everyday." As Ian Watt observes, "The various technical characteristics of the novel . . . contribute to . . . the production of what purports to be an authentic account of the actual experience of individuals."[3] Watt refers to this as formal realism, the common denominator of the genre. He also points out something of supreme importance for the historian. In seeking this effect, the novel's "formal convention forces it to supply its own footnotes."[4] Place and context. How things look and work.

Real life and its problems. What about Rio de Janeiro?

As we have seen, the Brazilian bildungsroman offers at least three distinctive solutions to the problematic individual. In *Sonhos d'Ouro*, José de Alencar portrays the struggles of Ricardo as a prolonged test of virtue against the corrosive mores of a corrupted society. The portrayed problematic individual, then, is an outsider unwilling to compromise in a novel of blocked ambition. Ricardo eventually is integrated when his love for Guida overcomes his stubborn pride and the couple is able to bring together wealth and honor in Alencar's golden dream. Machado de Assis offers no such solution in *Memórias Póstumas de Brás Cubas*. Brás is born integrated because there are no true dilemmas facing him as an individual. His *Bildung* is nothing more than the taken-for-granted mixed with volubility, with its tendency to incorporate and neutralize experience, and chance. There is no process of growth in the eternally childish world of the Brazilian elite, though there are many flashes of perverse worldly wisdom. In essence, to borrow from Margaret Cohen's profound studies of the European novel, Brás does not face the dilemma of balancing positive and negative freedoms—his freedom is one-sided and individualistic.[5] Finally, in *O Coruja*, Aluísio Azevedo presents characters fixed by heredity and social milieu on their stunted paths of growth.

In all three novels, despite their different outlooks on the prospects of growth and social integration, we see two common problems brought to the forefront: education and career on the one hand, and marriage and inheritance on the other. These are major problems, no doubt, at least for the middling and upper reaches of society, but not the only problems by any stretch.

In Chapters 4–6 the range of novels is expanded, and the problem solving extends beyond the core concerns of the bildungsroman. The basic lines of analysis follow two interlocking paths. First, there are problems of comportment and general attitudes toward life: how to act and feel in the changing circumstances of life in Brazil's capital city. Second, after learning how to live in society, there is the problem of social reproduction, particularly through the formal institution of marriage. Third, and the subject of the sixth and final chapter, there are problems of spatial practice: where to go and what to do. These are posed as imperatives here, not questions. That there is a normative side to the novel as a problem-solving genre makes it the critical genre par excellence and makes reading novels an act of criticism for contemporaries just as much as it does for us as historians.

Macrostructural Contradictions: Generic Considerations

In *Ao Vencedor as Batatas* Roberto Schwarz advances the thesis that the novel in Brazil harbors a basic contradiction at the moment of its birth in the nineteenth century. This contradiction is generated by the distance between the bourgeois ideology of the European novel and the local realities of a slaveholding society, which is both structurally and in practice antithetical to the bourgeois norm.[6] Thus Schwarz observes the incoherence and lack of fit between the peripheral elements in Alencar, where local color comes through, and the central plotlines, which attempt to follow the European model. This argument, taken further by Schwarz, identifies in Machado de Assis a kind of solution to this problem in which the contradiction is brought to the surface and its meaning (critique) is made through incoherence.[7]

Schwarz's observation marks one of those rare examples of creative illumination that forever changes the way we read a master novelist. The essential claims about the "peripherality" of Brazilian reality and the degree of difference in relation to European urban life nevertheless need to be assessed in light of the past three decades of social and economic research on the relationship between slavery and capitalism in general and on social life in Rio de Janeiro in particular. That is, whether or not Machado perceived contradictions and made them a formal part of his art is fundamentally different from saying that there are objective contradictions unique to Brazilian reality that cancel out the viability of conventional generic modes. The "Europe" in Brazil is no less real or substantial for all of its warping and contradictory elements. There is a bourgeois subject. Individuals and their problems of social integration exist. Slavery and client-patron relations do not dominate all social life. Schwarz never claimed the opposite, only that the gap was substantial, determinative, and genre defining.

Why is this historically important?[8] For two reasons. One is prosaic: *Sonhos d'Ouro* and *O Coruja* simply have not been given the detailed treatment they deserve. Taken together and placed in the generic realm of the bildungsroman with *Memórias Póstumas* alongside, the story of the Brazilian novel changes complexion in a nonnegligible way. The second reason is based on a difference in assessment: My reading of the nineteenth-century European novel sees the genre grappling with many of the same kinds of problems Schwarz identifies as more particular to Brazil. Here I follow the lead provided by Dain Borges in a recent essay.[9] Borges suggests that Machado's aims went far beyond satirizing the Brazilian upper class and extended into a critique of Western conceptions of the individual and society more generally. In other words, the interpretation of the Brazilian bildungsroman is also an exercise in world literature.

4 SENTIMENTAL EDUCATIONS

WHERE TO BEGIN and how to enter society? As humans, we are utterly dependent on others to provide us with the framework of meaning, to point toward and usher us through the right door. Yet the ideology of the nineteenth-century novel, and by extension the bourgeois ethos it often reflected, insists on an interiorization of frame and orientation—in other words, an authentic attitude toward life, which was internally generated and oriented toward independence despite the constraints of society. The novel of this era is conflicted because it traces out the concept of independence and authenticity at the same time that it lays bare the social structures that condition and inhibit the formation of independent bourgeois subjects.

The process by which individuals forge identities and garner the skills necessary for this composite role of socially integrated autonomy is through experience, through education—*Bildung*.[1] In this chapter I explore early passages from youth to adulthood—education, career, courtship, and sexual awakenings—as realms of experience and forms of social relations grounded in the specific context of Rio de Janeiro during the 1800s. Experience and social relations are understood here to be modulated by modes of comportment—by the stance, conscious or not, taken by the individual in the face of structural forces and social norms. In other words, it is not just the explicit content of action that marks out the dance between individual and society; it is also the implicit attitude adopted in the course of taking action that constitutes a critical component of social experience. *Bildung* is best defined, in this sense, as learning *how* to act.

By adopting attitudes or stances toward others, characters appear in novels as relatively independent or dependent. In this way (i.e., being depicted as acting from a certain stance), characters reveal both the possible frames and modes of comportment and the tensions produced by the insertion of individuals and their actions into social settings. I use the term *comportment* frequently throughout this chapter. The word connotes both action and attitude, which suits my purposes. I am interested in the way characters are presented as acting according to certain social scripts; comportment implies repeated and somewhat consistent action (even if the character is consistently inconstant). Through such repeated scripted actions, individuals signify their personality to others and social relationships are possible by reading surface actions and attendant attitudes.[2] The novels reviewed here probe the question of how one acts in order to live in society, weighing the internal and external dimensions along the way.

Erving Goffman's classic study, *The Presentation of Self in Everyday Life*, is particularly useful in this regard as an exploration of the relationship between comportment and social setting. Goffman shows how seemingly minor or inconsequential actions, attitudes, and situations reveal profound information about the microstructures of self and society. This is not because it is clever to read great things into small acts; on the contrary, the small things matter far more than we generally assume, and the unspoken or gestured can tell as strongly as words in creating impressions and staking out positions. For instance, Goffman contrasts expressions given with expressions given off. The latter refers to "theatrical and contextual" communication, which is often nonverbal.[3] I seek to use a similar distinction when I refer to explicit acts and implicit attitudes represented in novels.

Goffman's theories also point back to George Santayana's *Soliloquies in England*. Inasmuch as literature describes realistic characters in action, it can be said to be like life itself, not only descriptively but also substantively. As Santayana puts it, "We do not merely live but act; we compose and play our chosen character . . . our deliberate character is more truly ourself . . . we become 'persons' or masks."[4]

We wear masks and play roles, but not just any mask and not every role. Our masks are learned, and there are social limits to the kinds of comportment and public roles that are acceptable.[5] Perhaps it would be better to say kinds of comportment and public roles that are legible. Novels explore the acceptable range of comportment and the variation in social identities generated by the mixture of individual character and social setting—the combination of which results in Goffman's "definition of the situation." To this we might add an idea from Kenneth Burke's *Attitudes Toward History*. Burke's concept of the "acceptance frame" offers a useful way to think about the way that attitudes toward life operate to translate between individuals and societies through interpretation and action. Frames of acceptance are "strategies for living."[6] They are composite, containing "what is" and "what is to be done."[7]

The upshot of this combination of theoretical approaches to issues of comportment and socialization is not to provide a theoretical template or key to reading novels. Rather, it offers a subtle nudge toward focusing on certain aspects of the novels, reading in an idiosyncratic manner that deviates from both the historical and the literary critical modes. It highlights the importance of everyday tactical actions and positionings rather than traditional elements of character and plot—or perhaps, rather, a microhistorical perspective on character and plot: what to look for and a different set of questions, placing the activities of characters as they pass through key stages of experience in dialog with one another and with the history and literature of the era more broadly.

Problems of comportment (that mix of action and attitude), then, arise in the face of experience. There are many dimensions to human experience, and any attempt to approach the historical process of education and socialization through reading novels will necessarily edit and truncate the range of situations and possible attitudes. In what follows I focus on three critical passages or forms of experience depicted in the early years of the lives of fictional protagonists: education, career, and sex, although not always in that order. These passages are analyzed in light of two problematic axes representing the modes of interaction or comportment available to individuals according to a mixture of internal characteristics (personality and attitudes) and external factors (class position and setting). The external axis runs from the pole of independence to the pole of subordination. The internal axis might be thought of as running from ingenuity and sincerity to cynicism and volubility. Taken together, the personal and the contextual offer a distinctive window through which to view social history by way of fictional representations.

I begin with the question of independence: Can one be integrated into society and retain a modicum of autonomy and authenticity? This is obviously going to be a major problem in a patriarchal society characterized by patronage and elite caprice.[8] What stance toward this problem do characters in novels take, and to what degree does the question of independence break along gender or class lines? How do our authors account for their attitudes and the outcomes of their choices?

Next, I consider an urban attitude identified by Georg Simmel as emergent in nineteenth-century urban capitalist settings: the blasé and the voluble. Here, we get closer to the Goffmanesque analysis of the presentation of self as a method for living in society. Attitudes regarding independence and subordination connect to the question of the blasé and the voluble through the comportment associated with education, work, and marriage. In following this line of analysis, I trace a path to social integration (or the lack thereof) from questions of independence, through specific stances toward life, to the brink of marriage, the ultimate sign of integration for both men and women in nineteenth-century Rio de Janeiro. Doing so means both attending to the local context and simultaneously deprovincializing Brazilian fiction.[9] The social-historical specificity of Brazil does not negate the universal commentary on social integration under an evolving capitalist society. Thus it is vital that the literary historical dimension broaden to include European novels, both as models for stories and as common depictions of the urban experience and its problems relating to social integration.

The reader should be aware that the sixth and final chapter of this book focuses on spatial practices, thus addressing this same set of issues from a different direction. In Chapter 6 I explore the way fictional characters move through the physical spaces of the city and the way these spaces both enable and constrain the social space of encounters. Let us return to comportment for now.

Independence, Subordination, Competition

A classic passage from youth to adulthood for male protagonists is found in the first forays into the competitive world of work. Education, up to this point, provides young men with credentials necessary for entry into the game. For the middle and upper echelons of society, this education includes some kind of university degree, most often in law or medicine. Lower down, education might be limited to the equivalent of secondary schooling, as in the case of André in Azevedo's *O Coruja*. Formal education, however useful in real life, is of limited importance to male protagonists' career trajectories in most versions of the Brazilian bildungsroman. Careers in journalism, business, or politics did not require formal university degrees. Education for female protagonists of middling and upper status, to the extent that it is referred to at all, is informal and involves learning to dance, draw, play the piano, drop French phrases, and otherwise adorn a drawing room.[10]

The higher the class origin of the male protagonist, the lower the propensity to seek formal employment in a vocation determined by formal educational credentials. Teobaldo never finishes his medical studies and Brás never makes explicit use of his degree. So it went among the rich and well-born. Conversely, poor André used his secondary education to find work as a schoolmaster, and Ricardo used his law degree to embark on a career at the bar. In all cases entry into the world of work was negotiated through social relationships. There was no such thing as an impersonal, neutral labor market into which young men were launched. In other words, the passage to the world of work required social capital and involved choices of comportment—attitudes toward the idea of a career and the necessary social subordination required at the outset.

For the young man of some talent in nineteenth-century Rio de Janeiro, the crux of the problem was the gap between a world of bourgeois competition, which provided the motive force in one direction, and the world of seignio-rial power, which floated above and around the emerging capitalist society, in-troducing an element of caprice, which cut against the grain of the essentially meritocratic and individualistic bourgeois ethos.

The case of Ricardo Nunes in *Sonhos d'Ouro* provides an excellent starting point for analysis. As a young man from the provinces with a law degree, he enters the fray in Rio de Janeiro in the hopes of making his fortune. He arrives with his friend Fábio, who is in much the same circumstances. This doubling serves Alencar well. It underscores the quantitative aspect of a competitive capitalist society. But, it turns out, there are many young men on the make. The salience of two more lawyers, Guimarães and Nogueira, lends further weight to the sense of numbers, of competition. This is not meant to suggest that com-petition did not exist for previous generations in Rio de Janeiro. The theme of surplus lawyers appears as early as 1844, in Martins Pena's play, *O Diletante*: "Every year they come by the hundreds. . . . You run into them on every corner" ("Todos os anos chegam-nos aos centos. . . . Encontras em cada canto").[11] What has changed is the *quantity* of competition (the numbers of lawyers increased by a factor of 3 on a per capita basis between 1849 and 1870) and the *quality* of the competition (because the economic stakes rose with financial capitalism).[12]

As Moretti points out with regard to Balzac, this discovery of the "mecha-nism of competition" as a motive force for narrative shifts the register in the novel from the individual to the social: "Here it is not the hero who generates the story, but rather the world, with its many-sided and endless conflict."[13] Thus Jacques Collin says to Rastignac in *Père Goriot*:

> There are fifty thousand young men in your position at this moment, all bent as you are on solving one and the same problem—how to acquire a fortune rapidly. . . . There are not fifty thousand good positions for you; you must fight and devour one another like spiders in a pot.

> Une rapide fortune est le problème que se proposent de résoudre en ce moment cinquante mille jeunes gens qui se trouvent tous dans votre position. Vous êtes une unité de ce nombre-là. Jugez des efforts que vous avez à faire et de l'acharnement du combat. Il faut vous manger les uns les autres comme des araignées dans un pot, attendu qu'il n'y a pas cinquante mille bonnes places.[14]

Ricardo, a poor orphan (fatherless), must fight without weapons and *without protection*, a fight he is structurally determined to lose. Antonio Candido is only half-right in observing a lack of drama associated with the struggle for social ascent in Alencar. True, the solution to Ricardo's problem comes from the subtle help provided by Guida and her father, as Candido notes regarding Ricardo Nunes directly in this connection. However, this help comes late, and in the meantime Alencar shows, even if negatively, what Candido terms "the difficult choice facing a sensitive man in entering the world of bourgeois competition" ("a dura opção do homem de sensibilidade no limiar da competição burguesa"). Candido continues:

> He lacked, however, the Stendhalian or Balzacian sense of the drama of the career, neither his rise, nor the society in which he lived demanded the bitter struggle of a Rastignac or a Julien Sorel.

> Não tinha, contudo, o senso stendhaliano e balzaquiano do drama da carreira, nem a ascensão, na sociedade em que vivia, demandava a luta aspera de Rastignac ou Julien Sorel.[15]

This is only true in the sense that Ricardo refuses to play by the rules of the game; the game itself is on display from the very first chapter.

In *Père Goriot* Rastignac also begins with a certain reticence, if not scruples, regarding his mode of entry into the higher spheres of society. The difference is that he gives himself over completely to the game.

> The southern brain was beginning to scheme for the first time. Between Mme. de Restaud's blue boudoir and Mme. de Beauséant's rose-colored drawing-room

he had made three years' advance in a kind of law which is not a recognized study in Paris, although it is a sort of higher jurisprudence, and, when well understood, is a high-road to success of every kind.

Le méridional en était à son premier calcul. Entre le boudoir bleu de madame de Restaud et le salon rose de madame de Beauséant, il avait fait trois années de ce *Droit parisien* dont on ne parle pas, quoiqu'il constitue une haute jurisprudence sociale qui, bien apprise et bien pratiquée, mène à tout.[16]

Rastignac concludes, "Henceforward I shall have two protectresses."[17]

Protection is the other side of the coin. Competition for position and the related search for protection. These elements are fused in Balzac's rendering of Rastignac. He must win, playing the game with his mother and sister's money: "Yes! Success at all costs."[18] For Lucien, in *Illusions perdues*, it is much the same story, though the outcome could not be more different in his first foray into the social battlefield of Paris.[19]

In Alencar's creation, Ricardo refuses to play, first by declining an invitation (eventually accepted, to be sure) to Comendador Soares's mansion, later by turning down the offer of money from the Visconde de Aljuba, and finally by turning down Guida's offer of marriage. If he were to act like Balzac's creation, he would have contrived an invitation, accepted the money, and jumped at the chance for a rich marriage. Alencar's romanticism and its defects, which according to Candido tend to save his heroes from the taint of interest by keeping them at a distance from the fray, do not prevent him from describing a valid social type in the person of Ricardo. The fact that Ricardo refuses to enter the *luta áspera* points to the tension produced by his "ideas out of place." The urban world of competition is not made up solely of Rastignacs and Sorels. It also includes the obstinate and bitter men who court failure by adhering to an idealized sense of individual honor and independence. In this regard, who is to say whether Balzac or Alencar is more true to life?

Two observations. First, it is clear in Balzac that the world of competition is hardly free from the arbitrary intervention of protectors. It is not merely the struggle of 50,000 men for a limited number of positions; it is the fight to obtain protection from a limited number of sponsors. Second, the chief idea out of place in *Sonhos d'Ouro*, the bourgeois ideal of individual independence, yields two divergent trajectories for the novel's protagonists: Ricardo rejects the search for protection at the same time that Guida dons a protective carapace of volubility and caprice.

An additional point is worth considering regarding competition: Not only does it differentiate, separating winners and losers, but it also *integrates*. According to Bourdieu:

> Competitive struggle is the form of class struggle which the dominated classes allow to be imposed on them when they accept the stakes offered by the dominant classes. It is an integrative struggle and, by nature of the initial handicaps, a reproductive struggle, since those who enter this chase, in which they are beaten before they start, as the constancy of the gap testifies, implicitly recognize the legitimacy of the goals pursued by those whom they pursue, by the mere fact of taking part.[20]

This may be an accurate assessment of the role of competition in integrating and reproducing a social order, but the portrait painted by the Brazilian bildungsroman complicates matters in several ways. First, there is the question of competition among members of the dominant class. What kind of integration or reproduction is entailed in the competition between Brás Cubas and Lobo Neves, to give one example? Second, in *Sonhos d'Ouro* the plot hinges on the central characters' rejection of the rules of the chase; if participation in the game integrates, what happens when characters refuse to join in? What emerges from these novels is a sense of the composite nature of competition, wherein the economic, social, and political spheres are contested in an overlapping space, extending from the stock exchange through the salons of society to the Chamber of Deputies, forming a common arena where distinctions between private and public, independence and dependence, love and interest, blur. Thus, being fully integrated through the mechanism of competition in nineteenth-century Rio de Janeiro implies a domination-subordination that cuts across multiple spheres. Reciprocally, this means that the most successfully integrated characters compete using all the weapons and tactics that such a mixture implies: seeking protection from social contacts for economic ends, marrying for money, and leveraging wealth to bid for political power.

The foregoing description of "successful" integration through competition by means of a no-holds-barred approach fits Teobaldo nearly perfectly. He marries in part for money; he uses his beautiful wife as a weapon in the game of society, or she uses herself to further his political chances. Other success stories abound. In *Memórias Póstumas* Cotrim trades in contraband slaves all the while using his money and his marriage to the well-born Sabina to cut a respectable figure in society. In Machado de Assis's follow-up novel *Quincas Borba*, Cristiano Palha, the scoundrel hiding behind the mask of friendship, appropriates Rubião's money and uses Sofia's beauty to succeed in business. In *Dom Casmurro* Escobar trades on his friendship with Bento Santiago to obtain the capital he needs, from Bento's mother, to enter the world of business. Miranda, in Azevedo's *O Cortiço*, marries for money and uses wealth to buy a title of nobility. Aurélia, in Alencar's *Senhora*, uses her great wealth to buy a husband. In every case, success implies the mixing of spheres, leverage, and compromise—all of which Bourdieu would lead us to expect. To compete, one must compromise the values of one sphere for the sake of another. Independence compromised by protection opens a path in business or politics. Marriage compromised by interest offers the financial resources needed to play the game. Using every weapon and making every compromise—this is the bitter struggle Candido refers to in his critique of Alencar's tendency to protect his protagonists from the inevitable taint of competition *under the terms available* in Rio at the time.[21]

In *Sonhos d'Ouro* Alencar sets up binary oppositions between characters who compete no-holds-barred and those who, by holding back, signal a lack of consent to the rules of the game. By refusing to compete according to the terms given by society, this latter group is not thereby integrated through competition. Rather, it is distinguished by an alternative world of virtue and strictly separated spheres: marriage for love, not money; and autonomy rather than protection. Comendador Soares is rich without having made ethical compromises in his business; the Visconde de Aljuba is wealthy through usury and shady deals. Ricardo's interest in Guida is independent of her wealth; Bastos in the end consoles himself with a partnership in Soares's business, betraying his underlying financial motives.

The difference in this respect between *Sonhos d'Ouro* and *Memórias Póstumas* or *O Coruja* ultimately comes down to an external versus an internal critique of the dominant social order, the rules of the game. In Alencar's version of the Brazilian bildungsroman, there is a path, however arduous, to social integration without making compromises in fundamental values for the sake of advantage in the competition for social position. The characters that follow this path offer an external critique of the dominant order. By opting out, they offer an alternative predicated on a rejection of the dominant conventions of social integration. In Alencar's world it is possible to imagine honest businessmen and virtuous young men and women marrying for love rather than money. In the case of Guida and Ricardo, the characters show a degree of autonomy that cuts against the dominant integrative forces of society. Ricardo refuses to play according to the terms set forth by the dominant classes in Rio de Janeiro by turning down various offers of protection and rejecting the offer of an advantageous marriage. Guida defies the social norms surrounding proper feminine behavior and the rules of the game in the marriage market. In both instances we can say that the characters defy the legitimacy of the social order by withholding their consent to playing by the rules and according to the stakes. If this interpretation holds, then *Sonhos d'Ouro* offers an impressive critique of the integrative social forces in an emergent capitalist society. That is, the withholding of consent and the rule breaking evinced by the central characters as cardinal values upheld in their youth and entrance into society cut deeply against the dominant grain of acquiescence in the dominant social order.

These possibilities are denied in the version of *Bildung* offered by Machado and Azevedo. The critique turns pessimistic: Rather than show exemplary alternatives, the novels dwell on the self-deception and ethical lapses of the central characters. Society's rot is revealed not by contrast with idealized virtues but rather through an exaggerated dissection of the rotten tissue itself. Characters tend to give in to circumstance. The struggle for independence is subordinated to getting ahead or getting along, though this does not mean that agency is banished from the stage or that characters do not form projects. As Sidney Chalhoub points out nicely in an essay on the role of dependents in Machado de Assis, dependents play chess. They operate strategically as well as tactically.[22]

In a different register, tactics can become strategy in the picaresque version of lower-class life. The canonical example is the little masterpiece *Memoirs of a Militia Sergeant*, by Manuel Antônio de Almeida. Not so much a novel of growth, Almeida's narrative skips and jumps through the lower and middling reaches of Rio de Janeiro during the "time of the King," that is, 1808–1821. This book might marginally be termed a bildungsroman. It certainly contains many basic elements: the youth and adventures of the protagonist, finding a way in life, and so forth. Perhaps the reason it is not read this way is because the goal of the protagonist, Leonardo, is not integration into society, which is closed to men of his birth and education, but rather mastery of the means of survival (even pleasure) in the world of the lower classes. In this we can follow Antonio Candido and note how the moral universe of Leonardo is open and unstructured: "For him there was neither fortune that was not transformed into misfortune nor misfortune that did not end up as fortune."[23] He learns the ways of the world, but he does not really grow or change. Thus the story is picaresque and not an exercise in *Bildung* in the classic sense. It is important, of course,

both for the reasons Candido adduced—as a revelation regarding social structure (not as a depiction of social life)—and because it introduces the humble
language of the everyday into the Brazilian novel and explores the social topography of patronage and subordination in a funny and profound way.

Independence and Women

If the bildungsroman offers several modes of independent comportment for
male protagonists and several typical forms of dependence on protection, the
case of Guida suggests a more limited range for women. For her, independence
is vouchsafed at the level of comportment in terms of her caprice. The big game
is marriage: an end that can be postponed but not avoided, lest she become
a spinster or a fallen woman. A woman's independence within the bounds of
"good society" was limited and fragile, dependent to a considerable extent on
the strength of her will—that is, subjective rather than objective, internal autonomy opposed to external domination, although for a rich young girl like
Guida a fair degree of external freedom was also possible, even if usually under
the gaze of family dependents and chaperones.

What of fallen women and spinsters? Both categories could live outside the
boundaries of male control. Not surprisingly, the male novelists of the nineteenth century have much more to say about fallen women than spinsters. The
problem-solving genre was fixated on these dangerous and beguiling creatures.
Read against the grain, these stories of sophisticated courtesans and desperate
girls tell a tale of the struggle for independence and selfhood against the rigged
social structures and hypocritical patriarchal mores of the nineteenth century.

Alencar's portrayal of women is generally sympathetic, if, admittedly, sometimes fetishistic.[24] Not only is the hypocrisy of the sexual double standard laid
bare, but women are also shown to be resourceful and independent actors despite their social constraints, even if, in the end, Alencar's realism demands that
those constraints be made binding. In his critique of the double standard, Alencar follows in a venerable tradition of novelists, which we can trace back at least
as far as Richardson's *Pamela*, where, as Ian Watt notes, readers cannot help
but see the gap between the normative world governing Pamela's conduct, her
overriding constraint, where "The woman no redemption knows / The wounds
of honour never close" and the rules of the chase are set out for Mr. B.[25] This
theme dominates several of Alencar's works, both fiction and theater. Pamela
holds out. Many of Alencar's heroines do not. Yet there is a profound sympathy
in his portrayal of these wayward and wronged women.

By way of contrast, Machado, at least in *Memórias Póstumas*, in adopting the point of view of Brás, offers a devastatingly cynical perspective on women as sybaritic mistresses and blasé adulteresses. The view broadens out in the other mature novels, particularly *Quincas Borba* and *Dom Casmurro*, where the reader meets female characters of depth in Sophia and Capitu— women whose power of independent action leads directly or indirectly to the destruction of their male protagonist counterparts. But Sophia and Capitu are married women, and for my purposes in this section, my interest in them is confined to the period leading up to marriage. In particular, Capitu's "olhos de ressaca" and her clever ways of maneuvering Bento into a love affair interest us precisely because they depict the tactics of courtship used by a girl with the wherewithal to play for high stakes in the long game—tactics in service of a grand strategy.

To examine the theme of women's independence and passages through sexual experience, I turn the spotlight first on a group of characters representing the quintessence of subordinated agency: kept women, courtesans, and ladies of "easy virtue." In doing so, I intend to show how modes of comportment and forms of experience relating to sex reveal a complex mixture of tactical opportunities and traps for (especially) women and men during the passage from youth to adulthood in cases in which female protagonists are depicted as operating independently but from a weak social position. Here the issues of independence and subordination are transcribed on another register and given particular valence owing to the dominant gender norms of the era.

Passages to Sexual Experience

Sexual awakenings play a critical role in the bildungsroman. For male protagonists the love interest often serves to focus (or deflect) efforts in other realms of social integration. Whether or not the love interest corresponds to the initiation into sexual experience depends on the position and attitudes of the character. Rich and capricious young men, like Brás and Teobaldo, experience sexual initiation with (unmarriageable) mistresses. Ricardo is chaste with women just as he retains his honor in the face of suborning capital. Importantly, whether chaste or not, all these men retain complete freedom to enter the marriage market. Previous sexual experience does not disqualify men. It will come as no surprise that things worked differently for the women depicted in these novels.

Among women the terms of sexual initiation created two fundamentally opposed classes: those whose sexual initiation consummated their marriage and those whose sexual activities were not concurrent with matrimony. The social norm, often called law by Alencar's characters, dictated that sexual activity on the part of unmarried women precluded subsequent marriage in society.[26] As we know, stable unions between unmarried women and men were probably as common as formal marriages in Rio de Janeiro at the time. Fiction is largely silent on the much more numerous population of women involved in stable unions with men under what might reasonably be translated as common law marriage. Presumably, for these women and their partners modes of comportment would, mutatis mutandis, mirror those of the conventionally married. The social norm referred to in the Brazilian novels of the 1870s and 1880s is that of bourgeois society, and it is clearly an idealization rather than a depiction of the real sexual behavior of the rich and well-born. With these distinctions and caveats in mind, it is nonetheless possible to extract valuable information about sexual experience and initiation among young men and women, degrees of independence and subordination, and the scope of alternative female agency (within and beyond the traditional marriage market) associated with this realm of life.

Mistresses

One of the most common figures in the nineteenth-century Brazilian novel is the kept woman, whether depicted as a rich courtesan or a semi-prostitute. Young (and not so young) men with money and education expected to have sex with available women. Women, trading on beauty and/or availability, could, according to our male authors, play this game willingly, as was the case presumably with Marcela, or unwillingly, as with Lúcia.[27] For our novelists the fate of the willing was to grow old, ugly, and unwanted; the unwilling, in contrast, were doomed to wither and die young in the harsh light of a repentant conscience.

Who are the willing? Marcela from *Memórias Póstumas*:

> At first I could not clearly distinguish the features of her yellow, pockmarked face; when finally I was able to do so, I found it a most curious spectacle. One could see that she had been pretty, more than a little pretty; but premature old age and illness had destroyed the flower of her beauty.

> Cujo rosto amarelo e bexiguento não se destacava logo, à primeira vista; mas logo que se destacava era um espectáculo curioso. Não podia ter sido feia; ao contrário, via-se que fora bonita, e não pouco bonita; mas a doença e uma velhice precoce destruíam-lhe a flor das graças.[28]

And Leonília from *O Coruja*:

> And now? . . . She was a fat old hag, face covered with poorly disguised wrinkles, tired eyes, thin lips, stained teeth, lusterless hair, bad breath. What a difference!

> E agora? . . . Uma velhusca, muito gorda, o rosto coberto de rugas mal disfarçadas pelo alvaiade, os olhos cansados, os lábios descaídos, os dentes sem brilho, o cabelo reles, o hálito mau. Que diferença![29]

Who are the unwilling? Lúcia from Alencar's *Lucíola*: "A pallid smile still bloomed on her colorless lips: sublime ecstasy illuminated the pale transparency of her face" ("Um sorriso pálido desfolhou-se ainda nos lábios sem cores: sublime êxtase illuminou a suave transparência de seu rosto").[30]

AOS MEUS ANTIGOS APRECIADORES.

Ainda um sorriso encantador.

ILLUSTRATION 8. "To My Old Admirers. Still an Enchanting Smile."
SOURCE: *Semana Illustrada* 21 (1861): 165.

There is an intriguing inversion of this situation in *O Coruja*, as Branca's illusions regarding Teobaldo melt away. She withdraws from him, but it is he who is prostrated with sadness and ultimately dies the kind of death usually reserved for women. Teobaldo feels the loss of his former love: "He wanted her that way—a companion, friend, together and inseparable" ("Assim é que a queria—companheira, amiga, unida e inseparável").[31] But she is lost to him, and in his last moment of life, as he reaches out to embrace her from his sickbed, she cannot stifle her instinctive revulsion. She shrinks back; Teobaldo's head drops back onto the pillows. She moves toward him, now mastering her feelings. It is too late; he vomits blood all over the clean white sheets and dies.[32]

But where do kept women come from? According to the stories told in nineteenth-century Brazilian novels, we have seen that they are willing or unwilling. Yet there is a complicated matrix of context and choice that governs this realm. On one axis there is the continuum from ingenuity to worldliness. On another axis are the poles of circumstance, of good fortune or bad luck—that is, external and structural forces like those we have explored among male protagonists in earlier passages. The third dimension is an amalgam of physical appearance and temper—beauty and social grace at the peak, homely awkwardness in the trough.[33] This world of kept women is, of course, in large part a fiction drawing on European literary conventions, most obviously in the Camille complex. It would be a mistake, however, to stop at this. The stories about kept women also adumbrate a realistic and ambiguous space in which agency and victimization hang in the balance and women can operate in strategic as well as tactical ways.

The stories are realistic because the pool of ideal women marriage candidates was restricted. Consider the ideal: virgin girls, between the ages of 15 and 18, with rudiments of social polish, and a large dowry.[34] Most women, by definition, did not meet these criteria. Under these circumstances, elite men could look to keep a mistress while holding out for an opportunity to marry a girl in the ideal category. Conversely, ambitious but impecunious women could enter the game of sex and submission in ways that echoed the calculated entry of the male parvenu into society, by accentuating their attractions and procuring strong (rich) protectors. The actual results of these gambits were ambiguous, because the "spoiled" reputation of a fallen woman served, inversely, to open a path to a relatively autonomous existence, even the prospect of independent security—if not marriage material, why not make oneself secure through other means? Marcela and Leonília, doomed as they were to an ugly old age (according to their ex-lovers), lived for quite a while in splendor. Both possessed considerable fortunes at one point in time. When Brás meets Marcela again on his way to his fateful meeting with Virgília, she is ugly and apparently poor, although she has a local married man on a string. Brás observes that despite her terrible appearance,

> I began to suspect that she had suffered no great misfortunes (except the illness), that she had money enough to live very comfortably, and that she was in business only to further her lust for wealth, which was like a worm gnawing at her soul.

> Entrei a desconfiar que não padecera nenhum desastre (salvo a moléstia), que tinha o dinheiro a bom recado, e que negociava com o único fim de acudir à paixão do lucro, que era o verme roedor daquela existência.[35]

Marcela is subordinated to greed, in Brás's admittedly unreliable opinion, not men. In this, she is not so very far removed from Cotrim, the other purely venal character in the novel. Yet, given that families like Brás's would never countenance a marriage with a woman like Marcela, it is also certainly the case that she has made the most of her opportunities in terms of relations with the upper-class male.

Both Leonília and Marcela represent the demonic, man-destroying, high-class courtesan. Leonília churns through a banker's fortune before leaving him high and dry in Italy.[36] Marcela loved Brás "for fifteen months and eleven contos; nothing less" ("durante quinze meses e onze contos de réis; nada menos").[37] Nothing less and, it goes without saying, nothing more. Time is money for the courtesan; she must capitalize on her fleeting good looks and social reputation as high-class goods. In this regard, it seems safe to say that these characters bear the stamp of a common nineteenth-century European cliché. Clichés are not false. They are powerful ideas to live by. Can there be any doubt that some women in Rio de Janeiro operated according to these ideas, taking advantage while being taken advantage of? But what of the more common cases, the everyday compromises and arrangements entered into by unmarried women as they attempted to carve out a life in society and develop relations with men of wealth and social standing?

The outsized role of mistresses and fallen women in the Brazilian bildungsroman is, to be sure, an exaggeration and distortion of social reality introduced for generic purposes more than any other. The hero needs to be tested. Dangerous women, the *francesas* and courtesans of the metropolis, lurk along his pathway of experience and social integration. Bearing in mind this aspect of the novels, much genuine information and insight into modes of comportment and forms of agency or subordination remain embedded in the stories of these women. Perhaps most of all, the stories underscore the admixture of vulnerability and possibility associated with sexual experience in Rio de Janeiro at the time. Sex could be the pathway to love. It could be the source of money and gifts. It could be the source of disgrace and ostracism. Mostly, and here our authors' realism shines, it was fleeting and, in the end, disappointing. Sexual acts are more tactical than strategic, although the consequences of a single act can have massive strategic consequences.

Alencar: Fallen Woman Redeemed

Of all the nineteenth-century Brazilian novelists, José de Alencar hews most closely to European models when dealing with the theme of the fallen woman. He sets out self-consciously to reproduce the ideological critique of the sexual double standard found in works like *Camille*. For Alencar, a woman's virtue is not reducible to her sexual continence, nor were lapses in chastity permanent or fatal marks on her honor. To embody this argument, he creates female characters in both novels and plays who, despite sexual lapses, prove to be honorable and worthy. For this kind of logic to work, Alencar depends on two interlocking concepts, both of which relate to issues of independence or subordination and the sentimental education of young women.

The first concept is that of mitigating circumstance: Lapses can be explained by situations, such as poverty and desperation. The second concept is more firmly located in the ambit of *Bildung*: the idea that inexperience leads to miscalculations just as the fruits of experience lead to moral growth. In the end, Alencar remains conventional in his treatment of fallen women. They tend to be martyrs in service of an ideological critique and mimicry of European models. Recall the final lines regarding the tragic protagonist of Alencar's *Lucíola*.

> A palid smile still bloomed on her colorless lips: sublime ecstasy illuminated the pale transparency of her face. The weightless beauty of angels must be like her divinely limpid countenance.

> Um sorriso pálido desfolhou-se ainda nos lábios sem cores: sublime êxtase illuminou a suave transparência de seu rosto. A beleza immaterial dos anjos deve ter aquela divina limpidez.[38]

Readers of this passage would recognize unmistakable traces of what we might call the Camille complex, based on the ideology of female regeneration through death. This idealization was made enormously popular by Alexandre Dumas in his 1848 novel, which was adapted for the stage in 1852 under the title

La Dame aux Camelias.[39] Instead of traditional marriage and pure earthly love, the courtesan or fallen woman opts for withdrawal and self-abnegation, leading to premature death and the apotheosis of "sublime ecstasy" offered by a fundamentally misogynistic culture. Such a fate was not limited to fallen women. As Bram Dijkstra shows in his study of fin de siècle images of feminine evil, married women could also find themselves painted into this corner of quiet withdrawal and consumptive withering away.[40]

Historical details lift Alencar's version of the Camille story above the level of mere imitation. In *Lucíola* the backstory of the young girl's fall is anchored in the all too realistic context of the devastating yellow fever epidemic of 1850. The precariousness of life for the lower reaches of the free population of Rio de Janeiro are brought to the fore in this short profile of a woman written by Alencar at a pivotal moment in his own artistic development. As with *Camille*, the question asked in *Lucíola* is twofold: Can honest women fall and, if so, can true love redeem them? The first part of the question is crucial, because the dominant patriarchal response was a categorical no. Women fell because, at root, they were weak or, worse, because they wanted to. As we will see in the next chapter, Alencar was inconsistent in his own understanding of this question. In the play *As Asas de um Anjo*, written four years before *Lucíola*, the female protagonist falls of her own, admittedly naïve, accord.[41] In the reworking of *Camille*, Alencar's *Lucíola* offers a different story.

We first meet Lúcia in her splendor as a courtesan. She is, as Alencar self-consciously admits, a Brazilian *La Dame aux Camélias*. Accepting though never asking for gifts of jewels, she lives in high style, out in society. She is, as Dr. Sá, a friend of Paulo (the Brazilian Armand), says, not a "lady" but a "beautiful woman," surrounded by admirers just like her French counterpart.[42] Paulo senses something deeper in Lúcia, something honest and even chaste beneath the carapace of sensuous glamour. Like Armand, he falls in love, has his love tested, and eventually learns the truth about her circumstances.

Things are not always as they seem. In Lúcia's own words in closing her first meeting with Paulo and his friend Sá, "Even so, I have the right to be believed. Appearances often lie! Isn't that so?" ("Portanto tenho o direito de ser acreditada. As aparências enganam tantas vêzes! Não é verdade?").[43]

The truth is that Lúcia has not fallen. She has been pushed by terrible circumstances. Having moved with her family to Rio de Janeiro in the late 1840s when her father obtained a position in the Department of Public Works, she enjoyed a few years of relative happiness in the bosom of her family—in this,

the theme of provincial arrival and the testing of life in the great city is extended to a major female protagonist. She was reading and learning a smat-
tering of French; in other words, she was developing the rudiments of polish
that would make her a viable bride in her latter teens according to the expectations of middling society at the time. Her father's position can be taken to have
been on the low end of the scale of public employment; his income was barely
enough to maintain the family in a decent state. Low expectations, then, but
not null. When yellow fever struck in 1850, it not only killed several thousand
outright but also sickened many thousands more. Lúcia's parents both fall ill,
as do her brothers. A neighbor who had visited and tried to minister to the
sick members of the family soon fell ill herself and died. Panicked residents
of the city stopped visiting the homes of the sick, in just the way described in
the novel. Lúcia's family become pariahs in the neighborhood, and what little
money remains is soon spent on ineffective medicines. Adding to the scale of
the disaster, Lúcia's aunt, the only adult who had been spared up to that moment, also falls ill. At just 14, the girl is alone and responsible for caring for
and trying to save the lives of her whole family. At this critical age, her *Bildung*
becomes an exercise in survival and degradation.

Desperate to save her loved ones, she calls out to a passing neighbor named
Couto. He offers Lúcia consolation and beckons her to come with him to his
house. In exchange for the money she needs to get medical attention for her
family, Lúcia allows Couto to force himself on her.[44] Too late to save her mother
or brothers, the money helps her father survive the epidemic. In her innocence,
when pressed by her father to account for where she found the money, Lúcia
admits what she has done. In spite of her noble sacrifice, the father she has
saved from certain death repays her by casting her out of his house.[45] From this
point on, she prostitutes herself to obtain money to support her father and her
little sister, who, having also survived the epidemic, will need a dowry to have
hopes of a decent marriage.

The prostitute with a golden heart, the late dawning of love and rediscovery
of human dignity, the implicit critique of the sexual double standard—all of this
is ripped straight out of Dumas, notwithstanding Alencar's clever disavowal, in
the words of Paulo: "Let us leave off thinking once and for all of Camille. Neither
you are Margarida nor I Armand" ("Deixamos em paz A Dama das Camélias.
Nem tu és Margarida, nem eu sou Armando").[46] Yet Alencar's historical sensibility and humane view of women, however complicated and prudish, shines
through here in an authentic manner. The creaking joints of the plot, the hidden

identities, and the romantic pathos cannot hide this quality. No doubt, we have here our explanation for the continued popularity of this little book. This is a prime example of Schwarz's astute observation that it is Alencar's local color that lifts his fiction above the simple mimicry of French models. Where I depart from Schwarz is in the value of the French model for Brazil. Was there not a sexual double standard in 1850s Rio de Janeiro? If there was, as surely was the case, it seems that *Camille* is a perfectly good weapon to wield in the fight against it.

Moreover, in humanizing the fallen woman, *Lucíola* highlights the matrix of significations that surrounded female comportment in Brazil's capital during the nineteenth century. An unmarried woman out alone in society was not a lady but a beautiful object of desire. The male gaze, which Alencar writes of so disconcertingly, is not merely a reflection of his odd hang-ups. It is broadly representative, if not in its language, then in its intensity and ubiquity. Out there in the streets, men (and women) *were* looking. A "lady," especially if married (or hoping to be married), needed to guard against appearing as an "available" woman in the street.

A newspaper satire from the same period tells the story of a man and woman on a public tram. They flirt, although the man is forward and the woman feigns reticence. She worries about the gaze of others; he does not. Outside, their respective wife and husband walk by together, unseen.[47] We can take this kind of story as being dispositive of the temper of the time. The strategic imperative is to maintain one's reputation as a lady. The tactical maneuver is to feint and dodge while moving back and forth across the invisible line. Appearances *do* matter, and a single glance *can* lead to something more. Walking down the street could signify the battle at the start of a long campaign.

Likewise, comportment, not essence, determines the tone of encounters among mixed company. Lúcia herself is an act, a fiction just like her name. Seated at her piano, in her tasteful rooms, she is the picture of a decent woman.[48] Splayed out nude on a dining table at an orgiastic party, she is the demonic man-eater Paulo has been warned off from.[49] There is a famous scene in the novel, which is usually cited to emphasize Alencar's alleged taint of misogyny, where Lúcia transforms before Paulo's eyes from a chaste girl to a sexually potent and frightening woman in response to a misunderstanding caused by her reaction to his clumsy kisses. This transformation, however, is ironic. The point is that by changing her demeanor from shy and chaste to ardent and available, she delivers the equivalent of a slap in the face to the hapless Paulo, who has come seeking a lover and found love instead. When he misinterprets her shyness and blushing, which arise from her honest affection, for coquetry, she throws his masculine social expectations back on him. Her comportment reflects the truth behind his gaze: It is not an unmasking of Lúcia; it is an unmasking of Paulo. It is his mind that is filled with big felines and snakes, not Alencar the narrator's. Her caresses are "irritable," and he understands that she is not a "pleasure machine," that she "feels." He is horrified. Alencar *is* a realistic writer. Paulo sees but does not comprehend; he tries to shame her by tossing money at her but ends up leaving with his tail between his legs.[50]

Azevedo: Pathos and Passion

It is to Aluísio Azevedo that we owe one of the most affecting, if ultimately pathetic, depictions of the kept woman. As the reader will recall from Chapter 3, Teobaldo and André take a room upstairs in a house purportedly owned by a woman named Ernestina when they first arrive in Rio de Janeiro. At first, Teobaldo hardly notices Ernestina, absorbed as he is in setting up house and deciding what to study while in the Corte. Indeed, his indifference is part of his charm, and the poor girl is soon falling in love with this feckless son of a baron. She is described succinctly in the following short paragraphs, each of which warrants close analysis:

> Dona Ernestina, as the lady was known, was a good natured girl of twenty and some years, full bodied, but a bit mysterious with regard to her private life. By appearances, she had some money of her own and was an honest woman.

> D. Ernestina, assim se chamava a senhora, era uma rapariga de vinte e poucos anos, cheia de corpo, muito bem disposta, mas um tanto misteriosa na sua vida íntima. Pelo jeito possuía alguma coisinha de seu e era mulher honesta.[51]

Twenty-something and living independently meant a girl of ambiguous provenance. What was her situation, the narrator asks?

> Widowed, married or single?
> A widow, she might be; married, not so much, for in that case she would not be the master of the house, as her husband would hold that place. Single . . . but there are so many kinds of single women . . .

> Viúva, casada ou solteira?
> Viúva, podia ser; casada é que não, porque em tal caso não seria ela a senhora da casa e sim o marido. Solteira . . . mas há tantos gêneros de mulher solteira . . .[52]

Two points: The narrator sees fit to inquire after Ernestina's marital status immediately after observing that she appears to be an honest woman; and he (the gender of the narrator could not be more obvious and less naturalistically neutral than here) goes on to deduce that she must be a widow or a single woman, because there is no man of the house. The clinchers are the damning ellipses. If she is single, she is more or less assumed to be something other than an honest woman.

> Nevertheless, no one could question her conduct. She passed all the sainted day occupied with tidying around her house and only showed herself at the window or went out to walk in the garden on hot afternoons, when the body needed fresh air.

> Contudo ninguém podia dizer mal de sua conduta. Passava todo o santo dia ocupada com os arranjos da casa e só se mostrava à janela ou saía a passear no jardim nas tardes de muito calor, quando o corpo reclama ar livre.[53]

But, in the next paragraph we find out that she entertains an older man in her rooms at odd hours and alone. Not an honest woman after all.

The situation develops gradually, as Ernestina first offers Teobaldo and André meals in her rooms for a monthly fee. Eventually, Teobaldo takes to spending afternoons in her apartment, playing the piano and performing little sleight-of-hand tricks. Familiarity breeds contempt on his side; love grows on her side.[54]

Eventually, Teobaldo becomes linked to Ernestina through an informal sale offered by her former lover, Mr. Almeida. In this pivotal scene Teobaldo hears Ernestina's story filtered through the voice of her middle-aged lover. Almeida describes being led by a rented domestic slave girl to a shoddy room where Ernestina lies prostrate on the ground, having been beaten by her drunken husband. Seeing a pretty girl in distress, Almeida decides to act. He is both charitable and self-interested. There can be no doubt that the girl is hurt and possibly in danger. Taking her away and offering protection *is* charitable. However, Almeida is also stuck in a loveless marriage to a woman closer to his own age. He wants a younger mistress, and Ernestina appears ripe for the picking. She is vulnerable and needy at the same time that she is still an honest woman.[55] Almeida installs her in the house in Matacavalos, tucked nicely away on the outskirts of the city, and enjoys several years of nightly visits to his mistress.

As events unfold, Teobaldo is the proverbial loser of this game of musical chairs. The music stops and he is left standing with the unwanted commitment to keep Ernestina as his lover. His honor will not allow him to throw Ernestina to the wolves—that is, to deny his protection when Almeida is threatening to withdraw from the arrangement. Despite agreeing to take up her maintenance, Teobaldo has no interest in a romantic connection. Ernestina, having "won" Teobaldo through this episode, attempts to press her advantage and begins to cling to the object of her desire, moving uninvited into his rooms and refusing to leave. The young man, still in his teens, is forced to flee his rented apartment for the expensive sheets of the Hotel da França, located in the city center at the corner of the Largo do Paço and the Rua Primeiro de Março (formerly Rua Direita).[56]

Despite this episode and its vulgarization of sex, Azevedo is at pains to show the human side of the kept woman. Ernestina genuinely loves Teobaldo, worships him even. His disregard for her affection leads her to a half-accidental immolation, leaving behind her charred remains, bits of flesh streaking the walls, and a small inheritance she has bequeathed to Teobaldo.

Leonília, Teobaldo's other lover is, as we saw in Chapter 3, more worldly and resourceful than poor Ernestina. With this pair, we can assume that the attraction is mutual and that the sex is good. Leonília is presented in the novel as a predatory female. She is the most "beautiful creature of the era in the world of bohemian affairs." Nearly 30, she looks more like 20. Teobaldo is a mark. She picks him out by chance at the theater and asks a friend for an introduction. Teobaldo's blasé attitude only increases her attraction, and she sets out to conquer him.[57] He uses women; she wants to be loved and adored. In a key passage the two discuss the question of whether a carnal fallen woman can ever be truly loved. Teobaldo, echoing the ideology of the age, says no, there are only two kinds of women: virtuous and not virtuous. He characterizes the distinction as a social law. She is of the second kind. Leonília counters with a much more humane categorization: Women are either malicious or simple (there is no perfect translation for the Portuguese *simples*, but it can be taken to mean, in this context, naïve and uncalculating). A simple woman might fall and be seduced, but her core being may retain a redeemable goodness—Camille redux. She asks again, Can he not love her, if she "employs every means (to reform) . . . if I make myself your slave, your friend, your lover, only yours?" Teobaldo's response is categorical: "Impossible."[58]

Leonília, in desperation, moves out of her luxurious love nest and takes up housekeeping in a modest cottage on the outskirts of town. Spatial practices are important in this case. The house on the edge of town is a symbolic space, removed from the world of the theater, hotel dinners, champagne, and kept women. By taking on the external signs of an honest woman, replete with plain clothes, a sewing machine, and a wedding band, Leonília hopes to prove to her lover that she is worthy of true love. Teobaldo, unmoved, strips off her mask. He cannot see Leonília as a wife any more than Ernestina.[59]

There is a final act in this story of unrequited love. Leonília, scorned, does not slink away quietly. She may be weak relative to Teobaldo, but she is not without weapons. When she hears that her former lover is planning a rich marriage to a "virtuous" young girl all of 15, she acts to derail Teobaldo's plans, planting seeds of doubt in the mind of the girl's father. She extorts a cash payment, which Teobaldo's friend André pays her from his own meager resources, to go away for a time. On her return, she spies on Teobaldo and conspires with Branca's cousin Aguiar to unravel the marriage. In the first place, this shows that men did not always get a free pass as they moved from sowing wild oats to settling down as serious men and heads of household. Past behavior could compromise a man's plans and cast him in a bad light in the eyes of a future father-in-law. The sexual double standard was real enough, but male comportment was not hermetically sealed off from social norms. In the second place, the fates of fallen women in Azevedo's works point to a realistic sense of consequences. Sex and desire are combustible. In a small world like nineteenth-century Rio de Janeiro, where both society and the demimonde were looped together in a network of relationships, conflict and complication rather than easy movement from one state to the other would have been the rule rather than the exception. Even Brás, who seems to move through society with a Teflon coating, runs afoul of these entanglements. He encounters Marcela on the way to Virgília and the delay costs him a wife. Billiard balls are more likely to collide on a small table.

This observation sharpens the sense in which courtship among the city's elite and would-be elite was fraught with an unstable mixture of connivance and chance. Courtship required an engagement in social life, the navigation of social spaces with all the chancy elements associated, and throughout this the conscious (or unconscious) choice of comportment. Wooing was not, according to the stories told in these novels, a simple matter of men selecting women from the ranks of marriageable girls in society. It was a two-way street and not entirely dependent on wealth and status considerations, although in the aggregate these concerns tended to weigh heavily on marriage choice (see Chapter 5).

Teobaldo wooed Branca's father as much as he did the young girl herself—at least until his rival poisoned the budding relationship with the merchant. Courtship involved complex negotiation with the extended families of the two parties to the prospective marriage transaction. Thus, just as Teobaldo attempts to ingratiate himself with the rich father of Branca, Capitu, in Machado de Assis's *Dom Casmurro*, does something similar, and to greater effect, with Bento's mother. There are other cases in which women are depicted as the initiators of the marriage dance, either as the prime mover, in the case of Guida Soares in *Sonhos d'Ouro*, or as an avenging angel, as in the case of Alencar's *Senhora*.

Indifference and Volubility

The problem of social integration is not, merely, a question of finding a protector or enacting modes of masculine or feminine comportment in conscious ways. It is not simply a response to structure, engaged with tactically or strategically. Integration is conditioned by unconscious traits that may be considered typical of individuals of a given class and social position as well as the ticks and tendencies of inherited manners.

Brás Cubas is a loser in the structural position of a winner. On the contrary, perhaps he is structurally determined neither to lose nor to win. Brás's father urges him to "flee the common, seek the great." But his father's definition of greatness is merely a derivative of public opinion—which he takes as the greatest value of all.[60] Yet Brás's accomplishments, if we may call them such, are canceled out by the vacuity of the world in which he operates. It is not only Brás who is ultimately indifferent; it is the world of society and politics in Rio de Janeiro. Georg Simmel provides a diagnosis for Brás's affliction in the general effect of urban life on the individual: the genesis of the blasé outlook. Simmel's description of the process by which the complexity of metropolitan life and the predominance of the money economy engender a blasé outlook fits Brás Cubas almost too perfectly, as though Machado's creation foreshadowed the German sociologist's findings point by point.[61] If we remember, however, that Simmel's observations were first published in 1903, the correspondence takes on an even greater sense of validity. These two great observers of urban life are describing what is in essence the same conjuncture.

To begin with, Simmel writes, "The metropolitan type . . . creates a protective organ for itself. . . . Instead of reacting emotionally, the metropolitan type reacts primarily in a rational manner, thus creating a mental predominance through the intensification of consciousness, which is in turn caused by it." Furthermore, "Money economy and the domination of the intellect stand in the closest relationship to one another. They have in common a purely matter-of-fact attitude

in the treatment of persons and things."[62] Now, recall Brás's various pronounce-
ments regarding Dona Plácida: her purpose in life drawn in harsh rational tones,
the equation of her utility with Brás's ends, her acceptance of the 5 contos. Consider too, Brás on the true nature of his relationship with his courtesan lover:
"Marcela loved me for fifteen months and eleven contos; nothing less." Utterly
blasé and calculating and perfectly fitting Simmel's lapidary observation that "to
the extent that money, with its colorlessness and its indifferent quality, can become a common denominator of all values it becomes the frightful leveler—it
hollows out the core of things, their peculiarities, their specific values and their
uniqueness and incomparability in a way which is beyond repair."[63]

Finally, crowning the sense of commonality in Machado's fiction and Simmel's diagnosis of the mental life of the city, we have this: "The mental attitude
of the people of the metropolis to one another may be designated formally as
one of reserve." What is more, "The inner side of this external reserve is not
only indifference but more frequently than we believe, it is a slight aversion,
a mutual strangeness and repulsion," from which Simmel concludes that we
modern urban types are "saved by antipathy which is the latent adumbration of
actual antagonism since it brings about the sort of distantiation and deflection
without which this type of life could not be carried on at all."[64]

Antipathy and distantiation, then. Brás Cubas harbors a sense of dislike
of or distance from Dona Plácida, Lobo Neves, Marcela, Prudêncio, Cotrim,
Eugênia, Eulália, his sister Sabina, even Virgília. Toward everyone in his life.
There are many examples. Two will suffice. On Eulália, the flower he thought to
"pluck from the swamp":

> It is enough to know that she died. I might add that it was during the first epi-
> demic of yellow fever. I attended the funeral. It made me sad but it did not cause
> me to cry; from this I conclude that I had not really loved her.

> Ficam sabendo que morreu; acrescentarei que foi por ocasião da primeira en-
> trada da febre amarela. Não digo mais nada, a não ser que a acompanhei até o
> último jazigo, e me despedi triste, mas sem lágrimas. Concluí que talvez não a
> amasse deveras.[65]

And, upon hearing that Dona Plácida is sick and dying and needing to go to the
hospital: "Why must a dying person be taken to a hospital? You can die anywhere.
. . . What a nuisance! I won't go" ("Morre-se em qualquer parte. . . . Que maçada!
Não vou").[66] He goes. And going, he observes that Dona Plácida's purpose in the
world had been to facilitate his affair with Virgília. Utterly blasé, Brás assiduously

maintains his distance and cuts himself off from strong emotional attachments. He is surrounded by calamities but sails along on an even, numb keel.

Here, the contrast with Rubião, the hero of the next of Machado's novels, is especially revealing. Rubião is a poor provincial schoolteacher in Minas Gerais before inheriting Quincas Borba's fortune. His friend and philosophical mentor, Quincas Borba, explains the underlying principle of all human life in the phrase "ao vencedor as batatas" (to the winner, the potatoes). The parable describes two tribes fighting for survival. One tribe must vanquish the other in order to harvest the potatoes needed to survive and cross the mountains to the valley below, where there are potatoes aplenty. There are not enough potatoes for the tribes to share and survive together. Collaboration results in a pure Pareto pessimum.[67] Rubião, upon receiving his friend's fortune, takes this to mean that it is time to go to Rio de Janeiro and harvest potatoes in the big city. He is, however, manifestly ill-equipped despite his new wealth to flourish in Rio. He lacks, more than anything, Brás Cubas's blasé outlook. Rubião believes in friendship, in the promise of romance behind Sofia's seductive eyes; his naïveté leads him to discount and vacillate in irrational and unproductive ways. He does not read the city, and lacking the sense of antipathy and distance required for self-protection, it reads him to the tune of free meals, unpaid loans, and ultimate abandonment. The successful city types, Palha and Carlos Maria, share Brás Cubas's blasé outlook. They calculate, weigh, and maintain distance in their relationships.

The "excessive lucidity that destroys the illusions necessary for life" ("excesso de lucidez (que) mata as ilusoes indispensáveis a subsistência da vida")[68] that Augusto Meyer identifies in Machado's work is transformed through Simmel's optic into a tactic for everyday life. An intelligent, if warped tactic, as "it is not likely that stupid persons who have been hitherto intellectually dead will be blasé."[69]

Intelligent, ironic, calculating, indifferent: the voice of Brás Cubas, perhaps the voice of Machado himself, with the difference, certainly, that the novels serve a dual purpose. They represent society in a blasé voice, and in doing so they contain a kernel—a smirking, winking kernel—of acidic critique. This stance calls to mind Walter Benjamin: "All decisive blows are struck left-handed."[70] To which Machado adds: The horrors of (urban) life are best told as jokes.

Heredity and Environment

Significant differences can be found among nineteenth-century Brazilian novelists when it comes to the role of heredity and the environment in determining comportment and the prospects of successful social integration. The distance from Alencar to Azevedo is probably greater in this regard than is the distance from Balzac to Zola. In Balzac we get intimations of hereditary forces and phrases about the "Southern brain"; in Alencar, these forces are largely absent. Azevedo, for his part, is nearly as committed to the intertwined concepts of environmental and genetic determinism as his French master, Zola, although it cannot be said that he developed a coherent project along the lines of *Les Rougon Macquart* as a vehicle for exploring these beliefs across several generations.

The problem of environmental or hereditary factors in the formation of individuals (or groups for that matter) was of increasing prominence during the last third of the nineteenth century, particularly as the influence of Darwin and Spencer spread throughout the West. In this regard, the novels of the era, particularly those written in the realist or Naturalist modes, represent a literary engagement with an unsettled science of human evolution and social development. It should be obvious that such questions are relevant to the process of *Bildung*. Machado de Assis and Azevedo certainly thought so. By way of contrast, Alencar's characters evince only a tenuous degree of internalization of *original* environmental forces; they are more apt to evolve in response to internal change and hence their perception of their environment; they more likely bear within themselves essential and individual characteristics that do not necessarily derive from environmental causes but cannot, at the same time, be reduced to heredity. Call this romanticism, even unreconstructed romanticism.

"The child is the father to the man." "Of such land, fertilized by such manure, this flower drew its substance."[71] As is often the case, Machado conceals something behind the mocking tone of these clichés. Yes, clichés: not to be taken at face value, but not necessarily to be discounted too heavily. In Machado, the external determinants have a tendency to become internalized. Character is relatively fixed in a hereditary, genetic sense. Recall Augusto Meyer's astute observation: There is a terrible constancy in much of Machado's work.[72] Brás stays true to his word. He hews to his original "substance" to the end. *Dom Casmurro*. The title says it all: Sir Stoneface. Paulo and Pedro, frozen in position in *Esaú e Jacó*. The cynicism of Machado's later novels resides, in no small degree, in the extent to which the major protagonists often embody this dual sense of emplacement, by both heredity and environment, in fortified and internally stable positions. Born and bred to be as they are, by no means consistent or happy, but fatally—hence, and ironically, caprice and chance play the greater role in the lives of these men and women.

Given his Naturalist inclinations, it is no surprise to see Azevedo putting great stress on the formative power of heredity to shape the destiny of an individual in a given social environment. In *O Coruja*, André and Teobaldo are virtually unchanged in their core personalities despite the great swings in their social positions. If the environment is an independent variable inasmuch as it changes in ways that are autonomous from the perspective of the individual, then hereditary disposition is a constant term from which Azevedo derives the coefficient concerning a given personality's interaction with a specified milieu.

Here we are, then: romanticism, cynicism, determinism. It is easy to see why Machado's position proves the most enduring in its appeal to us latter-day sophisticated readers. He caught the temper of the twentieth century (and the twenty-first) in 1880. Winners who are losers, buffeted by chance and caprice, all-seeing and blind, ineffectual . . . Prufrock, Bloom, Herzog . . .

Notwithstanding the contemporary appeal of Machado's fictional treatment of heredity and environment, it is worth returning to the nineteenth century and inquiring into the romantic and deterministic versions of this interaction. To begin with, how, if at all, did Alencar address the interaction of genetics and milieu? The answer is, obliquely, through his concept of character. Character for Alencar is both inherited and shaped by the environment. Guida is naturally independent and capricious, but she has also learned to be so through her experiences as a rich sole heiress. We can assume that Ricardo is stubborn and hardworking by birth, but it is his provincial education in São Paulo that has made him suspicious and withdrawn.[73]

For Machado and Azevedo, the new science heralded by Darwin's theories and Taine's historicism and modulated in the case of Azevedo through Claude Bernard by way of Zola, offers both an opportunity and a challenge to go beyond the romantic portrayal of the origins and growth of a personality. Readers of Machado de Assis have long detected the influence of Darwin on the deterministic world depicted in the great novels of his mature period.[74] Raimundo Magalhães, in discussing the cast of Machado's thought in the year before the publication of *Memórias Póstumas*, points to an essay published in 1879 in which the author exhorts the young generation to reread its Spencer and its Darwin.[75] Why did Machado want the young poets to read Darwin? What had he learned from the new science? Basically, he discovered the concepts of natural selection, the struggle for life, and survival of the fittest. This "universal law" was beyond right and wrong, untouched by morality.[76] It was both an explanation (why people acted the way they did) and a source of irony (the unfitness of the fit, the real Cotrim).

Azevedo's determinism begins with genetics, with blood. Blood is both culture and race. Characters with Portuguese blood carry Portuguese culture. Mixtures of blood are unstable—both internally, because mixture undermines the integration of personality, and externally, because the social position of a person of mixed blood is ambiguous. This internal instability is ascribed by Azevedo to Teobaldo's father and therefore to the son by extension. Emílio Henrique de Albuquerque, the future Barão do Palmar, was the son of a Portuguese *fidalgo* and a beautiful *cabocla* from Paraná.

> From such antagonistic elements was formed his hybrid and singular character—aristocratic and rustic at the same time, because the veins of Emílio de Albuquerque coursed with the refined blood of nobility and the barbaric blood of the Tapuias.
>
> De tais elementos, tão antagônicos, formou-se-lhe aquele caráter híbrido e singular, aristocrata e rude a um tempo, porque nas veias de Emílio de Albuquerque tanto corria o refinado sangue da nobreza, como o sangue bárbaro dos tapuias.[77]

Machado's determinism gives no consolation to his time and place. It reflects something beyond repair because it is not even broken. In this sense his position is conservative, like that of Flaubert: artistically, a triumph, but normatively null, except in the limited sense of negation of received ideas, including, it should be emphasized, the received ideas associated with Darwin, Positivism, and so on.

Faced with Azevedo's proto-eugenics, we shiver at the touch of the leathery bat wing bearing future concentration camps. To a lesser degree, we also turn away from Azevedo's implicit progressive call for reform of the environment, for cleaning up the slums, for fixing what is broken in the lives of others. We have read Foucault. We think we know where this kind of thinking ends.

Ironic fatalism or earnest fatalism. Which will it be? Are these the only choices? No.

It is possible to stand with the defeated without irony. Hardy manages it with Tess and with Jude.

Alencar's volunteerism reads like Stendhal without the cynicism. Life is there to be seized. Heroes are possible. Nothing is determined. For some, this will sound like *Reader's Digest*. For others, it will sound like hope.

≈

The period of *Bildung* often ends, symbolically, at the wedding altar. Men and women, upon entering into marriage, are complete; they are socially integrated and now fully capable of fulfilling the process of social reproduction in bourgeois society. Or so goes one of the core ideological givens of the time.

Novels tell a different story. They sometimes end with happy marriages, but more often than not, marriage is neither the end of the story nor a happy condition. It turns out that the conflicts between individual autonomy and authenticity and between social structure and integration are far from finished with the exchange of vows. Getting and staying married were difficult.

MARRIAGE AND MONEY

IF THE BILDUNGSROMAN is focused on the reconciliation of the individual to society by means of the pathways of work and career, its classical form often ends with the social integration that comes through marriage. As we have seen, for a young woman like Guida Soares, her *Bildung* is all about creating an individual personality and using it to attempt to influence the terms of her marriage. She learns how to play the game in order not to play it according to the established rules. In the end, marriage to Ricardo offers the reconciliation promised by the genre. In contrast, Brás Cubas never marries, never fully reconciles, and leaves behind no children. Yet in social terms this is not seen as an indelible failure; it does not define Brás as a man.

To marry or not to marry? This is a very different question when posed to a young woman rather than a young man. In a society where two out of every five babies were born to unmarried mothers and where "proper" eligible women were outnumbered by their male counterparts, the question takes on a particular cast with quite different valences depending on gender and class position.

According to parish records, the rate of natural births was high and relatively constant over the second half of the nineteenth century in Rio de Janeiro (see Table 3).[1] The small decline apparent by the 1880s can be seen, perhaps, as the growing acceptance of marriage and the bourgeois norm filtering through a broader segment of society—but this kind of data, on its own, is inconclusive. The proportion of births to unmarried mothers during this era was much

TABLE 3. "Natural" Births in Rio de Janeiro Compared with Other Locations

Location	Period	Rate of "Natural" Births	Rate of "Natural" Births Without Alforrias
Baptized free			
Rio de Janeiro[a]	1854–57	40.7	39.2
Rio de Janeiro[a]	1870–71	42.0	39.2
Rio de Janeiro[a]	1887–89	32.3	
Free or slave?			
Cuiaba, Mato Grosso[b]	1853–90	43.5	
São Cristóvão, São Paulo[b]	1858–67	33.9	
Curitiba, Paraná[b]	1801–50	27.4	
São José del Rei, Minas Gerais[c]	1799–1807	34.0 (including slaves)	11.7 (free only)
London[d]	1855–64	4.2	
Urban France[e]	1879–83	10.1	

SOURCES: (a) Sacramento Parish, Livros de Registro de Batismos, Arquivo da Curia, Rio de Janeiro; (b) Praxedes, "A Teia e a Trama da Fragilidade Humana: os Filhos Ilégitimos em Minas Gerais, 1770–1840," in *Anais do XI Seminário sobre a Economia Mineira* (CEDEPLAR: Universidade Federal de Minas Gerais, 2004), 10; (c) Libby and Frank, unpublished data, collected 2004–2013; (d) *Annual Report of the Registrar General* (London, 1879), xxii; (e) Baldwin et al., "Moral Statistics," in *Dictionary of Philosophy and Psychology* (London, 1902), 108.

higher in urban Brazil than in European centers. Social-historical data like this can add substantially to our understanding of why certain European ideas appear out of place. It is not only a story of slavery and seigniorial power out of synch with bourgeois ideals but also a quite different configuration of family structure, at least in this realm, than was contemplated in the fictions of Dickens or Balzac.

In addition, the cultural coordinates mapping sex, love, family, and money were in flux. Dowries were in decline; parental control was ebbing; capitalism was transforming social structures and reshuffling social relations.[2] The novels of the era cast light on this complex subject, but it is a flickering light and the shadows are deep. Social-historical methods can help place these fictional stories of the marriage market in context.

The metaphor of the marriage market needs fine-tuning. What kind of market is this? How competitive and how segmented is it? Certainly, the marriage market in Rio de Janeiro strayed far from the level playing field of a frictionless and open system. The dramatic (or melodramatic, as the case may be) heft of the marriage plot in nineteenth-century Brazilian fiction derives in no small part from the historical difficulties known to readers from experience and the strands of gossip concerning this evergreen theme.

Marriage was costly, especially for the middle and upper classes, for whom it was expected as an outcome capping off entry into the adult world: costly in the moment, by way of finery, food, and festivities; and costly in the more profound and potentially positive sense of commingling family wealth and future prosperity—that is, spouses laid claim to future inheritances, as did, of course, any children who issued from the union. In this respect, the quality of the match was of paramount importance. Under these circumstances the clear prediction is class endogamy in marriage. Like will marry like more often than not. Social history can begin to tell us the strength of these forces.[3]

Let's begin with the question of who ultimately ends up married in this society. We can approach this issue in several ways, beginning with simple tabulations provided by the census. Digging deeper into the archives, voter qualification lists, and parish records of births and marriages tells a more subtle and detailed story. All the evidence points toward a strongly segmented marriage market. Ironically, this state of affairs probably exacerbated the sense of competition in the middle and upper spheres of society. Far from a faceless crowd of thousands, the marriageable subset of young men and women was delimited and essentially knowable—and thus subject to gossip and manipulation.

The strongest information regarding the marriage market comes from marriage records themselves. Although these records contain little direct information about the bride and groom, two indirect measures help to define the social position of the couple. The first of these is simply whether or not the mother of the bride or groom is listed in the marriage register with the honorific Dona. In an analysis of 817 marriage records taken from Sacramento Parish for the 1850s and 1860s, class endogamy appears in the strong correlation between brides and grooms who share mothers with honorific titles. The coefficient of correlation in this case is 0.61 and is statistically significant. The same rules appear to have applied to a lesser degree (coefficient of correlation 0.25, also significant) at the opposite end of the social spectrum, with respect to brides and grooms born as "natural" children. In other terms, like married like according to family background.

Occupations with higher status are clearly associated with much higher rates of marriage. In the legal field, counting lawyers, notaries, and *procuradores*, the census for Sacramento Parish indicates that 47% of Brazilian males in these professional categories were married circa 1872. Medical doctors were married, according to the census, at an even higher rate of 61%. Public employ-ees, another group of moderate to high status, stood at 44%. Meanwhile, among Brazilian-born artisans, a mere 14% had married at the time of the census.[4] Similar trends can be seen in the other core parishes of the city. Because mar-riage entailed costs, it comes as no surprise that higher status individuals were more likely to enter formal unions.

Men with professional standing were more attractive as marriage partners. Their class also shared a cultural predisposition to formal unions in keeping with bourgeois norms. For these men there was the added attraction of gaining formal control of women's wealth. Marriage, particularly for the middle and upper groups in the city, was a social and economic transaction—the pecuni-ary aspects of which so often came in for criticism in the literature of the era.[5]

Lack of money can stymie plans for marriage; inequality in economic posi-tion can block or poison a union; great wealth can complicate the relationship between parents and children with regard to the timing and circumstances of marriage. Marriage did not just bring wealth and distinction through dowries and inheritances. It also conferred social and economic advantages of its own. By using records from voter qualification rolls, it is possible to begin to trace out an additional piece of the marriage puzzle and answer the question of who, among men, was likely to be married at some point in his life. Crucially, these rolls include information on occupation and *income*—two factors that can be assumed to weigh rather heavily on the odds of making a match. As such, the voter rolls underscore the somewhat impressionistic information derived from the census records regarding occupations and marriage.

Disentangling the dependent from the independent variables in social-historical settings is notoriously difficult. Causality is murky. From Table 4 it is reasonable to conclude that part of the income premium associated with ever being married is an artifact of the social and cultural expectation that, in order to marry, one must have a decent income and that having a decent income might well be expected to correlate with coming from a family of similar ante-cedents. So the marriage variable is not truly independent. Still, the coefficient is large and statistically significant. It is equally impossible to conclude that the entire marriage premium is explained by the causal chain money—marriage. Married men earned higher incomes, controlling for age, occupation, and le-gitimacy of birth. The large negative coefficient on men who did not list the names of their fathers in the voting rolls is also a strong indication of the eco-nomic value of marriage in Brazilian society during the 1800s. Children of mar-

TABLE 4 Exploring the Determinants of Income: Occupation and Family Background

Income Regressed Against:	Coefficient	Standard Error	t	P > t
Public employee dummy	30	216	0.14	0.89
Business dummy	−110	120	−0.92	0.36
Artisan dummy	−764	101	−7.60	0.00
Ever married dummy	514	82	6.25	0.00
Natural child dummy	−355	81	−4.39	0.00
Age	20	4	5.65	0.00
Constant	803	148	5.43	0.00
Number of observations	1,400			
Adjusted R^2	0.198			
$F (6, 1,394)$	58.6			

SOURCE: "Lista dos cidadãos votantes da freguesia do S. S. Sacramento," Cod. 66-4-4, Arquivo Geral da Cidade, Rio de Janeiro.

ried couples did better when it came to incomes later in life, partly owing to greater expectations of inheritance and attendant resources and partly owing to a better social position, all other things being equal.

The data in Table 4 can be interpreted along several lines. First, I want to briefly explain the method used. The question at hand is, What variables seem to influence reported incomes in the voter qualification rolls for Sacramento Parish? Using ordinary least-squares regression, we can measure the effect of a variable and simultaneously control for the effects of other variables. The model includes three kinds of variables.

The first kind has to do with occupation. It is reasonable to assume that one of the chief factors determining income is the kind of occupation an individual pursues. Interestingly, after controlling for age and variables associated with birth or marriage, only the artisan variable shows a large and statistically significant coefficient. Taking into account other factors, such as age, artisans were associated with incomes that were 764 mil-réis lower than the rest of the qualified voters in this sample. Most artisans were relatively poor. We can also explain the lack of significance for the business and public employee variables on account of the heterogeneity of earnings in these groups; public employment, for instance, ranged from humble receptionists to powerful ministers.

The second kind of variable includes a dummy variable (1 or 0) for whether the individual has ever been married (including widowers) and a dummy variable for whether their record suggests natural rather than legitimate status at

birth. Both of these variables are significant and point in the expected directions. With everything else in the model accounted for, a voter whose birth
status was natural can be predicted to earn 355 mil-réis less than otherwise.
The marriage-money nexus thus can appear under different guises. Remember,
these are just statistical predictions based on a fairly large number of observations; they do not mean that all children born with natural status earned less
than their legitimate peers. What is more, although the effects are statistically
significant, they are by no means overwhelming.

Age provides a third kind of variable and an additional control for our es-
timates. This variable is critical because incomes are expected to rise with age.
Moreover, age is expected to be positively correlated with the ever-married
variable.

Why go through all this trouble rather than report some simple averages
(e.g., married voters earned x mil-réis). The answer is that income is a complex
variable and simple averages often do not show us what we think they do. Ultimately, the data reinforce and illuminate the sense of importance attached to
career and money with respect to marriage.

Yet, if social structures and norms governed at the level of aggregate experience, there remained ample room for maneuvering and for uncertainty in the
marriage search. Novels and the stories they tell of courtship and marriage suggest the range of strategies and tactics involved in this crucial aspect of social
life. They suggest that women's agency in marriage can be understood through
the lens of comportment and everyday tactics and through the more conventional metrics of wealth and social position. Women played the game as active
participants and not as passive receptacles of patriarchy. They did so by adopting attitudes toward the marriage market, creating a persona, and manipulating
expectations. Novels offer evidence concerning the experience of the marriage
market that cannot be approached satisfactorily from a social scientific perspective. Beyond this, as I argue in this chapter, fiction opens up the history of
marriage itself as a complex, lived experience: not just who gets married, then,
but also what marriage was like.

Volubility: Not Just for Elite Men

Volubility is associated, through the classic studies of Roberto Schwarz, with
the character of Brás Cubas and, by extension, the Brazilian elite during the
nineteenth century. As we have seen, Teobaldo, the protagonist of Azevedo's
O Coruja, provides another example of elite volubility. However, the term's as-

sociation with a privileged male member of the elite can obscure as much as it illuminates, because this correlation seems to suggest that volubility and caprice are quintessential weapons of the strong.[6] When it comes to women, things are more complicated. Elite women in particular were in an odd position that combined strength of position with subjugation to fathers and future husbands. Their power was concentrated on a single point, in theory: the marriage choice itself. Women could be forced to marry against their will by domineering men or desperate circumstances, but the dominant ideology of the time insisted on the somewhat unlikely combination of marriage for love *and* money, thus injecting a degree of autonomy in the choice of partner that ceded significant power to young women. This autonomy produced a field of signifying action. A woman's comportment, if voluble, could hinder marriage, whether purposefully or unconsciously. Several important points follow from this.

First, we can see that this situation was common across much of bourgeois culture throughout Europe and its offshoots. Literary examples abound. For instance, in Eliot's *Middlemarch*, Dorothea is considered less of a catch than her less beautiful and talented sister Celia. Why this is so comes down to Dorothea's comportment, which is considered dangerously voluble.

> And how should Dorothea not marry?—a girl so handsome and with such prospects? Nothing could hinder it but her love of extremes . . . a young lady of some birth and fortune, who knelt suddenly down on a brick floor by the side of a sick laborer and prayed fervidly . . . such a wife might awaken you some fine morning with a new scheme for the application of her income which would interfere with political economy and the keeping of saddle-horses.[7]

Dorothea's comportment, her love of extremes, is one kind of volubility. Eliot presents it as arising from a mixture of innate character and intensely held personal religious feeling. Her odd mixture of openness and monomaniacal ardor proves volatile. She marries poorly thinking she has married well; she remains true to herself and thereby subverts her own successful social integration; her *Bildung* is problematic. The point here is that Dorothea's comportment is constitutive of her opportunities and difficulties in life. Attitude is a form of agency.

Second, it is clear that all three of our canonical Brazilian authors grappled with the significance of female power in marriage choice and the role that a woman's comportment played in shaping her marriage options and ultimately the success or failure of her marriage. Alencar can be said to have been obsessed with the theme. It appears in simple form in *A Pata da Gazela*. It recurs notably in *Sonhos d'Ouro* and *Senhora*. It dominates in the last finished novel, the neogothic *Encarnação*. Let us take *Sonhos d'Ouro*, which should be familiar by now to the reader, and juxtapose it with *Encarnação*.

Recall that whether as narrator or in the voice of Ricardo or Guida, Alencar typifies the young female protagonist as capricious or the like a score of times. As I have argued, this caprice and volubility give Guida the space to maintain her independent personality and repel her unwanted suitors without the need to withdraw into self-imposed social exile. Acting like a ditz, she undermines the seriousness of situations that would otherwise be taken dead seriously as moments of courtship. In adopting this comportment in selected situations, Guida is able, in Goffman's terms, to shift the definition of the situation. In the moment, this is a tactic; repeated over time, it becomes a strategy. Guida cannot change the larger social conventions within which she moves, so there is no grand strategy available. Weapons of the weak can be the weapons of the strong. A rich girl keeping suitors off balance through her erratic comportment is another example of feint and indirection more often associated with the poor and dominated. Rich, but a girl. Rather than being a prelude to a marriage offer, an encounter with a man can be defined as a lark.

Serious courtship, as we have seen and will see again, was considered the point of no return for a woman and her honor. Once a woman allowed herself to be courted in earnest, she was committed and, in a perverse sense, already damaged goods from the perspective of other would-be suitors.

Keeping suitors at bay was a serious, full-time job, even if it required a lightness of touch that appeared, in social settings, as caprice or volubility. What were the internal coordinates of this universe? Alencar gives few hints in *Sonhos d'Ouro*, but for good stylistic reasons, he leaves these hints implied and indirect, making Guida a more satisfying fictional character than her mouthpiece-like counterpart Ricardo. Certainly there are stronger hints, really more in the form of negative examples, in *Senhora*. In *Encarnação* the hints about the internal mental state of young girls in peril of being courted become overt proclamations.

The story in a nutshell is a bit of a gothic potboiler. The scene takes place in a countrified setting at the outskirts of the city, in São Clemente. Two wealthy households in neighboring properties are home to a widower, Carlos (a.k.a. Hermano), and a young woman in "flower," Amália.[8] The widower has lost his wife and one true love and now walks about in a torpid daze, keeping a place for his beloved set at the dining table, never touching or moving any of her effects in her old bedroom. The young girl, meanwhile, has no interest in Hermano at first. She is too busy playing Guida's game to perfection: avoiding entanglements while enjoying life out in society.

Sonhos d'Ouro is a remarkably chaste novel. Independence cancels out both power and sex, at a cost of losing a chance at happiness, leaving aside the contrived happy ending in the postscript. Everyone remains virginal and even the young men, Ricardo and Fábio, sow no wild oats in the sinful metropolis. Brás Cubas, in contrast and probably more realistically, given his gender and class position, is sexually initiated at a young age by the beautiful courtesan Marcela. All his sexual activity happens outside marriage, whether in youthful trysts or in middle-aged adultery. Virgília's miscarriage saves him from the common fate of fathering an illegitimate child. In *O Coruja* Teobaldo seduces and then kidnaps Branca, obtaining her body and her money in a middle-of-the-night marriage. André, his friend, cannot marry owing to a lack of money. These three novels alone offer a wide range of possible outcomes, if not necessarily solutions, to the marriage problem and suggest different attitudes toward sex. Let us take a look at the whole range of novels written by our three authors and see what broader patterns emerge with respect to the theme of marriage.

Wives and Husbands

If it can be said that marriage is the end that most nineteenth-century bildungsromans seek, even if to lay bare the difficulties, then most of Brazil's canonical novelists in the genre offer a rather thin description of what life was like in matrimony. Alencar's plots mostly involve the period of courtship, not the aftermath. Machado wrote four indisputable masterpieces.[9] Only one, *Dom Casmurro*, truly delves into the lives of characters in marriage as a central aspect of the plot. Happy families are boring subjects for fiction.[10] The thrill of the chase soon succumbs to tedium after a happy marriage. No reader would have wanted to follow Guida and Ricardo into their long and happy years raising a family. Boring or not, what was marriage like according to novels? What were the routines and expectations and fault lines of tension?

After the glow of the honeymoon, which generally meant a trip abroad or at least out of the city to a quiet country retreat, the couple would need to set up house and find a new register for comportment in public as well as private life. This might involve, for wealthier couples, being seen at the theater and hosting occasional dinner parties. In the domestic sphere proper, a new blended arrangement regarding home economics would need to be settled on. Money issues would inevitably crop up. Married women were legally subordinated to their husbands in most financial matters. This is sometimes taken to mean that they gave up all financial autonomy. Such an impression is mistaken. Through formal legal and informal cultural means, women were able to keep their hands on some of the financial levers in the household.[11]

To make things more explicit and to foreshadow a canonical example discussed in greater length later in this section, consider the question of domestic expenses associated with keeping house. The woman was expected to be master of the house in these matters, attending to shopping for food and linens and the like. A classic division of labor was the ideal within the house, with the wife supervising the domestic servants and meting out petty cash for running expenses. For this she might receive an allowance; from this, she might accumulate some small savings. Readers familiar with the story of Brazilian slavery will note an eerie resemblance here to the way slaves who worked for hire were able to skim off small savings toward eventual self-purchase. Money is always two-faced this way. It is a tool of domination and a potential source of individual emancipation. The difference is in the asymmetry. As domination, money is social and omnipresent in any version of capitalism, nineteenth-century Brazilian capitalism included; emancipation is personal, incomplete, and fleeting.

What *is* marriage, after all? It is many things: affection, sex, money, children, family.

Start with Alencar. His answer to the marriage question was fundamentally vexed by the problem of reconciling the positive values of independence and love with the potentially corrupting power of money and interest. Sex, for Alencar, is threatening and destabilizing. Given the aim of *Bildung*—toward marriage (and career for men)—sex threatens to defile young women and to divert young men. Alencar's other strong novels of urban life, *Lucíola* and *Senhora*, offer further evidence of both the fear of sex and the concern with the corrupting power of money. In *Lucíola*, written early in Alencar's career, power meets powerlessness and sex is the result of domination and self-abnegation. The heroine is, as Antonio Candido argues, preserved to an extent by the fact that her abjection and subsequent embrace of the life of prostitution is so complete as to suggest that an equal and opposite dignity hides behind the appearance of disgrace.[12] In *Senhora*, power trumps sex, giving Aurélia the bittersweet revenge of buying her husband and negating the natural sexual attraction of husband and wife through the debasement of the relationship through the transmuting power of money, which allows people to be treated like things, bought and sold.

If Alencar's attitude toward sex before and during marriage is prudish, it will probably come as little surprise that the treatment is quite a bit more explicit and ribald in the naturalistically inclined Azevedo. In *Filomena Borges* (1883–84), Azevedo offers up a comical scenario in which sex is withheld and thus wielded as a weapon in a battle of wills between a young wife and an older wealthy but rustic man.[13] Filomena is the lovely but secretly poor "flower of Catete," daughter of Dona Clementina, a vain and scheming woman who scrimps and saves in order to maintain a decent front in society, essentially so as to display the girl to men of means. Her props include a piano and a novel by Tolstoy.[14] To her credit, the girl is repulsed by the idea of marrying any of these older men procured by her mother. Then her mother dies and, fearing her marriageable years are coming to an end, she capitulates and marries Borges, a rich building contractor.

The wedding goes off according to plan, and Borges, portrayed as simple, rough, but good hearted, is practically drooling with desire by the time it comes to consummate the marriage that night. Meanwhile, Filomena is completely revolted by the presence of midnight revelers waiting about half-drunk to congratulate Borges on his conquest. She enters her bedroom and locks the door. Borges, too polite to cause a scene, ends up disappointed. Morning comes

ILLUSTRATION 9. "Barometer of Love: Cold Woman." In this illustration love's barometer hits a low. The woman turns her back, cold (*frio*), to her kneeling suitor.
SOURCE: *Semana Illustrada* 43 (1861): 340.

and finds Borges sprawled on a couch outside Filomena's bedroom. When she finally emerges, he asks, naturally, what is going on. Filomena tells her new husband that he is going to have to prove his love in order to unlock her heart and breach her chastity.

In what follows, the novel explores the many comical lengths a man might go to so that he can conquer his finicky and romantically inclined wife. Ultimately, Filomena turns her husband into a dandy rake and convinces him to stage a kidnapping (of her, of course) in order to abscond with her into the countryside (of Spain) and there, finally, ravish her. Having gone so far, it comes as no surprise that Borges is willing.

Despite the tone of the book, which clearly has Filomena marked out as foolish, if not villainous, Azevedo's story suggests how women could use the original weapon of the weak to manipulate their partners. The surface ideology is that behind every honest man turned fool there is a foolish and scheming woman. The undercurrent: Women do not like to sell themselves to the highest bidder and then subject themselves to witnessing the backslapping congratulations of his friends and acquaintances. Filomena turns the tables. She, who was treated essentially as a thing to be traded by her mother (all with the best intentions, of course!), locks her bedroom door and thereby begins to operate *on* Borges, working from the outside in, first changing his table manners and dress, then his speech, and ultimately his character.

Azevedo must have seen some harrowing wedding parties in his day, because the theme of gross voyeurism associated with the wedding night recurs in the novel *A Condessa Vesper* (1882; 1901), published immediately before *Filomena Borges*. Two friends, Gaspar and Gabriel, arrive late to the wedding party. The big house is trashed; everything is strewn around save for the little sugar doll bride on top of the remains of the cake. In short: an orgy of food and revelry. The young men ask where the new bride has gone and are informed, "The bride? She just left to go with her groom to the little pink pavilion prepared for them. . . . Look! Look! Sir! You can still see them from this window! There they go!" ("A noiva? Acaba, neste instante, de retirar-se com o noivo para o rico pavilhãozinho cor-de-rosa que lhes foi preparado. . . . Olhe! olhe! meu senhor! Aqui desta janela aindo os pode ver! Ali vão eles!").[15]

These scenes illustrate the transactional and public nature of sex in marriage, particularly among the middle and upper groups in society. It seems that the spirit of the village, of the *charivari*, lingers on in the metropolis—as though the womenfolk somehow belong to all the men vicariously.

Capitu: Getting Married Versus Being Married

Capitu is the second most famous character in all of Brazilian literature, over-shadowed only by the colossal Brás Cubas. Is Capitolina Pádua—Capitu—a manipulator and adulteress, or is she a misunderstood victim of a jealous husband? And those unforgettable, undertow eyes, like a tractor beam pulling the male gaze in and down. My concern here is not with the traditional questions of her guilt or innocence;[16] rather, I focus on comportment and Capitu's strategy and tactics read against the backdrop of what we have learned from reading the Brazilian bildungsroman.

To begin with, Capitu is poor. Thus her fate, barring remarkable good fortune, is to remain single or to marry badly. In tricking fate, she presents us with a realistic depiction of the clever tactics of a young girl; Machado's realism of assessment insists on following this comportment and attitude toward life to its conclusion. That is, her manipulations and open stance toward life and relationships come back to haunt her marriage to rich and jealous Bento Santiago.

No reader of *Dom Casmurro* can fail to see that an unreliable and self-serving individual narrates the book. In light of this fact, how far can we go with an analysis of Capitu's comportment and attitude toward life? It is all secondhand and distorted by Bento's post hoc justifications. The answer, I think, is pretty far. Here are some things we can say with some degree of confidence:

> Capitu, though poor, lives in a wealthier part of the city, in the Rua Mata-cavalos.
>
> Capitu's neighbors are rich and have an only son about her age.
>
> Growing up in this neighborhood, Capitu's frame for reading the world and defining her desires is wider, filled with more possibilities, than it otherwise would have been.

Given her gender and class position, Capitu's best prospect for obtaining a richer, broader life, in keeping with that frame, is a good marriage. The alternative would be the path of the kept woman.

Her best chance at a good marriage is the rich boy next door. In order to win the boy, Capitu must manipulate him and his family, using everyday tactics in the interest of a grand strategy of marriage.

If we take the point of *Dom Casmurro* to be about the incompatibility of open and closed attitudes toward life, particularly in the context of a marriage, then the significance of particular aspects of comportment and discrete acts rises to the foreground. *Dom Casmurro*, then, is about the difference between getting married and being married. What Machado is able to show masterfully in the novel is the way that overcoming external barriers does not necessarily portend the dissolution of real internal divisions. Bento is saved from the seminary by a substitute, his mother is won over, and all the external obstacles fall relatively easily. It is the internal barrier that rises up and destroys what should have been by all accounts a happy marriage. As René Girard suggests in *Deceit, Desire, and the Novel*, both internal and external forms of mediation generate the triangles of desire and transform fictional selves. In *Dom Casmurro* both elements are present, but it is the internal mediation, the triangulation between Bento, jealousy, and Capitu, that drives the narrative in the end.[17]

Before digging into the details of Capitu's attitudes and actions, let me emphasize one more point. She is not alone in her open attitude toward life. In *Dom Casmurro* the other great open character is, ironically, the Santiago family dependent (*agregado*), José Dias. The closed characters are Bento and his widowed mother, Dona Glória. The similarity between Capitu and José Dias is significant because it underscores the way poor people with open attitudes engage the world opportunistically, as master tacticians playing long games that result in strategic outcomes despite the lack of a fixed position.[18] The difference between the girl and the dependent—the independence of the one and the subordination and social integration of the other—drives the plot. Machado's achievement in *Dom Casmurro* resides in no small part in the way that the book depicts the bridge between tactics and strategy in such a realistic and nuanced manner.

Told in the first person, by Bento Santiago, *Dom Casmurro* is silent as to Capitu's internal mental states. We must read her attitude toward life from Bento's problematic ramblings. Better, we must read her attitude by her actions. These are consistent and realistic. As facts, we can take them as the most honest things Bento has to say. As to their interpretation, we need not limit ourselves to Bento's ideas.

Being married, Capitu and Bento head up to Tijuca for their honeymoon. The chapter title says it all: Heaven. Up above the clouds, in a love nest, from which Bento would rather not descend.[19] Capitu is eager to go back down the mountain to take up her life in society. She has made the leap, through a fortunate marriage, from shabby gentility to opulence. Her eagerness is understandable. Bento has been rich all his life.

Married life starts out well for the couple. Capitu takes up her role with aplomb, learning to play the piano (the fact that she did not learn as a child is a sign of her poor upbringing), going to the theater, and starting the round of visits to friends.[20] Money enters the equation innocuously at first. Bento gives his wife a monthly allowance for household expenses. She is frugal in her spending and manages to save the equivalent of 10 pounds sterling. Bento is proud of her economy, though the worm of doubt creeps in with the discovery that Escobar, Bento's childhood friend, has served as Capitu's broker in exchanging her little savings from mil-réis to libras.[21] Nothing is made of this at first, but the fact that his wife has gone behind his back and had financial dealings with another man comes back to haunt him when he begins to doubt Capitu's faithfulness. Machado is astute in planting this seed. It is one thing to be an economical housewife; it is entirely another to show this degree of autonomy, which in a perverse way creates a different kind of connection and possible obligation to a third party. Capitu's stance is open to the world. She acts independently and her independence threatens the delicate fabric of a traditional marriage. When Capitu asks Bento what to do with the money, he responds: It's yours. She replies: It's ours.[22] There is no argument, but the thin wedge of misunderstanding enters the relationship.

After setting up house and getting in the swim of married life, the next step for most couples is having children. Cue the next page in the novel. Bento and Capitu's child Ezekiel proves their undoing. The boy has a tendency to imitate others. His imitation of Escobar is all too real, down to the eyes. When Escobar drowns a few chapters later, Bento observes Capitu's reaction, and another seed of doubt is planted. As the boy grows, he seems to morph (in Bento's mind) into Escobar. Here, the everyday aspect of married life becomes insupportable. Bento tries to avoid contact with his "spurious" son, to no avail. He considers suicide. After attending a performance of *Othello*, he considers murder.[23]

Much of what has been written about *Dom Casmurro* hinges on the question of Capitu's purported guilt. That is a reasonable question, but it is not the question I want to ask here. Rather, it is Bento's ultimate choice to exile Capitu and the boy to Europe that interests me. This solution offers a way out of an impossible marriage without physical violence. Because Bento Santiago is rich and respectable, it is Capitu and the boy who must go.[24] There are many ways out of an unsuccessful marriage. The most common, as we shall see, is quiet withdrawal within the relationship. The surface remains unruffled. A perfect example of this process is Teobaldo and Branca. Spousal abandonment, of which Capitu and Ezekiel's exile is of a piece, is another means. More often, according to both the literary and historical sources, it was the man who simply left.[25]

If marriage closes the classic bildungsroman, then adultery peels away the veneer and prolongs the period of exploration. In *Sonhos d'Ouro*, marriage literally closes the novel in the postscript. In the last paragraph, headed "A ultima hora" (the final hour), Alencar writes, "The marriage of Guida and Ricardo would take place anytime these days" ("O casamento de Guida com Ricardo efetua-se qualquer destes dias").[26] The last remaining suitor, Bastos, has been given the consolation prize of partnership in Soares's firm. Society, embodied in the sycophantic Benicio, is there to watch. This conclusion implies an end to exploration and growth—from here on out there will be stability and each character will be given his or her just desserts.

By way of contrast, Brás never does marry, failing first to carry out his father's double plan and later losing a fiancée to yellow fever; his great love, which in hindsight was not really so great after all, is Virgília, with whom he carries on an adulterous relationship that ends with a whimper. Like Frédéric Moreau, he never completes the journey to marriage; like Flaubert's hero, he never truly grows up. Teobaldo, after a period of affairs and dissipation, kidnaps 15-year-old Branca and makes her his wife in the dark hours before the dawn. Love and admiration turn to suspicion and eventually to hate, as Teobaldo betrays his friends and eventually Branca. His self-regard mixes with the impressions and expectations of his milieu, and he never is reconciled to himself or to the world, although on a superficial level his charm and his self-regard do result in a modicum of conventional success; his *Bildung* is incomplete or, perhaps better yet, fatally flawed. His rival, Aguiar, says it best:

> Teobaldo could never be a good husband; he'd never be capable of dedicating himself for a lifetime to one person, even if she were the most adorable creature in the world. He only thinks of himself; everything that is not about him, everything that doesn't speak to his precious individuality, has no value to his eyes. Everything beyond him is merely public and comprises the rest of humanity, which, in his mad pretension he considers a mere adjunct to his person. Therefore, in his feverish desire to give the right impression and never give offense, he is never frank with anyone: if you ask him a favor, he never says no, promising always and the next moment forgetting everything he just said. If a woman gives him a provocative smile, he returns it, even if he detests her; he has no friends—he has an audience; he has no love—only lovers. It is a simple question of vanity, in the objective sense of the word.

> Teobaldo nunca poderia dar um bom marido; nunca seria capaz de dedicar-se durante a vida inteira por qualquer pessoa, fosse esta a mais adorável das criaturas. Todo ele é pouco para pensar em si mesmo; tudo que não for ele; tudo

que não for a sua querida e respeitável individualidade, nenhum valor tem a seus olhos; tudo que não for ele, é público e faz parte do resto da humanidade, a quem, na sua louca pretensão, ele considera um simples complemento de sua pessoa. Então, na eterna febre de armar ao efeito e não desgostar seja lá a quem for, jamais tem franqueza para ninguém: se lhe pedem qualquer obséquio, ele nunca diz que não, promete sempre, ainda que um instante depois já nem se lembre de semelhante coisa; se uma mulher lhe lança um sorriso de provocação, ele responde com outro, ainda que a deteste; não tem amigos—tem auditório; não tem amor—tem amantes. É uma simples questão de vaidade, no sentido positivista da palavra.[27]

And the crux:

When he speaks, he doesn't address himself to the person with whom he is talking, but rather to those who are watching him speak, only concerning himself with the effect that he produces in them. And just as in conversation, so too in all the actions of his life.

Ele, enquanto fala, não se dirige à pessoa com quem conversa, mas sim às que o observam de parte, só preocupando com o efeito que está produzindo sobre elas. E, como é na conversa, é em todos os atos de sua vida.[28]

Ricardo, in contrast, discovers and stays true to himself. Guida grows up into herself and away from society. *Sonhos d'Ouro* is written *against* the solution offered by the postscripted marriage, yet for Alencar the concept of the happy marriage can ultimately resolve the seemingly intractable problems he has thrown up for his protagonists throughout the body of the book. Brás holds himself apart, maintaining role distance—an old soul wedded to childish caprice. Teobaldo embraces himself through the eyes of others, burning up in the fever of a corrupt society. If marriage is the end to which the classic bildungsroman points and if reconciliation with the world is the larger point of youthful exploration, why is it that the happy ending is so elusive in these novels?

Schwarz provides us with part of the answer, having to do with the Brazilian dilemma of ideas out of place. Flaubert and Machado flirt with another element: The combination of chance and personality conspire against any lasting equilibrium. Nineteenth-century novels, especially the bildungsroman, are about youthful lives, not limited episodes; the only way for marriage to provide an ending is for the ceremony to take place in the last pages. Otherwise, marriage is just a point where transecting trajectories cross. Lives imply projects, strategies, interests, that project backward and forward in space and time. George Eliot, again, offers an astute observation regarding the place of marriage embedded in the narrative of episodes of *Bildung*. As narrator, she interjects at the very end of a long book, "Marriage, which has been bourne of so many narratives, is still a great beginning. . . . It is still the beginning of the home epic—the gradual conquest or irremediable loss of that complete union which makes advancing years a climax."[29] Discovery of this union requires a different kind of growth than that contemplated in the classic stories of *Bildung*. It requires a mutual exploration and a move away from the egocentric pathways of self-discovery. Hence we have the abiding power and interest of *Dom Casmurro* as an attempt to narrate the irremediable loss of love and faith occasioned by jealousy.

Money and Inheritance

A discomforting thought: Money is everything. In the emerging space of commerce and finance emanating from the Rua Direita and environs, stretching south to the mansions of Botafogo, and far west into the hills studded with coffee plantations, there is a sense of domination by money. The old rules are no longer in effect. Men who begin life as rustic *tropeiros* (muleteers) can become barons—men who pay 4 contos per letter for a noble title. Perhaps it is better to say, the pace of change and turnover has picked up significantly since Brás Cubas's ancestors' gradual ascent from coopers to *fidalgos* (noblemen).[30] Ricardo's intonation "Gold, gold . . . you reign and govern" is echoed cynically by Teobaldo's friend/rival Aguiar in *O Coruja*.

> Ah! There's nothing like business for making money! And nowadays, say what you will, money is everything! With it one gets everything—glory, honor, pleasure, esteem, love! Everything! Everything!

> Ah! Nada há como o comércio para fazer dinheiro! E hoje, deixem falar quem fala, o dinheiro é tudo! Com ele tudo se obtém—glórias, honras, prazeres, consideração, amor! tudo! tudo![31]

For Ricardo, the reign of gold is a problem to be solved. His own social integration depends on the marriage of virtue and wealth, which is in distinct contrast to Aguiar's idea of money as a value-free medium for obtaining everything, including honor, love, and consideration—three things that money is not supposed to be able to buy in Ricardo's view. Brás Cubas is much more Aguiar than Ricardo. He buys the love of the beautiful Marcela for 11 contos; the honor of a poor woman, Dona Plácida, is suborned for 5 contos and a pack of lies.[32]

Too much money, too soon, leads to the undoing of weak spirits by prof-ligacy. The worry that money corrupts recurs throughout the novels of the period. Alencar explores this theme directly in the short profile of a woman, *A Viúvinha*. The protagonist, Jorge, inherits 200 contos and promptly runs through his fortune in three years of high living, ending up in self-imposed exile in order to rebuild his fortune and reputation.[33] As ever, Alencar keeps the light on at the end of the tunnel. Brás Cubas, meanwhile, uses his wealth to underwrite a mediocre existence of affairs and dilettantism. To an extent, his aristocratic temperament suits him to his wealth and his world; having money is not a problem, per se, for Brás. Teobaldo, undone first by having too much money and thus freedom, is later tormented by the lack of money and his de-sire to continue living a life of decadent luxury. He thus represents the dark side of aristocratic tastes. If, like Teobaldo, Brás had suddenly found himself poor . . . Put another way: Teobaldo's sudden poverty interrupts the natural progression of his *Bildung*. Unlike Brás, he will not bend to his father's will and put an end to his dissipation, having sown his wild oats and sated his appetite. The *Bildung* of a rich and vain young man, interrupted so brutally, effectively freezes his development; he never grows up.

Money corrupts. The difference in attitude toward money among the three novelists is subtle but worth exploring. Machado de Assis would never preface a novel with the following lines from Azevedo's *A Condessa Vesper*: "Mothers and fathers! If you should hope to leave a rich inheritance—look at my life and consider the danger of excess money for a twenty year old" ("Pais! que pretendes deixar um rico testamento—olhai para a minha vida, e considerai o perigo do dinheiro em excesso aos vinte anos").[34]

In *Quincas Borba*, the one novel of Machado's where the moral of the story might appear to be "money corrupts," it is easy to see that this misses the mark. Left to his own devices Rubião would not have been "corrupted" by his unex-pected inheritance of 300 contos. The moral of the story is more like, Choose your friends wisely.[35] And the corollary would be, Mediocre spirits are no match for the meat grinder of society. Rubião is naïve and impressionable. He wants to fit in, to find his way in the world of 300-conto legacies, but he does not have the cultural capital it takes. This leads him to imagine conducting great affairs with beautiful married women, to make poor business deals with shady characters, and to be susceptible to the suggestion of distinction implicit in the list of titled men in the *Almanak Laemmert*.[36] By way of contrast, con-sider how comfortably Brás Cubas fits into this world, into which he was born and from such "manure" his flower bloomed. Azevedo comes close to this position in *Filomena Borges* in his treatment of Borges himself. Money is not the issue; it is people, a social environment, ideas about money.

As Antonio Candido observes, money in Alencar's novels comes either to those who work or to those who subordinate the spirit to the goddess of financial success: an idealized wealth accumulated by Comendador Soares's Midas touch or the shady dealings of the Visconde de Aljuba, known for lending money at high interest to "pretos quitandeiros."[37] Wealth also comes as inheritance. There are three ways, then, to get rich: work, speculation, and inheritance. The last two terms are intimately related when considering the disposition of the wealth of a sole heiress, such as Guida.

Inheritance law in nineteenth-century Brazil is a complex subject beyond the scope of the present study. In basic terms, readers should bear in mind two main points. First, the talk of vast dowries in the Brazilian novels of the era is surely an artistic exaggeration. Dowries were in decline throughout the century and were rarely even mentioned in estate inventories. There were certainly no dowries worth hundreds of contos in the 900-plus estate inventories that I examined. The dowry, or *dote*, in novels is probably better read as a shorthand for inheritance. Marriageable girls were, according to this logic, the daughters of men and women of means. These parents would, eventually, pass along substantial resources to their children. The death of just one parent would occasion a transfer of that parent's share of the community property to the necessary heirs, including, in this case, daughters who happened to be married. The husband in these instances would, as head of household, govern the use of these funds. A sole heir like Guida, with just one surviving parent, was guaranteed a fortune as her eventual inheritance. In a regime of equal inheritance and forced heirs, there was no need for special treatment of particular children. Dowries, to the extent that they existed, were about providing independent means to the daughter (and her husband) while they waited for what was presumably a much larger inheritance in the future.

In reality, the historical record suggests that for most middle- to upper-status children, the expected inheritance, even in cases of substantial family wealth, was likely to be quite modest. A sample of 227 heirs listed in estate inventories from the 1850s to the 1880s reveals that the average heir received just over 6.5 contos (around $3,500 dollars at the time). For the top decile of heirs, the average inheritance was a more substantial 40 contos, the next decile made due with 9.5 contos—roughly what Brás reputedly blew through in his affair with

Marcela. This is a far cry from the hundreds of contos thrown around as values in the novels of the era. Indeed, the bottom 50% of heirs inherited just under 1 conto, suggesting that for the vast majority of inhabitants of the city, the quantitative dimension of these novels was more fantastical than fictional. This observation goes for the gentry as much as for the poor. When Maximinano Pereira de Magalhães died in 1853, he left an estate worth 59 contos. This was a major sum at the time—if not a fortune, then certainly a sum that placed his family in the top 5% of wealth holding. Yet, once divided with his surviving spouse, the ten surviving children shared an inheritance that dwindled to 1.6 contos each.[38]

Inherited wealth plays an outsized role in the novels of Machado de Assis. Brás Cubas, Rubião, Bento Santiago, and the twins Pedro and Paulo are all rich heirs. In every case save Rubião's, the inherited money is old, or at least it has been passed through the hands of more than one generation. This provides the key to understanding the placid complacency and confidence of a Brás Cubas or a Bento Santiago. New money in Machado is nearly always hopelessly corrupt: tainted by the slave trade, as in the case of Cotrim, or derived from speculation and the fleecing of innocents, such as Palha. Old money comes from land, slaves, and buildings.[39] It is traditional, which is not to say that nothing can go wrong. Consider the case of Teobaldo. In the story of the rise and fall and rise again of that ill-starred man, Azevedo touches on the theme of the fragility of old money in new times as well as, of course, the theme of rich marriage as the solution for a poor man of distinction.

Old money and new times. The action in *O Coruja* takes place during a period in which many old *fazendeiros* made rich by coffee were falling on hard times. Teobaldo's father, the baron, commits suicide in 1862, crushed by debts.[40] Capital flowed up into the hills of Rio and Minas Gerais in the form of credit to planters; it also flowed back in the payment of debts with interest. As Fragoso shows convincingly in his study of the late colonial and early national economy of southeastern Brazil, great wealth was anchored in three sources: land and agriculture, slaves and the slave trade, and commerce, both internal and international—all of which were dominated in a fashion by merchants and their capital. The merchants were the common denominator; and the more successful, the more likely they were to have interests in all three areas.[41] In the 1860s, a crisis of labor and land rolled through the rich coffee uplands. Slaves were more expensive after the suppression of the illegal Atlantic trade. The land itself succumbed to overplanting and soil depletion. As the coffee frontier moved on, it left behind more than a few bankrupted planters cut from the mold of Teobaldo's father.[42]

New Times and Easy Money: Speculation and Commerce

Despite the decadence in the Paraíba Valley, coffee would reign supreme for several more generations in southeastern Brazil. It would, in time, help fuel an urban financial and industrial boom in the great cities of Rio de Janeiro and São Paulo.[43] Like any boom, this process challenged the social order and, by extension, the imaginations of the writers who sought to narrate a society undergoing drastic change. Arguably, it was the financial boom that came first and inspired an artistic response. Banking, the stock and bond markets, and informal credit networks had all expanded mightily by the 1860s, with attendant scandals and panics sufficient to suggest something rotten or needing correction in the core of economic life. The most important of these events was the collapse of the banking house of A. J. A. Souto & Company on September 10, 1864. This event, still relatively fresh in the collective consciousness of Rio de Janeiro, must have been imprinted strongly in Alencar's mind. It helps explain the author's motive in writing a story in which provincial virtue marries *licit* metropolitan capital. The Souto crack-up is worth recounting here in a few lines, because it furnishes an example of the fragility of speculative capitalism, the interdependence of economic and political elites, the order of magnitude of speculation during the period in question, and, in the person of the Visconde de Souto, an appropriate villain and foil for the fictional Comendador Soares.

According to the government's investigative report published in the aftermath of the Souto collapse, the firm was the largest informal banking house in Rio de Janeiro (and, by extension, Brazil). After the bankruptcy, it was found that "its system of financial administration was the absence of a system."[44] Souto, the millionaire *visconde*, had begun his career as a humble broker in 1833. It was not until 1858, during the booming period of financial growth of that decade, that he constituted the firm that was to shake the foundations of Brazil's financial system in 1864. The firm grew rapidly with what was later discovered to be loose, risky, and even fictitious banking practices. In this, it was helped by many powerful friends in government and banking. By the time of its demise, it owed over 14,000 contos to the Bank of Brazil, from which it drew what seemed, until September 10, 1864, to be a bottomless pit of credit. On that fateful morning, creditors started a run on the bank. By 10 a.m. Souto & Company had closed its doors and suspended payments. The *visconde* himself left the premises and did not return. Crowds of creditors accumulated in front of the firm offices in the Rua Direita. Runs on other banks got underway, and four other large firms went down in the course of the crisis. Police had to be stationed in the doorways of the banks, and guards were sent to protect the lives and property of Souto and other bankers.[45] The government report reads at times like an Alencar novel.

> The banking house of A. J. A. Souto & Co., overly favored by the Government, and by the Banks, supported by a confluence of happy circumstance, surrounded by friends, and by gratified clients, at the height of power and force, became fascinated by the splendor of its brilliant star, [and thereby] abandoned the good counsel of science and experience, abused everything, and thus arrived at the point where it could no longer honor its promises.[46]

It is against this backdrop of transformation and crisis that José de Alencar attempted to write a bildungsroman in which financial capitalism could be reconciled with provincial virtue. In *Sonhos d'Ouro* Comendador Soares is presented as a prodigy of the marketplace, a man who mints money through "a series of licit deals" and rises to the ranks of the richest men in Brazil in a single generation; his honesty and the firm foundations of his wealth make him the opposite of a historical figure such as the Visconde de Souto. Candido observes, "In the time of Alencar, clerks and muleteers . . . ended up barons and *comendadores* in old age" ("No tempo de Alencar, os caixeiros e tropeiros . . . terminavam barões e comendadores de maturidade").[47] The idea that some men of humble origin could rise by honest means to the heights of wealth is, of course, a fundamental tenet of the liberal creed and bourgeois ideology. The competitive market, then, serves as an arena for talent—but it must be honest and not abusive or corrupt.

Providing contrast to Comendador Soares, villains such as the Visconde de Aljuba build fortunes on speculation and by charging usurious interest rates to those unfortunate enough to fall into their clutches. These two visions of great wealth rest uneasily side by side in Alencar. A key to understanding *Sonhos d'Ouro* from the perspective of its internal structure, which, as Candido suggests, bears the stamp of the logic of the social structures of the time, is to see the sequence through which Alencar traces an ideal transformation of wealth into something stable and virtuous. First, there is the period of honest accumulation during which Soares, through his talent for business, makes his fortune. Second, there is the moment of danger during which Guida's suitors threaten to undo both the honesty of Soares's money and the sanctity of disinterested marriage based on love. Third and last, there is the marriage of provincial virtue and urban wealth, which closes the circle and ensures that Soares's justly gotten gains will not be dissipated or perverted in illicit speculation. By positing a character such as Soares, Alencar offers a way around the dilemma facing Ricardo and every other honest but poor man of talent facing the choice between easy money and virtue. Soares's purpose is, in effect, to launder the money and pass it on clean and free of taint to Guida and, by extension, to Ricardo. The fact that Ricardo rejects Guida's offer of marriage until the postscript proves that he is not marrying out of interest.

Alencar's effort to narrate the marriage between provincial virtue and metropolitan capital reads marriage through the lens of financial transaction, even as the plot and the characters disavow this explicit connection and its undertone of interest and corruption. Contrastingly, for Machado's characters, marriage and money are read not through the lens of corruption but rather the corrosive effects of jealousy. Marriage, in this view, solves nothing. Azevedo carries things to their naturalistic conclusions but blends his sober critique of opportunism and selfishness with elements of the gothic and the sentimental. The fact that Alencar and Azevedo end two of their strongest novels on weak notes—both dealing with the question of marriage and married life—suggests that this, of all subjects, remained ideologically and artistically unsettled throughout the latter decades of the nineteenth century. Greater novelists, including Machado, but extending to the likes of George Eliot and Tolstoy, found ways to write about the problem of the individual and his or her social reproduction through the institution of marriage in more convincing manner.

6 PROBLEMS OF SPATIAL PRACTICE

SPACE IS A USEFUL—and problematic—term for historical analysis. Its use can easily take on the form of an incantation. Use the term enough and it seems to conjure a sense of flaccid weight bearing down on any substantial meaning. Space is everything, so it is nothing. The concept of spatial practice helps maintain analytical focus, but it too must be framed cautiously. It is easy to write the words *space* and *practice*; it is difficult to use them in a consistent and illuminating way.

In Chapters 4 and 5 I focused on the problems of comportment or attitude, from education and career through marriage and married life, that face characters in novels set in Rio de Janeiro. I now turn to the dimension of spatial practices. Here, the problem is how to move through the domestic and public spaces of the city and how to utilize the material and cultural significations of space as part and parcel of a strategy for living. Spatial practices can be thought of as consisting of four basic elements: ritual, material, front and back regions, and open and closed spaces. These elements overlap and are mutually reinforcing. Together, they knit the social spaces of the city.

By ritual, I mean the signification of space generated by repeated social scripts. Social meaning—the interpretability of action—is generated by repetition, which allows for the reproduction of the *given* social world. Going to the theater, for instance, is a ritualized spatial practice (among other things) that produces a social space. Material refers to the built environment and its furnishings made social by cultural significations. The placement of a living room and the disposition of its contents, furniture, and piano create a stage for specific kinds of action. All space is relational. People acting according to scripts in a given material context are positioned such that there are front and back regions defined by their relations to the space and to other occupants. Front and back regions are therefore dynamic and contingent. Front regions tend to be visible and monitored; back regions tend to be veiled and only partly accessible. The last element, open and closed space, is related but not reducible to front and back regions— open and closed not in the literal sense, though that may come into play, but in a social sense: accessible and fluid versus constrained and static. Ritual is the verb tense of spatial practice, material the noun, back/front and open/closed the adjectives. These last dyads are also referred to here as relational spaces.

A simple paradigmatic example suffices to parse this grammar. Consider the girl at the window. Ritual provides the social script for the spatial practice of young women standing at windows. The signification is clear: The girl is making herself visible, available. Ritual also explains the repeated presence of her paramour in the street below. The materiality of the house and street create the stage for enacting this spatial practice.[1] The window is liminal. It is the front region of a closed house. In the back region, the young woman's family and her material possessions—her dresses and her piano—lurk in a supporting or complicating role. Perhaps her parents disapprove. The window is thus a transgressive membrane, combining hope with danger. The admirer has access to the front region but is not yet welcome in the back. The street is open. He moves freely there but is also observed, perhaps the subject of gossip or envy. Standing in the street at her window is a public declaration of love.

In what follows, I analyze each element of spatial practice in a series of connected examples drawn from a range of novels. The analysis is micro rather than macro; it focuses on practice rather than plot. In dividing the analysis across two chapters, first dealing with comportment (Chapter 4) and second with spatial practice (this chapter), I do not mean to suggest that there is a separation between these aspects of experience. These dimensions are mutually constitutive. The division is symptomatic of the difficulty in developing any holistic analysis of human experience, fictional or otherwise. It is extremely hard to see everything at once. Pierre Bourdieu may have come closest in his concept of the habitus, but modesty demands that I recognize my limits.[2]

Let us begin with ritual and build from there. Start with Roberto Da Matta:

> We can now conceptualize the realm of ritual as being totally relative to the
> day-to-day world. A banal and trivial action in the everyday world can take on

exceptional meaning and become a "rite" when it is put in focus in a certain environment through a certain sequence.[3]

Da Matta is referring here to the big events in social life, but there is no reason to limit our definition of ritual to festivals and ceremonies. The important thing is the environment and sequence, which together make for spatial practice. Novels tell us a great deal about the rituals of nineteenth-century Rio de Janeiro. These rituals can be further differentiated along a continuum from domestic to public, from intimate to impersonal. At one end are everyday domestic rituals involving dressing, cooking, eating, and the like. In the middle we find mundane activities associated with work, shopping, and leisure. At the other end are rituals tied to the calendar of life, private or public, such as birthdays, weddings, carnival, and elections.

Novels are engines of this complex simultaneity. They weave ritual, materiality, and relational space into the fabric of human experience. Perhaps more than anything else, the intricate spatial practices of domestic life emerge most clearly in fictional accounts. A favorite example from *Senhora* is illustrative.

The plot centers on an inversion of power. A poor girl named Aurélia becomes rich and buys a man, Fernando Seixas, who once spurned her, resulting in a prolonged struggle of wills and an eventual reconciliation in the form of an odd ransom motif. An intriguing plot, no doubt, which explains why criticism fixates on this dimension of the novel. But the plot tells us nothing about spatial practice. We need to look closely at the early passages of the novel, in the mode that Erich Auerbach applies to the pension in Balzac's *Père Goriot*, to see how brilliantly Alencar succeeds in revealing a whole complex matrix of ritual, materiality, and relational space—an indirect representation of a way of living.[4]

Chapter 5 of *Senhora* begins:

In the Rua do Hospício, near the field, there once was a house that has since disappeared with the latest reforms.

It had three windows facing the street; two belonged to the parlor and the other to an adjoining office.

The exterior of the house, as with its interior, displayed the poverty of the habitation.

The furniture in the parlor included a sofa and six chairs and two consoles of rosewood, which retained no vestige of their original polish. The white wallpaper was yellowed and one could see where in places it had been carefully repaired.

The office gave off the same appearance. The wallpaper, once blue, had taken on a brownish hue.

All of this, if it had the same air of decrepitude as the furniture in the parlor, was like those pieces carefully cleaned and dusted, giving off a sense of scrupulous care.

Havia à Rua do Hospício, próximo ao campo, uma casa que desapareceu com as últimas reconstruções.

Tinha três janelas de peitoril na frente; duas pertenciam à sala de visitas; a outra a um gabinete contíguo.

O aspecto da casa revelava, bem como seu interior, a pobreza de habitação.

A mobília da sala consistia em sofá, seis cadeiras e dois consolos de jacarandá, que já não conservavam o menor vestígio de verniz. O papel da parede de branco passara a amarelo e percebia-se que em alguns pontos já havia sofrido hábeis remendos.

O gabinete oferecia a mesma aparência. O papel que fôra primitivamente azul tomara a côr de fôlha sêca.

Tudo isto, se tinha o mesmo ar de velhice dos móveis da sala, era como aquêles cuidadosamente limpo e espanejado, respirando o mais escrupuloso asseio.[5]

Clues to life: a house that no longer exists is tenuous; yellowed but repaired wallpaper represents a mixture of poverty and tenaciousness; a visiting room with chairs and consoles, old but of noble wood, suggests vestiges of social hopes, of having visitors; and above all else, the space is meticulously clean. Why, if there are no visitors? What gives rise to the ritual of cleaning and polishing this shabby space? The answer is not long in coming. There is a visitor of sorts in the person of Fernando Seixas. This house is his back region. It is the front region of his mother and sisters.

Beyond the unusual cleanliness, another incongruity marked this part of the house—the sharp contrast between the poverty of the furniture and certain objects spread about for the use of the inhabitant.

Thus draped on the back of an old rosewood chair one saw at this moment a black suit jacket, which by the fine fabric, and above all by the elegant cut and superior tailoring, was recognizable as the chic style of the house of Raunier, the most fashionable tailor of the era.

Alongside the jacket were the rest of an evening outfit, all of which came from the same fashionable source—a beautiful collapsible top-hat hat from the best milliner in Paris, straw-colored gloves from Jouvin, boots from the house of Campas made only for the most favored customers.

Outra singularidade apresentava essa parte da habitação; era o frisante contraste que faziam com a pobreza carrança dos dois aposentos certos objetos, aí colocados, e de uso do morador.

Assim no recôsto de uma das velhas cadeiras de jacarandá via-se neste momento uma casaca preta, que pela fazenda superior, mas sobretudo pelo corte elegante e esmêro do trabalho, conhecia-se ter o chique da casa do Raunier, que já era naquele tempo o alfaiate da moda.

Ao lado da casaca estava o resto de um trajo de baile, que tudo êle saíra daquela mesma tesoura em voga; finíssimo chapéu claque do melhor fabricante de Paris; luvas de Jouvin côr de palha; e um par de botinas como o Campas só fazia para os seus fregueses prediletos.[6]

The description of these objects continues, almost cinematically, as the narrator's gaze travels through the shabby rooms of the house. There is a box of fine Havana cigars, a shelf of novels, cigar boxes of various styles, strangely shaped ashtrays, a shelf of colognes and soaps like a display case in a perfume shop, umbrellas and canes with distinctive and expensive handles. Everything a young dandy needs to be seen in the right places about town. Unlike Teobaldo, who in his salad days furnished his rooms with the same style as his fine clothes, Fernando is limited to maintaining a distinctive front outdoors. He carries his front with him and, upon returning home, leaves it strewn about for his womenfolk to tidy up.

Summing up, in the words of Alencar's narrator:

An observer would recognize at once the striking material difference between the exterior and domestic life of the occupant of this part of the house.

If the house and furniture signaled an absence of means, if not extreme poverty, the clothing and objects of display indicated a social profile only possessed of the finest gentlemen of the Corte.

The appearance of the dwelling was repeated in its occupant, Seixas, splayed out at this moment on the sofa of the living room, reading one of the daily papers on his knees.

Um observador reconheceria nesse disparate a prova material de completa divergência entre a vida exterior e a vida doméstica da pessoa que ocupava esta parte da casa.

Se o edifício e os móveis estacionários e de uso particular denotavam escassez de meios, senão extrema pobreza, a roupa e objetos de representação anunciavam um trato de sociedade, como só tinham cavalheiros dos mais ricos e francos da corte.

Esta feição característica do aposento, repetia-se em seu morador, o Seixas, derreado neste momento no sofá da sala, a ler uma das folhas diárias, estendidas sobre os joelhos erguidos.[7]

Alencar's prose is richly evocative in these passages. It caresses the beautiful objects like a scene from Balzac, the master. Taken together, the clothes and accoutrements tell more than a story of incongruous luxury—they tell a spatial story, which comes into clearer focus as the chapter progresses and we are introduced to the human inhabitants of the house. Fernando, we discover, is a young man of limited means but some taste and education. He frequents the theater and the Cassino Fluminense. The materiality of spatial practice extends to the trendy cut of Fernando's suit and the fine hat he wears when he steps out of his poor abode and into the social worlds of the street and theater. Material objects, especially when distinctive, such as French-style hats, are proleptic. They anticipate social activity and call to mind particular venues. Fernando's hat and gloves and umbrella and cologne are out of place in these poor rooms. They contrast with the peeling wallpaper. Yet they conjure up the whirl of the casino and box seats at the theater. Material objects, spaces, and activities compose a field of social signification, which in this instance can be characterized as the realm of social distinction. Stealing a page from Bourdieu's style of representation, social distinction in nineteenth-century Rio de Janeiro can be comprehended as a simultaneous arrangement of tangible and intangible components, most of which can be glimpsed in the passages quoted from *Senhora*.[8]

Figure 3 expresses the multidimensionality of the spatial practice of the good life in Rio de Janeiro as revealed in novels. The description of objects and places in *Senhora* and other novels of the era map onto a symbolic system—a shorthand guide for how to live and where to do it. In Fernando's case Alencar is playing with the symbolic and spatial fields. The young man has objects that gesture toward Paris and nocturnal habits that converge on places like the Cassino Fluminense, yet he is described as splayed out in a shabby room in the Rua do Hospício. He does not dominate the field; he has cultural capital and appropriate possessions, but he is poor and well outside the space of living well.

Figure 3 can be read in several ways. For instance, moving from the bottom left to the upper right, we see the tangible symbolic representations of abstract European (bourgeois) living. Similarly, moving from the bottom right to the upper left, one travels from the space of the drawing room, best located in a fine neighborhood, such as Botafogo (best filled with the tangible objects from the bottom left), toward the social spaces in the center of bourgeois life, and onward, ultimately, to the abstract symbols and practices of European culture.[9]

As Chapter 5 of *Senhora* unspools, we learn more about Fernando's activities. His sister Mariquinhas enters the room and offers him his morning coffee. He accepts her services like a sultan, giving no thanks and taking her for granted. She asks if he enjoyed himself the evening before, noting that he did not return home until 3 in the morning. Where was Fernando? At a big dance in the Cassino Fluminense, resplendent in his beautiful clothes, running into his old flame Aurélia. Thus the central plot of the novel takes flight. Clothes, music, dancing, beautiful and rich women—the life of a dandy played out in a ritualized space that stretches like an elastic band from the poverty of home to the lights of the Cassino Fluminense and back again at 3 a.m.

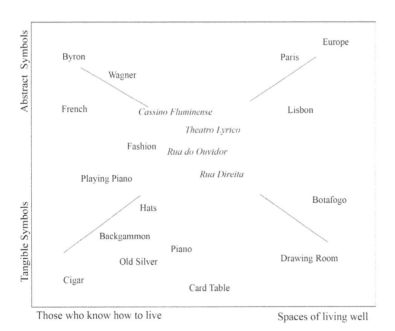

FIGURE 3. The spaces of good living in nineteenth-century Rio de Janeiro.

SOURCES: Alencar's *Lucíola*, *Senhora*, and *Sonhos d'Ouro*; Azevedo's *Casa de Pensão* and *O Coruja*; and Machado's *Dom Casmurro*, *Memórias Póstumas de Brás Cubas*, and *Quincas Borba*.

The plot is moralizing. It is about false fronts and living beyond one's means. The substrate of the chapter is about spatial practices—the mixture of ritual, material, and relational space. It is not just about the young dandy going out on the town wearing a top hat; it is about sisters who stay inside, cleaning and mending, serving coffee and fetching half-smoked cigars, and taking in sewing jobs to supplement the household's meager income. It is about the problem of spatial practice when the pieces of life cannot quite be made to fit together.

Published in the same decade as Alencar's *Sonhos d'Ouro* and *Senhora*, Machado de Assis's first novel, *Ressurreição* (Resurrection) (1872) portrays a similar set of spatial practices and underscores the contextual-spatial dimension of 1870s bourgeois culture. Tellingly, what begins as a whirlwind of movement through spaces of sociability ends with the heroine, Lívia, finding solitude in the crowded city. The narrator concludes, "Lívia knew how to remove herself from society. No one ever saw her again at the theater, on the boulevard, or at gatherings. Her visits were few and intimate" ("Lívia soube isolar-se na sociedade. Ninguém mais a viu no teatro, na rua, ou em reuniões. Suas visitas são poucas e íntimas").[10] This change in Lívia's comportment is remarkable in light of the descriptions of social life in the first chapters of the novel.

Machado de Assis's first novel contains many of the elements found in his more celebrated mature works. These include the elements of jealousy and bad faith, voluble characters, and, for our purposes here, a rich depiction of spatial practice. *Ressurreição* does not contain any of the core elements of the bildungsroman. This is not a story of youth finding its way in the space of the city and the complex networks of social relations found there. Rather, it is a story of love curdled by jealousy and fundamentally flawed internal characteristics. In other words, the problem is not how to enter society, compete, find protectors, and ultimately succeed in career and marriage; it is whether and how a voluble bachelor can overcome his self-doubt and suspicion and give himself over to the love of a young widow.

Still, despite the maturity of the protagonists in *Ressurreição*—he, a medical doctor (not practicing) of some inherited wealth, she a moderately well-to-do widow with a young child—their courtship and the complications of their affair need a spatial arrangement to take flight. The movements of the characters throughout the novel, including planned moves that are not executed and a concurrent set of epistolary movements, contrive to generate much of the narrative flow and suggest, through placement and comportment in place, something equally important about the interior lives of the protagonists and other salient characters.

As the novel unfolds, its spatial density ebbs and flows, as though Machado needed movement and spatial relations primarily in the first and last thirds of the book, where actions begin and finally end. The middle chapters are more static and closed to the domestic space of the house and the thoughts of the characters. Movement in these chapters is more likely to involve letters or emissaries. By spatial density, I refer to the extent to which specific locations and the movements of people play a critical role in the narrative itself and in the elaboration of fictional identities. Presumably, these spatialized identities can be assigned largely to the early chapters of any novel. Knowing where people live, where they are from, the places they frequent—all these things are crucial for knowing them in a realistic sense. The other kind of density of spatial reference is, in the case of *Ressurreição*, an authorial choice to foreground the *social* underpinnings of sentimental encounters. Dr. Félix has to meet the widow Lívia here, not there; she must be accompanied by he, not she. It is not so much that the fateful reencounter *must* take place at a dance held at a wealthy colonel's semirural estate—it is that encounters in *such places* are embedded in social relations and modes of behavior that give the origins of the relationship a particular valence and momentum.

The chapters immediately preceding and following the meeting of the future lovers at the colonel's dance provide a paradigmatic example of Machado's deft use of spatial practices to adumbrate characters and set in motion the gears of narrative in a realistic manner. In the first chapter we are in Dr. Félix's "semiurban, semi-sylvan" Laranjeiras house. This is the quiet, retired world of "an idle, unambitious" man. He is not inconsequential, but he is peripheral—perhaps by choice, perhaps by temperament. The place itself speaks to this peripherality. In the second chapter a trip into town takes us to the richly appointed rooms of the doctor's mistress, Cecília. He has decided to break off their relationship on New Year's Day. Feminine comportment is on display: tears and the piano as a prop to lean on. In the third chapter Félix goes to the colonel's house to attend a soirée—not a dance or a party, but a soirée. There, in the middle of a waltz, he literally collides with his future love interest as he tries to pick his way across the room. So far we have seen three houses, three stages of sociability. Then Machado does something unexpected. He removes Félix from the city and takes him for a time to his rural retreat in Tijuca—that reserve of peace and quiet where, at around the same time as most of the action of the novel takes place, the early 1860s, a real-life José de Alencar was thinking some of the thoughts that would be transformed eventually into his *Sonhos d'Ouro*.

In the fourth chapter of *Ressurreição*, Dr. Félix spends two weeks in the country and then returns to town. And what a return! This little chapter is replete with movement through different social spaces. Félix goes to the theater and, from the vantage of his orchestra seat, sees Lívia and her brother Viana in their box. As a single male, attending on his own, the orchestra is where he belongs. Invited to join the pair, he spends the last act watching Lívia watch the play. It is a comedic love story with a happy ending. Days later, Félix, now interested in the widow, travels across town to Catumbi to visit her, only to find that she is out. They meet again, two days later, by chance in the Rua do Ouvidor. They part ways after agreeing to meet again, and Félix runs into a young lawyer friend named Meneses, with whom he goes off to share a sherbet at Carceler's.[11] By the end of Chapter 4, we have been introduced to the space of the novel and the characters have become realistic inhabitants of a world that extends from the forests of Tijuca to the suburbs of Larangeiras and Catumbi, the theater, and the Rua do Ouvidor, with the obligatory references to objects of desire farther afield, such as Lívia's plans for a European adventure encompassing not only France but also Germany and Italy.

After the dense use of spatial references in the first chapters, Machado shifts the narrative toward the sedentary and internal states of mind of his characters. The middle section of the novel contains few references to theaters or the Rua do Ouvidor. The time of random encounters has been surpassed and with it the open space of society. Félix goes so far as to dream of living outside and beyond society, alone and uncomplicated, with his beloved: "When the two of us are together, removed from society, from contact with strangers, I'll find peace in my heart."[12] The final irony is found in the withdrawal of both Félix and especially Lívia from society—without having consummated their love.

This lengthy discussion of spatial practices (which, I reiterate, means something like space plus movement plus society) in *Ressurreição* underscores the importance of a particular set of locations and a limited range of possible characters and attitudes derived from social interactions associated with the rituals of courtship, friendship, and the quest for connections and favors in Rio de Janeiro. In the bildungsroman, loosely defined to include the novels studied in Chapters 1–3 of this volume, these places and interactions take on a different cast. The emphasis is on entry, experience, and the formation of identity through movement and social relations. In short: to learn, to grow, to master, to integrate, rather than to accommodate an existing character and system of life to the blossoming of love, as in *Ressurreição*.

Front and Back Regions

Seen through a spatial lens, Brazilian novels reveal a rich world of front and back regions, some of which are clearly spatialized with physical demarcations and others of which refer more to the visible realm of social performance versus the hidden work performed behind the scenes to maintain the front. In *The Presentation of Self in Everyday Life*, Erving Goffman elaborates a model for understanding the division of space as regions of performance.[13] As for the division of space, the house and garden are paradigmatic. In the front is the house, with its rules of decorum and the vigilant eyes of society; in the back, is the private garden, out of sight and therefore open to behavior that cannot take place in the front region. The front is closed, whereas the back is open. This is not as incongruous as it first appears. Goffman's definition of the front region stresses how controlled this space must be in typical middle-class settings.[14] Admitting the great differences between the 1950s society studied by Goffman and that of Rio de Janeiro a century before, the basic idea is supported in the literary sources under consideration here. Houses and gardens, not the house and the street, then. And gardens are the best place for secrets and for stolen kisses.

Consider Villaça and Dona Eusébia kissing in the garden at Bento Cubas's estate; Rubião and Sofia in the garden under the moon, Rubião grasping Sofia's hand and comparing her eyes to the stars; Bento and Capitu and the door linking the gardens behind their parents' houses, she scratching their names on the wall with a nail.[15] Gardens also offer space for the kinds of conversations that would not be authorized in the front regions, such as the house or the dinner table. For example, Nogueira takes Ricardo aside in the garden of Comendador Soares's estate to sound out Ricardo's intentions and to make clear his own designs.

Front and back regions can also usefully be thought of in more abstract terms as composite constructions involving people, places, and social conventions. Thus the little house in Gambôa where Brás and Virgília carry out their adultery is both a back region where secret love can flourish beyond social laws and at the same time a front region where the presence of Dona Plácida conveys an entirely different meaning with respect to Virgília's presence in the house. Front and back are grounds for performance, but they are also performed.

Extending this line of analysis, one can consider the many cases in which the difference between front and back is sustained by nothing more than the

—— Amo-te tanto que só um beijo pagar-me-ha tantos sacrifícios.
—— Um beijo assim em publico? Não posso.
— Bem vés que este jardim está deserto.
— E Deos que nos está vendo?
— Por isso é que eu trouxe este chapéo de sol.

ILLUSTRATION 10. "The Seductive Garden." The dialogue between the lovers trans-
lates to:
 —I love you so much that nothing less than a kiss will repay my sacrifices.
 —A kiss now, in public? I can't.
 —Don't you see that this garden is deserted?
 —And God, isn't he watching us?
 —That's why I brought along this parasol.
SOURCE: *Semana Illustrada* 55 (1861): 436.

verve (audacity, perfidy) of the performers. Goffman has this to say on the subject: "Commonly we find that upward mobility involves the presentation of
proper performances and that efforts to keep from moving downward are expressed in terms of sacrifices made for the maintenance of front."[16] In *Filomena
Borges* the eponymous heroine maintains a front as the "flower of Catete" with
the help of her socially ambitious mother and a backstage scheme predicated
on scrimping and privation that remains hidden behind the front—a situation

reminiscent of the passages quoted from *Senhora*. This strategy works because the stage on which Filomena acts out her role, in front, is physically and socially separated from the poor rooming house in back.[17] Keeping the two separate requires constant vigilance.[18]

In *O Coruja* Teobaldo's commitment to playing his role in front, even when he no longer has the means to do so, leads to a series of ethical lapses that utterly debase him and those around him. He attends the theater and eats fine meals when he does not have the money to pay for these activities; he borrows money from his poor friend André in order to bribe his former lover, Leonília, to leave town and avoid a potential scandal, that is, to maintain his front as a gentleman with Branca's rich father.[19] In this sense, he is like an amoral and protean version of Fernando Seixas.

These observations are not meant to suggest that front and back regions are synonymous with public and private or open and secret. The point to remember is the intimate relationship between the two regions. In this sense, every given front region has a back region. The front region may be public or private. In either case the front depends on a back region, where a different set of norms obtains and a whole range of materials is stored away for selective use in the front. What's more, a considerable element in any *Bildung* is the accumulation of these resources and techniques in the process of transformation from youth to adult, from provincial to parvenu to established member of society—that is, one must learn to inhabit and navigate through these regions. In Teobaldo's case, Azevedo suggests that a lack of fit can exist between the resources accumulated during the process of *Bildung* and the objective circumstances facing an individual owing to reversals of fortune. Conversely, we might consider the case of Maria Benedita, Sofia's poor country cousin in *Quincas Borba*. As Palha works to maneuver Rubião into considering the girl as a potential wife, he remarks, "You can't imagine what a good person she is. A fine upbringing, very strict. And as for the social graces, if she didn't have them as a child, she made up for the lost time amazingly fast. Sofia is her teacher" ("Não imagina que primor ali está. Boa educação, muito severa; e quanto aprendas de sociedade, se não as teve e criança, ressarciu o tempo perdido com rapidez extraordinária. Sofía é a mestra").[20] How she does this is instructive.

Upon first arriving at her cousin Sofia's house, Maria Benedita attends a dance and refuses to waltz, saying she is uncomfortable "to have a man hold my body tight against his." Her country manners are a hindrance to entering society, which, as far as Sofia is concerned, means marrying well. To compete for a good mate means learning to do precisely the things that Maria Benedita's conservative mother, with all her rural mores, opposes: "Oh, yes? Then it is French, piano, and love-making that she's going to learn?" Precisely, and Maria Benedita is a fast study. She practices piano for hours to "make up for lost time." She drops French phrases here and there. On a deeper level, she "had become adjusted to the milieu much quicker than her natural taste and life in the country would have made one believe," and she was "already in competition with the other woman."[21]

Heterogeneous Space

The domestic world of Rio de Janeiro was often no less mixed than the streets and theaters outside. A good example of this aspect of the domestic milieu is found in Aluísio Azevedo's *Casa de Pensão* (1884). The novel opens with the arrival of young Amâncio at the offices of Luís Campos in the Rua Direita. Campos is a successful merchant with a large three-story house in the prime business district. A vast warehouse takes up the first floor; the second serves as his office by day and his clerks' sleeping area by night; the third floor is occupied by the merchant himself, his wife Maria Hortênsia, and a niece named Dona Carlota.[22] Amâncio comes bearing a letter of introduction from his aged father, who lives in Maranhão. Campos is called on, through old social ties, to serve as the young man's sponsor and protector in the world of the Corte.[23] Azevedo, as is usually the case in his novels, is especially attentive to spatial practices and the way class and gender imbue movement with the weight of crossing social thresholds. In the small world of Campos's house, there is a whole microcosm of social life, which moves to the rhythms of commerce and according to the domestic rituals and relational spaces generated within the four walls and three floors of the building.

Consider the example of meals taken in Campos's house. On the third floor, in the owner's quarters, meals are served for family, guests, and functionaries at two large tables. At the head table sit Campos, his wife, niece, the *guarda-livros* (accountant of the firm), and any guests (who were frequent). Conversation is subdued, and the *guarda-livros* tell only carefully selected anecdotes chosen in advance. The *caixeiros* (sales clerks) sit separately, as though at the kids' table. The scene Azevedo paints is heavy with patriarchy and the sullen power of ritualized hierarchy. Each day, the *caixeiros* wake early and descend from the second floor to the first for work; they ascend to the third floor for lunch and dinner, which is ample and a source of pride among them when talking to employees of other firms; they descend from lunch to work and from dinner to the second floor, where their beds are made up in the office area occupied by Campos himself during the day.[24]

Heterogeneous spaces are tricky. The weight of patriarchy and ritual cannot fully suffocate human experience. In *Casa de Pensão* Amâncio's arrival in Campos's house sets off a cascade of events leading to a tragic end. The young provincial ends up falling for Hortênsia while keeping a young woman named Amélia as his lover. He is ultimately murdered by Amélia's brother, another medical school student, in the Hotel de Paris.[25]

Historical data regarding incomes and rents provide a deeper context for these literary examples. In Figure 4, the left-hand axis refers to incomes reported in voting lists and the right-hand axis refers to the range of rents reported in property tax rolls. To highlight the heterogeneity of domestic spaces, three in-

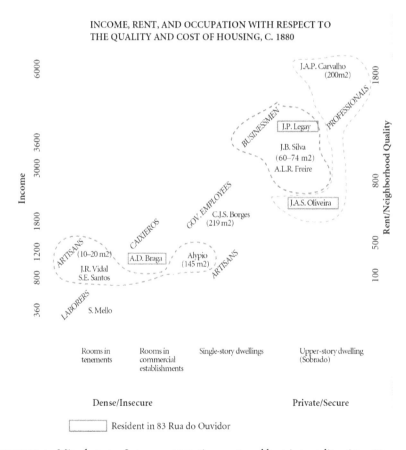

FIGURE 4. Mixed spaces: Income, occupation, rent, and housing quality, circa 1880.

SOURCES: "Décima urbana," 1870 and 1888, Arquivo Geral da Cidade, Rio de Janeiro; and "Eleitores," Sacramento, 1880, Arquivo Geral da Cidade, Rio de Janeiro.

dividuals resident at the same address in the Rua do Ouvidor are outlined with boxes: an artisan, a businessman, and a professional. Based on their surnames, they appear to be unrelated. Mixed occupancy was common in Rio de Janeiro during the nineteenth century. This fact turns interiors into complicated spaces marked by subtle rules of comportment and a set of spatial practices that do not correspond to a simple house versus street distinction of public and private space, or to a straightforward schematic relationship between income on the one hand and levels of privacy and security on the other. We have already seen many examples of the kinds of spatial practices that arise in heterogeneous domestic settings. Teobaldo descends to Ernestina's rooms to be waited on and entertained. Ernestina ascends to Teobaldo's rooms to lay claim to him as a lover. These situations aggravate tensions in and between front and back regions; they complicate the definition and maintenance of open and closed spaces.

In modified form, the same thing goes for domestic spaces that are not shared by several unrelated individuals. In wealthy households the presence of servants and slaves injects heterogeneity. The kitchen is the province of the servants; the boudoir the realm of the lady and her maid; the office, the refuge of the man of the house. Servants move in and out of focus; they spend most of their time in the back region, but they emerge into the front region with a silver tray during a dinner party. Sometimes, the servant or dependent even plays a leading part. In *Dom Casmurro*, when José Dias's intervention famously reveals Bento to himself—by telling Dona Glória, the boy's pious mother, that her son is spending too much time with Capitu, the pretty girl-next-door with gypsy eyes—his presence in the house and his point of view set in motion the plot of the novel.[26] The spatial practices revealed in *Dom Casmurro* are exquisitely rendered, showing how proximity and access to closed spaces give birth to infatuation. The doomed relationship between Bento Santiago and Capitolina Pádua begins innocently but turns furtive as they age.

These opening chapters are all about permeable spaces, about the way neighbors have privileged access to the closed space of the home and garden. Indeed, a garden gate through which the two children pass connects the two houses. It is in the garden, a liminal space that is neither open nor closed, that Capitu scratches her name next to Bento's with a nail. The infatuation is inscribed in space. Bento enters Capitu's room and combs her hair. He is the young boy from the neighboring house; his presence is ambiguous—a mixture of innocent everyday friendship and latent sexual longing. Both young people operate tactically, taking advantage of furtive moments together away from the watchful eye of the adults. In doing so, they develop a counter-strategy for living. Dona Glória has promised to send her son to the seminary. That is her strategy—the prerogative of parental power in determining a child's future. Capitu manipulates Bento and, through him, José Dias, to subvert Dona Glória's ends. José Dias has his own desires, which coincide obliquely with the wishes of the young lovers. Machado builds a web of manipulation from the homely building blocks of furtive caresses and overheard conversations, all of which are underwritten by the spatial practices associated with the neighboring houses.

These practices give *Dom Casmurro* a striking texture of realism. Instead of love at first sight, we have manipulation and infatuation taking wing and generating an inexorable motive force. The whole edifice is made possible by the little spatial details Machado is so careful to describe; the story would not be possible without the complex mix of people and spaces made up of the two houses and their gardens. When the narrator tells us, at the outset, that Dom Casmurro's house in the suburbs is an exact replica of the house in the Rua Matacavalos, he reinscribes the power of place. Bento's simulacrum is a failed bid for self-knowledge: "My end was to tie together the poles of my life and to restore adolescence in my old age" ("O meu fim evidente era atar as duas pontas da vida, e restaurar na velhice a adolescência").[27] The bid was a failure, but his instincts were right. Everything hinged on that particular place; but people change.

Social Spaces and Networks

Network diagrams are tools for analyzing complex social phenomena. They can also look like giant hairballs and be just about as useful. Two approaches are viable. One is to use network statistics, predicated on some kind of network theory, and extract quantitative information. The other is to shape the networks to show complex relationships in a legible manner. From the statistical point of view, the diagram itself becomes little more than an illustration. The important information is conveyed in numbers, such as network density, which measures the proportion of closed triads in the graph. Alongside the quantitative approach is a viable interpretive mode in which the graph itself, properly configured, is a tool for exploration. This really only works when the data in the graph are legible—not just literally legible (many graphs are simply too cluttered to interpret) but also figuratively legible, in the sense that the component parts are known to the reader. This is why I end my study with these techniques only after a detailed discussion of the novels in question. The two approaches of course can and should be combined. As Franco Moretti suggests, character networks (and I would add character networks embedded in spatial networks) turn time, the narrative flow of a novel or play, into space.[28]

To demonstrate what I mean by these techniques, I have quantified and graphed the network of relationships in *Sonhos d'Ouro*. To begin with, it should be recognized that network graphs generally present information in an abstract space. An algorithm places the nodes (dots with character or place names) and edges (denoting connections) in a particular arrangement on the page. Nothing demands that Guida be above and Ricardo below. The graph could easily spin around. What is (almost) constant is the distance between these two characters. Their web of relationships in this particular force-directed algorithm *must* place them at approximately this distance—they are drawn close by their dense and mutually overlapping social networks. Not so for the distance between Ricardo's office and Marechal Manoel. These characters, only slightly connected, can be moved around to different positions and the graph will still settle into a stable configuration. So when reading a graph like this, one should always be aware that the highly connected characters are most accurately placed and stable and the least connected are the most arbitrarily arranged. Before examining the graphical visualization of the network, what do the numbers tell us?

First, they tell us that the novel is relatively balanced in structure. Ricardo and Guida each sit at the center of subnetworks, which gradually become knitted together over the course of the novel. They are central by any measure, although it is Guida who stands most squarely in the middle. It is through her that Ricardo's path to social integration and eventual marriage must pass. Viewing the book in terms of social networks changes the way we see the balance between the two leading characters. Guida and Ricardo speak roughly the same amount of dialogue: 24% and 25%, respectively.[29] Yet Ricardo is *much less integrated* into the network of society. Basic quantitative measures relating to network position provide further information about the characters with spoken dialogue in the novel and their relative social positions in the imagined world of *Sonhos d'Ouro*.

The technical terms may be disorienting at first for readers unfamiliar with network analysis. Briefly, *degree* refers to the number of edges (connections to other characters by means of speech), both incoming and outgoing, associated with a given *node* (character). Higher degree simply indicates more relationships. The value can be an odd number if a character speaks but is not spoken to in a particular relationship. *Closeness centrality* provides a measure of how close a given character is to all other connected characters in the graph—the lower the value, the less distance needed to travel to the rest of the characters. *Betweenness centrality* quantifies things according to shortest paths; in this case, the higher the number, the more shortest paths across the network run through a particular character. *Modularity class* identifies groups within the network with internally dense connections relative to the entire network. The *clustering coefficient* (local) is fairly self-explanatory—higher values indicate location in a tight cluster within the graph, and lower values reflect a network position situated between several cliques. Finally, *eigenvector centrality* expresses a measure of influence—high values mean more connections to other highly influential nodes.[30]

According to the network statistics, Guida has a degree of 41—that is, 41 different incoming or outgoing partners in conversation. She is the most central character in every dimension of network statistics I measured. She is the central object of affection and concern in the novel. Of course, we can discover this by just reading the novel. Why, then, measure relationships in novels with these statistical tools? Quantification becomes useful in three ways. First, it reveals information about magnitudes. Human readings of novels are superior to computer readings in every regard save one: Computers count everything and forget nothing. With a quantitative approach, we supplement our subjective sense of the relationships specified in the novel and can read, in a brief table, orders of magnitude of difference knitted together but not necessarily perceived while reading on our own. Second, quantification provides a helpful scaffold for writing about baggy monsters full of words, such as novels, in structural terms. These structures can be expressed in only two ways: One can describe them in words, based on a subjective reading; or one can describe them (or graph them) in numbers, based on objective counts and algorithms. My approach argues for the value of doing both of these things. Third, quantification opens up new lines for comparative analysis. Novels can differ in many ways. This is one of them and is eminently worthy of exploration, particularly if we use these techniques to "read" several novels simultaneously—distant reading. Table 5 provides a summary of the quantitative measures of network relationships pertaining to the major characters in *Sonhos d'Ouro*.

The first thing that jumps out in Table 5 is the size of the gap between Guida and the rest of the characters, Ricardo in particular. The book, as narrated, takes Ricardo's point of view, yet he is a distant second in the world of social relations. When I first read the book, I was so caught up in the narrative, the plot of Ricardo's *Bildung*, that I did not notice this asymmetry. Reading the book

TABLE 5. Network Statistics for *Sonhos d'Ouro*

	Degree	Closeness Centrality	Betweenness Centrality	Modularity Class	Clustering Coefficient	Eigenvector Centrality
Guida	41	1.31	495	1	0.1	1
Ricardo	25	1.62	104	1	0.25	0.85
Comendador Soares	17	1.72	97	0	0.37	0.59
Visconde de Aljuba	15	1.83	63	0	0.31	0.54
Fábio	15	1.93	72	1	0.43	0.68
Guimarães	15	1.83	81	0	0.36	0.57
Nogueira	12	1.83	69	0	0.45	0.48
Benicio	11	1.93	8	1	0.60	0.51
Bastos	9	1.83	56	0	0.23	0.25
Dona Guilhermina	8	2.59	58	1	0.25	0.30
Mrs. Trowshy	7	2.14	0.9	1	0.75	0.25
Daniel	6	2.07	0.8	1	0.83	0.18

SOURCE: José de Alencar, *Sonhos d'Ouro*.
Character connections coded by Regina Coeli.

anew with this knowledge in mind heightened the sense of Ricardo's precarious and peripheral social position. Although Alencar consistently portrays Ricardo as a strong and capable young man, he is, structurally, a weak and ineffectual person on the margins of society.

A second insight derives from the interaction of modularity class with the other measures of network centrality. The social clique around Comendador Soares, modularity class 0, is relatively homogeneous. It represents the in-group, a tight knot of relationships that serves to repel Ricardo—the space where everyone knows everyone else's business, or speculates on that basis. It is also the claque of dowry chasers that Guida must flee to maintain her capricious autonomy. Her movement outward forges the connective tissue between the two groups, thus her overwhelming score in terms of betweenness. Meanwhile, modularity class 1 is much more heterogeneous. It contains the two protagonists in the marriage plot, but it also includes friends and confidants. This is precisely the point at which spatial practice intersects with networks of social relations and structures.

The space of *Sonhos d'Ouro*, when thought of in network terms, reinforces our sense of Ricardo's complicated position. He is outside looking in compared with Guida. Where exactly is "in"? Where Comendador Soares is embedded in a clique (modularity class 0) composed of the rest of Guida's suitors. This is the social space in which Ricardo feels most out of place, and it is a space of mansions and country estates. His connections to Guida, Mrs. Trowshy, Daniel, and Fábio first appear in the "open" space of the forest of Tijuca, although of course we know he is an old friend of Fábio's. Physical spaces and social networks taken together provide an alternative, distant reading of the novel. This combination can be rendered in a graph that blends relationships among people and the places where connections are made (Figure 5).

Ricardo's conundrum is summed up in Figure 5. He begins in the lower portion of the graph, out on horseback, and must end in the upper right, duking it out with the suitors. The epilogue moves once again to the periphery. The happy ending cannot be consummated in the center of Soares's world. The upper right is the space of social domination, and the upper left is the world of work and consumption. Ricardo cannot pry open the pathway to success in the world of work because he lacks or refuses the protection available in the upper right. Provincial and peripheral, his *Bildung* is thwarted by the networks of relationships and social spaces that his pride prevents him from embracing or entering.

The contrast in network structure is stark when looking at *Memórias Póstumas*. Obviously, a novel narrated in the first person is likely to have a much stronger central character. Brás is the egocentric sun around which the rest of the network revolves. As an experiment in visualization, I created, together with my colleague Erik Steiner in the Spatial History Lab, a linked two-part graphic depicting both the network space and the physical space of Brás Cubas's world (Figure 6).

The visualization in Figure 6a has been trimmed such that minor characters do not appear and not all locations are depicted. Locations, it should be emphasized are approximate and a certain amount of artistic license was used in laying them out. The basic points are clear enough. Brás sits at the center of a social network, and the network is built up over the course of the novel through encounters that embrace many distinct parts of the city. Machado uses the space of the city and some of its representative institutions and zones of activity both to render Brás's *Bildung* realistically and to provide opportunities for particular kinds of encounters, crossing paths, and moments of insertion into or withdrawal from the whirl of city life.

Open social spaces, such as the Passeio Público and the theater serve in the novel as the source of accidental encounters. But these are predictable accidents. They involve the same cast of characters making the rounds. Lobo

Neves is bound to be at the theater. Quincas Borba frequents the Passeio. Life, Machado suggests, is inevitably made up of one damn thing after another. One need do nothing more than move about, in and out of the open social spaces of the city; indeed, one can do nothing else. This fact gives the novel its strange propulsive force. As I have already suggested with my discussion earlier in this chapter of the spatial practices adumbrated by Machado in his first novel, *Ressurreição*, this process of moving about from country to city, from theater to street, from closed domestic space to the open space of domestic social events, serves both a narrative function, allowing for chance and conjuncture to work their whiles, and a structural function, generating a sense of the staging ground for social relationships.

Closed space has two faces. It can be claustrophobic, as in the setting for Brás's uncomfortable conversations; but it can also be snug, perhaps a bit melancholy, as in the time spent in Tijuca during the months after his return from Europe, or perhaps monotonous, as the love nest in Gambôa doubtlessly soon became.[31] In any event, closed space is depicted in the novel in typically domestic terms and the spatial practices are traced with extreme economy. The social network depicted in *Memórias Póstumas* grows in fits and starts, as a remembered series of encounters and movements in space and time, sometimes recounted out of sequence. In statistical terms there is but one central character, Brás, with a degree of 48 and other measures of centrality an order of magnitude greater than the rest of the characters.[32] Interiority and spatial practice, then, rather than social structure and networks. Machado could not have devised a better form with which to capture the peripatetic and unstructured volubility of Brás Cubas.

Given Azevedo's professed admiration for Zola and his Naturalism, it comes as no surprise that the social network depicted in *O Coruja* is richly complex, spanning social classes and a diverse set of public and private spaces (Figure 7). As one reads the novel, it quickly becomes clear that the book is primarily about Teobaldo (degree 54), not André (degree 40). Yet the novel's title is true to the way its title character sits at the crossroads of the social network depicted by Azevedo. *O Coruja* is a character stuck in-between several worlds. He is akin in many ways to a dependent, yet he tends to be the one who foots the bill. André is an odd mixture of free agent, confidant, go-between, and fixer. He is close to the center of the social network, yet he is not subsumed by it like his friend. Teobaldo's place in the graph can best be thought of as a point in a series of forbidden triangles.

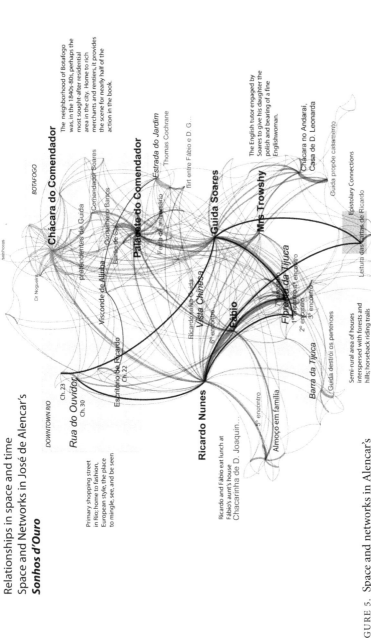

Relationships in space and time
Space and Networks in José de Alencar's
Sonhos d'Ouro

BOTAFOGO

The neighborhood of Botafogo was, in the 1840s-80s, perhaps the most sought-after residential area in the city. Home to rich merchants and rentiers, it provides the scene for nearly half of the action in the book.

Chácara do Comendador

pretendentes de Guida
Comendador Soares
Conselheiro Barros
Barão de S...

Estrada do Jardim
Thomas Cochrane

flirt entre Fábio e D. G...

Visconde de Aljuba

Palacete do Comendador

Festa de aniversário

Guida Soares

Mrs Trowshy

The English tutor engaged by Soares to give his daughter the polish and bearing of a fine Englishwoman.

Chácara no Andaraí,
Casa de D. Leonarda

Guida propõe casamento

DOWNTOWN RIO

Rua do Ouvidor
Ch. 30

Ch. 23

Escritório de Ricardo
Ch. 22

Primary shopping street in Rio; home to fashion, European style, the place to mingle, see, and be seen

Ricardo visita Guida
Vista Chinesa

Fábio

4º encontro

Floresta da Tijuca
1º encontro
2º encontro
3º encontro

Epistolary Connections

Leitura das cartas de Ricardo

Fábio diz que Guida ama ...

Casa de Ricardo

Dr Nogueira

solteironas

6º encontro

Ricardo Nunes

5º encontro

Ricardo and Fábio eat lunch at Fábio's aunt's house
Chacarinha de D. Joaquin...

Almoço em família

Barra da Tijuca

Guida destrói os pentelhos

Semi-rural area of houses interspersed with forests and hills; horseback riding trails

FIGURE 5. Space and networks in Alencar's *Sonhos d'Ouro*. Network diagram hand-modified from a force-directed graph drawn in Gephi.

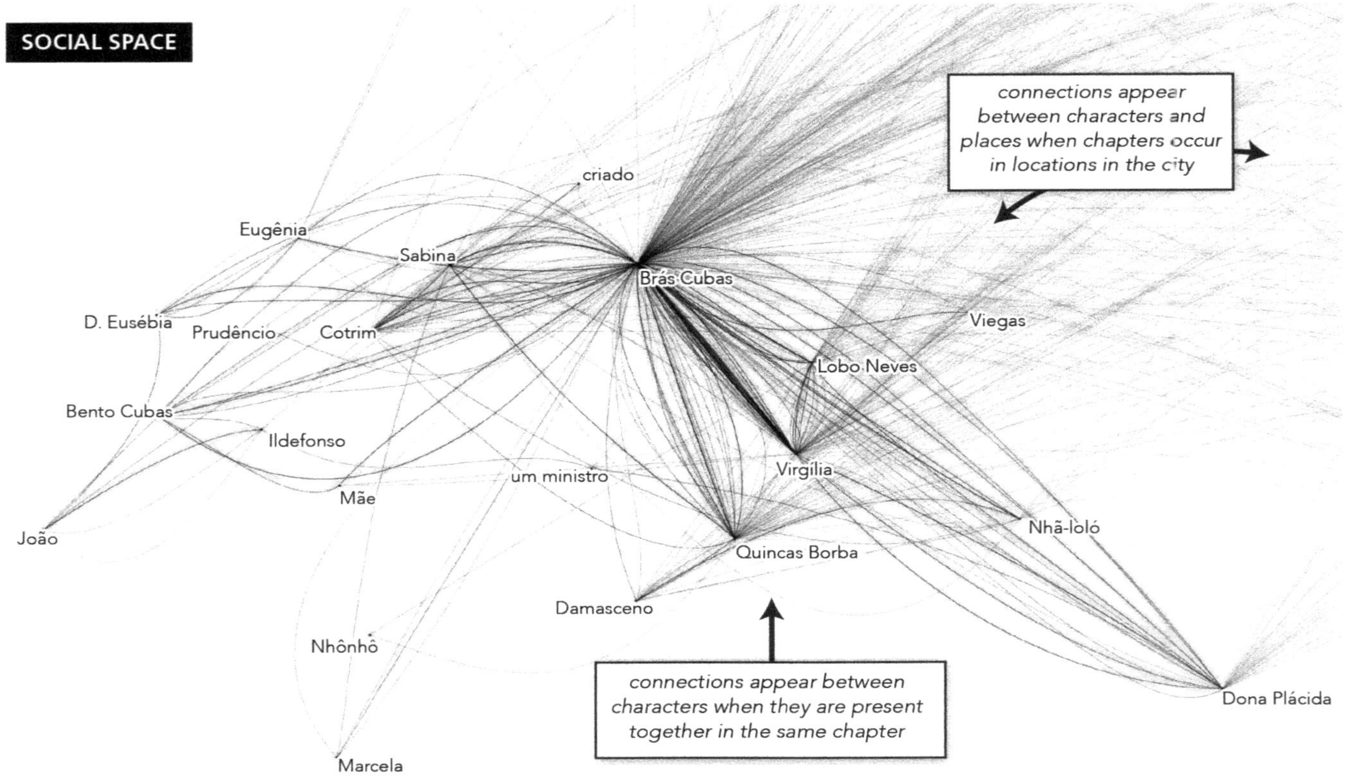

SOCIAL SPACE

connections appear between characters and places when chapters occur in locations in the city

connections appear between characters when they are present together in the same chapter

Dona Plácida

Nhã-loló

Viegas

Lobo Neves

Virgília

Quincas Borba

Brás Cubas

Damasceno

um ministro

criado

Sabina

Cotrim

Mãe

Nhônhô

Marcela

Eugênia

Prudêncio

Ildefonso

D. Eusébia

Bento Cubas

João

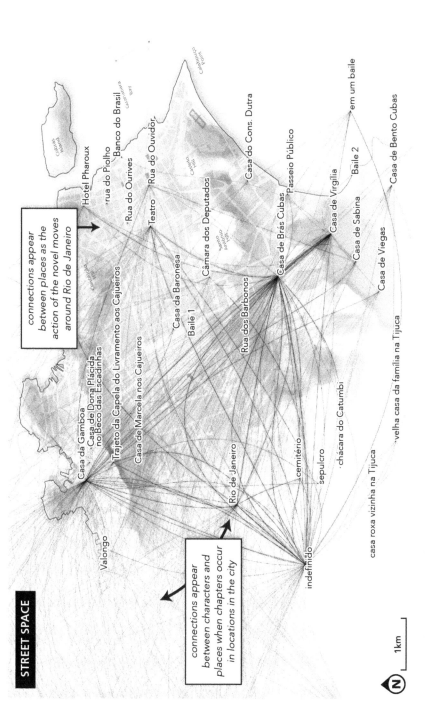

STREET SPACE

connections appear between places as the action of the novel moves around Rio de Janeiro

connections appear between characters and places when chapters occur in locations in the city

Corcovado Point

Corcovado Hotel

Guanabara Bay

Castello Hill

Santo Antonio Hill

Hotel Pharoux

rua do Piolho

Banco do Brasil

Rua do Ouvidor

Rua do Ouvidor

Teatro

Casa do Cons. Dutra

Câmara dos Deputados

Casa de Brás Cubas

Passeio Público

Casa de Virgília

Baile 2

Casa de Bento Cubas

Casa da Baronesa

Baile 1

Casa de Sabina

em um baile

Casa da Gamboa

Casa de Dona Plácida no Beco das Escadinhas

Trajeto da Capela do Livramento aos Cajueiros

Casa de Marcela nos Cajueiros

Rua dos Barbonos

Casa de Viegas

Valongo

Rio de Janeiro

cemitério

sepulcro

chácara do Catumbi

velha casa da família na Tijuca

casa roxa vizinha na Tijuca

indefinido

N

1km

FIGURE 6. The (a) social and (b) physical spaces of Machado's *Memórias Póstumas de Brás Cubas*. Graphic design by Erik Steiner, Center for Spatial and Textual Analysis, Stanford University.

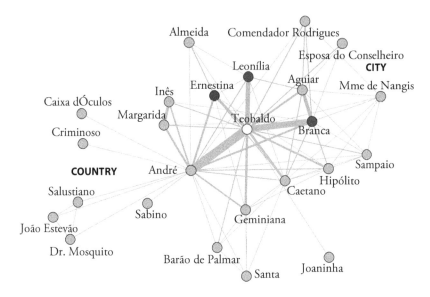

FIGURE 7. The social network in Azevedo's *O Coruja*. Hand-modified force-directed graph.

Azevedo's technique is quite simple: Connect two dots and then add a problematic third. Thus we get a whole series of uncomfortable threesomes. Teobaldo + Ernestina + Almeida. Teobaldo + Ernestina + Leonília. Teobaldo + Branca + Aguiar. He goes to any lengths, including taking his friend's last mil-réis, to avoid the fatal triad Teobaldo + Leonília + Branca. To no avail, of course, as Aguiar is happy to close that nasty little circuit. Meanwhile, note how with every woman in his life, there is a triad that closes with his friend André occupying the third position. André the enabler.

The network diagram depicted in Figure 7 reveals two distinctive poles around which relationships in the novel cluster. In the country we have the childhood relations of Teobaldo and André. In the city, where the action of the novel is concentrated, the dominant force is Teobaldo. He connects the major and minor characters of the city in a web of relationships, including several amorous triangles, at least two of which turn out to be fatal. Looking at the diagram closely, one can see how the characters of André and Aguiar pull Teobaldo from the poles of country and city. It is Aguiar, the friendly rival, who will provide Teobaldo's undoing, because he is the indirect but fatal connection between Branca, the naïve young bride, and Leonília, the once-beautiful courtesan and object of desire for Teobaldo. Aguiar, the city slicker in love with his cousin Branca, represents the integrated personality Teobaldo never becomes. He is at home in society and consistent and in control of his personality. Meanwhile, on the periphery is a cast of mostly older and wealthier men and women—grown-up society, which, in its norms, expectations, and distribution of resources, will make and then break the younger characters in the center.

For the reader now acquainted with these three novels through the analysis presented in Chapters 1 through 3, the network graphs and statistics provide a convenient summary of the characters and their interactions. The visualization of information serves to open up the text for a different sort of interpretation based on a holistic view. Reading is a linear experience, and it is not always possible to keep in mind all the intricacies of plot and action. Seeing things all at one glance changes the way we remember what we have read.

We can go further. The social networks in novels take shape in the social space of the city. Characters meet in open and closed spaces, and locations depicted in novels can be connected by people—indeed, this is the only meaningful way that connections exist between places. Typically, social network analysis presents relationships in abstract space. This is clearly incomplete. Looking back at the graphs for *Sonhos d'Ouro* (Figure 5) and *Memórias Póstumas* (Figure 6), consider the physical space of the city and its relationship to the social space of the network. Now look at an expanded collection of novels, combined in one graph to include locations (Figure 8).[33]

We are approaching the promised land of distant reading. Characters float about between locations, knitting together a social and spatial fabric. If the novels were somehow combined, these would be the places where the disparate characters might meet, the environments they would experience. Indeed, once we have read these novels, they are combined in our imagination precisely through these mutual spaces.

In broad strokes, the information in Table 6 can be translated in the following terms. First, there is the dominance of the interior world of the *casa*. Of all the possible characters, 133 appear at least once in a domestic setting. I retain the distinction between houses and country retreats (*chácaras*) in order to differentiate urban and rural domestic locations. Although the closed space of the house dominates, as we would expect in the genre, the street and theater both appear with connections to a great many characters. It is in the street where chance plays the greatest narrative role. The theater is the place par excellence for introductions and for complications.

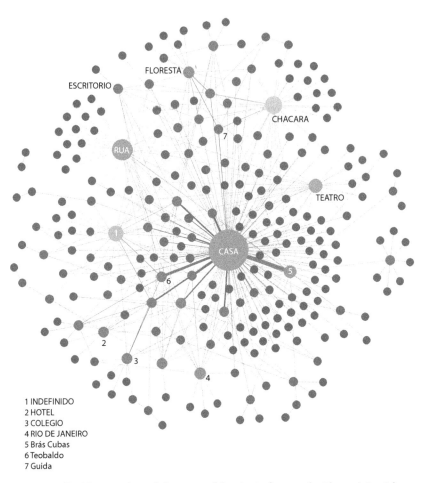

ESCRITORIO
FLORESTA
CHACARA
RUA
TEATRO
CASA

1 INDEFINIDO
2 HOTEL
3 COLEGIO
4 RIO DE JANEIRO
5 Brás Cubas
6 Teobaldo
7 Guida

FIGURE 8. Social networks and the space of the city in five novels: Alencar's *Lucíola*, *Senhora*, and *Sonhos d'Ouro*; Azevedo's *O Coruja*; and Machado de Assis's *Memórias Póstumas de Brás Cubas*.

Second, to the extent that people appear in the table, this should be read as a measure of their spatial practices and the diversity of locations in which they are depicted. Brás, peripatetic, is all over the city (and in plenty of imaginary places as well). Major characters such as Teobaldo, Lúcia (from *Lucíola*), Fernando (*Senhora*), and Guida (*Sonhos d'Ouro*) move about through a fairly wide range of spaces. Minor characters, as would be expected, appear seldom and in just one or two places. This is not likely to be a mere effect of their marginality in the narrative. Theaters, hotels, and forests were not frequented by fishermen,

criminals, beggars, old maids, or wet nurses—all examples of marginal characters who appear in just one or two settings in the novels. Even "open" spaces are
in essence closed to many urban residents.

Third, the world of work is almost completely absent. In the five novels used
for this analysis, only nine characters ever venture into an office, two enter a
bank, and four go inside a shop. To be sure, in the twenty-odd scenes set in the

TABLE 6. Networks of Places and People in Nineteenth-Century Brazilian Novels Set
in Rio de Janeiro

Label	Degree	Closeness Centrality	Betweenness Centrality	Eigenvector Centrality
Casa	133	1.83	20,741	1.00
Rua	53	2.47	5,468	0.45
Chácara	40	2.70	4,185	0.28
Indefinido	32	2.83	2,598	0.26
Teatro	25	2.77	2,072	0.20
Brás Cubas	19	2.15	6,167	0.21
Rio de Janeiro	16	2.87	1,236	0.12
Floresta	15	3.28	1,076	0.12
Colégio	12	2.93	1,401	0.08
Party	12	2.91	623	0.12
Paulo	11	2.44	1,128	0.18
Hotel	11	2.85	787	0.11
Teobaldo	10	2.36	1,182	0.19
André	9	2.41	1,374	0.17
Lúcia	9	2.52	799	0.15
Fernando Seixas	9	2.47	769	0.18
Escritório	9	3.09	301	0.10
Fazenda	9	3.28	636	0.06
Tijuca	9	3.12	615	0.07
Ricardo Nunes	8	2.39	731	0.18
Galera	8	3.09	1,750	0.02
Guida Soares	7	2.41	659	0.17
Aurélia Camargo	7	2.46	446	0.17
Virgília	6	2.48	635	0.15

SOURCES: José de Alencar, *Lucíola*, *Senhora*, and *Sonhos d'Ouro*; Aluísio Azevedo, *O Coruja*; and Machado de
Assis, *Memórias Póstumas de Brás Cubas*. Locations coded by Regina Coeli.

Rua do Ouvidor, shopping is going on, but the interiors of shops and the process of buying and selling are largely absent. Instead, the contents of the shops are generally described in the context of the interiors of houses or the clothes on the backs of the main characters. The main vestige of the world of work in these novels is the shadowy presence of slaves and dependents around the margins—as domestics, porters, ambulatory retailers, and the like. The only major character we see working with any real sense of the material conditions of labor and the cold necessity of earning a living is André, the schoolteacher in *O Coruja*. We might wish to add some of the fallen women in these novels to the list of workers. Certainly they earned their keep, and our male authors lovingly describe the settings and circumstances of their work. The contrast with the realistic novels of Balzac, Flaubert, and Zola could not be sharper. The first chapters of *César Birotteau*, scenes in the pottery factory in *L'Education Sentimentale*, laundry work in *L'Assomoir*—all give us more detail about the settings and processes of work than all five Brazilian novels in my little sample combined. To be fair, Azevedo does describe work in considerable detail in some of his other novels, with *O Cortiço* being the outstanding case. Still, as far as the bildungsroman goes in nineteenth-century Brazil, work is rarely described and almost never seen being done. Characters think about jobs and careers and money and sometimes the narratives tell us that they have indeed worked, but we do not see the work or the spaces where work takes place.

Read in this fashion, the characters and their movement through space provide strong support for one key aspect of Roberto Schwarz's interpretation of the Brazilian novel in the nineteenth century. As Schwarz points out, Brazil's social structure was riven with personalistic and capricious favor rather than neutral and impersonal forms of relationships, and the favor granting grew ever more prevalent in bourgeois Europe. This slave- and favor-based society had a stunted view of the world of work. The inability, for the most part, of Brazil's canonical novelists to depict a rich world of work is traceable to this fact.[34]

Throughout this chapter, I have insisted on interpreting space and spatial practice as fundamental concepts for reading Rio de Janeiro through novels. In Figure 8 the city itself emerged as a character drawing together the variegated plots and styles of five novels, inviting readers to see the novels and the city in a new light.

CONCLUSION

THIS STUDY IS AN ODD CONFECTION: a generous portion of literary history, a dash of economic and social history, a leavening of social theory, a large dose of close reading, and a sprinkling of distant reading. From literary history I took the central problem of the book: the individual in youth and early adulthood and the question of social integration. The central problem pointed clearly to the issues of education, career, and marriage—the questions, in other words, of *Bildung*. From economic and social history I garnered data and context—the why of it all. The scope and velocity of social and economic change in the second half of Pedro II's reign heightened the sense of competition and the fragility of the hopes of youth in the face of an emergent financial capitalism. Social theory offered concepts, means of interpreting the practices described in the novels. Close reading revealed the dense tissue of lived experience in light of the problem and context. Distant reading put literature in conversation with itself and with the context and concepts on an abstract plane.

In proceeding in this way, I willingly (willfully) ignored disciplinary rules and expectations. Simply put, I took risks and made rash assumptions. I assumed that readers could be made to understand and even to cherish largely unread books. I assumed a familiarity with European literature that is perhaps unwarranted. In either case, I elected optimism over pessimism and pedantry. This book truly is dedicated to the happy few with the sincere hope that their numbers will grow. Rather than go on justifying or qualifying my choices, I have saved two key ideas for final elaboration here. These are by no means the only conclusions to be drawn. They are, however, cumulative impressions and this is where they belong.

Dead Fathers, Dead Mothers

Without exception, every version of the Brazilian bildungsroman examined in this book centers on male protagonists with dead fathers. This is the case in *Sonhos d'Ouro*, *Senhora*, *O Coruja*, *Memórias Póstumas de Brás Cubas*, and *Dom Casmurro*. One need not be a follower of Freud to perceive the critical importance of this factor in the construction of the novels and the symbolic universe they represent. In some cases the father has died before *Bildung* can begin; in other cases, he dies in the middle of the education and socialization process. Thus in these novels we have young men without fathers and a desta-bilized economic and social order—present and future threatening to become unmoored from the past. Can a young man succeed under these conditions, complete his *Bildung*, and enter a stable adult world? For Alencar, the answer is a qualified perhaps, given the right character and the good faith of solid, hon-est people—older values hitched to newer realities. Machado's answer is that it makes no difference because there is never any stable adult society into which one can integrate. Azevedo seems to have concluded that the answer is prob-ably no, despite the possibility of superficial appearances to the contrary.

Most of the female protagonists in the Brazilian novels under consideration are also orphans, more often than not having lost a mother rather than a father. Guida, Capitu, Aurélia, Lúcia, Branca—orphans all. Only Virgília stands as an exception, and it is unexceptional that she is alone in contracting a conven-tional marriage under the usual terms. The absence of a mother places these young women's *Bildung* in jeopardy. Whether rich or poor, they must navigate through education, marriage, and wifehood without the advice and protection born of experience from their mothers.

The parricidal tendencies of nineteenth-century Brazilian novelists, par-ticularly when working in the genre of the bildungsroman, are of a piece with their European counterparts. A list of orphaned heroes in European novels of the genre would be interminable but might begin with Julien Sorel, Dorothea Brooke, Tertius Lydgate, Will Ladislaw, John Harmon, Pip, Lucien Chardon/Rubempré, and Frédéric Moreau. If, as Moretti suggests, the bildungsroman seeks to solve the problem of the integration of the individual into bourgeois society, this integration will be especially fraught for young men and women facing the world alone. In this sense, dead mothers and fathers resonate with a fractured chronotope—a particular kind of disinheritance, a rupture in time. Their struggles illuminate a subjective experience and, in doing so, reveal with terrible lucidity the rickety and incomplete structures of the world as it is given to them. Returning to Joshua Esty's concept of unseasonable youth, we can see the genre, in this guise, as grappling with the structural conditions underlying failed *Bildung*.

Casualties of War

The specific character of the Brazilian case blends into the universal nature of the problem of social integration. To compete, to integrate, one must master the rules of the game. Refusal leads to frustration or worse. When Rastignac, the greatest parvenu in world literature, proclaims "It's war between us now," he accepts the rules and enters the fray, unscrupulous and calculating.[1] Julien Sorel stops at nothing to attain success. On the other side of the ledger, Lydgate, no parvenu, misreads the signs, and his life becomes a slow shipwreck. The social war is one of competition and calculation, predicated on the cultivation of rich capitalistic sponsors. Examples of these powerful men and women abound in the European bildungsroman: Nucigen, Bulstrode, Dambreuse, de la Mole. War is also waged on the sentimental front. Marriage is conceived as a competitive market. It is another means to the same end—money, power, position.

What of the Brazilian case? As we have seen, the protagonists of the Brazilian bildungsroman are, as a lot, hesitant to play by the rules of the game. When they do, the result is either tragic, as in the case of Teobaldo, or voluble and ultimately pointless, as in the case of Brás Cubas. But our authors have taken pains to provide an ample assortment of secondary characters to play along according to the rules, to show what the players look like and what winning entails. The most flagrant examples are furnished by Machado: Escobar, calculating and cashing in on connections to the wealthy Santiago family; Palha, grifting his was through Rubião's unexpected fortune; Cotrim, moving smoothly from illegal slave trader to the financial speculation made possible by the Cubas inheritance. Alencar offers us Couto, the quasi-rapist cum capitalist, and the dog's breakfast of suitors hovering around Guida in the rich capitalist Soares's mansion and country estate. Without scruples and with protection, it is possible to play and win this game.

In any competitive social order, there are winners and there are losers. The losers can be further distinguished in two camps: those who lose because they choose not to enter the battlefield or enter (or exit) it badly; and those who are condemned to lose before the battle begins. In the former camp, we have Ricardo, Teobaldo, Fernando Seixas, Guida, Bento, and perhaps Brás (the small winner). In the latter camp (all born poor but resourceful), we have André, Lúcia, Dona Plácida, and Capitu. Perhaps between these camps are the survivors: Marcela, Leonília, Virgília—scarred but more or less still in one piece. Win, lose, or draw, the social battles depicted in the Brazilian bildungsroman are marked by carnage and loss. One of the chief findings of this study is the existence of this structure of feeling, this sense of disinheritance, disillusion, and obstinate refusal.

Quantitative evidence regarding economic and social change helped alert me to the possible existence of the social war and its scale and pace of development. Yet, without access to the literary sources, social and economic change appears as something quite different: Whether under the cover of terms such as "increasing dynamism" or "financial intermediation" or "capital deepening," or "sectoral transformations," there is no accounting for the experience of young lives caught up in the gears of the complex machine. Nothing in the published and unpublished statistics comes close to expressing the psychological depth and feeling reported so carefully and eloquently by Brazil's novelists during the era. The reporting in these novels is incomplete, focused mainly on the lives and problems of the middle and upper reaches of society. The authors spend relatively little time on that vast category of the defeated at birth. Those lives and experiences will, in large part, need to be approached from a different direction using other techniques. Fortunately, a vast literature continues to grow on the subject of slaves and workers and their urban experience in Rio de Janeiro.

I began reading Rio de Janeiro in search of local color and anecdote and ended up discovering a world. Along the way I was reminded of something that I already knew but had kept compartmentalized in my mind as I worked for two decades as a social historian: Human experience is many things, but it is always aesthetic and sentimental—how we see ourselves and how we see others. Historians pride themselves on writing about human experience and have developed many clever ways of approximating something akin to experience in their readings of primary documents. Pushed to the limit, the attempt to get close to the aesthetic and sentimental dimensions of experience approaches the practice of imaginative literature. Natalie Zemon Davis's brilliant and controversial *Return of Martin Guerre* immediately comes to mind. In that book Davis seems to be saying that we need to imagine our way into life in the past, to look for little clues and warrants in order to ascribe actual human sentiment to old transcripts—not only because we wish to color our histories with a layer of human feeling but also and more importantly because those aesthetic and sentimental aspects of experience are part of the explanation of how things worked and how people lived. For the experience of youth, education, career, and marriage in a time of economic and social change, the Brazilian bildungsroman offers historians the most complete transcription. I conclude with the exhortation: Read these novels, read more, and read these last words by Alencar and Machado.

Alencar:

You cleansed me, anointing me with your lips. . . . You sanctified me with your first glance.

I was your wife in heaven . . . in the end, I still loved her! She is my wife.

Leopoldo kneeled at the feet of his bride . . . the lion, releasing his claws, was overcome by the gazelle.

Finally, the marriage was to take place one of these days.

The curtains were closed, and the whispers of the night, caressing the breast of flowers, sang the hymn of our mysterious and sacred love.

We can rebuild our home and live here, where our love was born.

Tu me purificaste ungindo-me com os teus labios . . . tu me santificaste com o teu primeiro olhar.

Fui tua esposa no ceu! . . . Enfim, ainda a amava! Ela é minha mulher.

Leopoldo ajoelhou aos pes da noiva. . . . O leão deixou que lhe cerceassem as garras; foi esmagado pela pata da gazela.

A última hora, o casamento efetua-se qualquer destes dias.

As cortinas cerraram-se, e as auras da noite, acariciando o seio das flores, cantavam o hino misterioso do santo amor conjugal.

Podemos reconstruir a nossa casa e viver aqui, onde nasceu o nosso amor.[2]

Machado:

Adding up and balancing all these items, a person will conclude that my accounts showed neither a surplus nor a deficit and consequently that I died quits with life. And he will conclude falsely; for, upon arriving on this other side of the mystery, I found that I had a small surplus, which provides the final negative of this chapter of negatives: I had no progeny, I transmitted to no one the legacy of our misery.

Weep for the two recent deaths if you have tears. If you only have laughter, laugh! It's the same thing. The Southern Cross that the beautiful Sofia refused to behold as Rubião had asked her is so high up that it can't discern the laughter or the tears of men.

"Thou wast perfect in thy ways, from the day that thou wast created." I stopped and silently asked: "When would the day of Ezequiel's creation have been?" Nobody replied. Here is a mystery to add to the many others in this world. In spite of everything, I dined well and went to the theater.

Aires knew it was not the inheritance, but he did not wish to repeat that they had been the same, since the womb. He preferred to accept the hypothesis, to avoid argument, and he left, patting his buttonhole, which held the same, eternal flower.

They wanted to laugh and be merry but they could do no more than console themselves—console themselves with the sweetly melancholy remembrance of their own love.

Somadas umas cousas e outras, qualquer pessoa imaginará que não houve míngua nem sobra, e conseguintemente que saí quite com a vida. E imaginará mal; porque ao chegar a este outro lado do mistério, achei-me com um pequeno saldo, que é a derradeira negativa deste capítulo de negativas—Não tive filhos, não transmiti a nenhuma criatura o legado da nossa miséria.

Eis! chora os dois recentes mortos, se tens lágrimas. Se só tens riso, ri-te! É a mesma coisa. O Cruzeiro, que a linda Sofia não quis fitar, como lhe pedia Rubião, está assaz alto para não discernir os risos e as lágrimas dos homens.

"Tu eras perfeito nos teus caminhos, desde o dia da tua criação." Parei e perguntei calado: "Quando seria o dia da criação de Ezequiel?" Ninguém me respondeu. Eis aí mais um mistério para ajuntar aos tantos deste mundo. Apesar de tudo, jantei bem e fui ao teatro.

Aires sabia que não era a herança, mas não quis repetir que eles eram os mesmos, desde o útero. Preferiu aceitar a hipótese, para evitar debate, e saiu apalpando a botoeira, onde viçava a mesma flor eterna.

Queriam ser risonhos e mal se podiam consolar. Consolava-os a saudade de si mesmos.[3]

Machado de Assis offers not reconciliation with the world but desolation or consolation, which he would say, in the voice of his narrator, is the same thing. In this way, his endings, as Moretti suggests, "train us without our being aware of it for the unending task of mediation and conciliation."[4] If Roberto Schwarz is right and Machado's great novels reflect a kind of solution to the puzzle posed by a slave society on the periphery of capitalism—a brilliant solution because it solves by not solving—it is nonetheless equally true that their endings challenge us here, now, in these times.[5]

NOTES

Introduction

1. In using the term *modernity* in this context, I follow the path staked out by David Harvey in *Paris*.

2. Moretti, *Way of the World*, 15. See also Moretti, *Signs Taken for Wonders*, for a lucid statement of the role of literature in generating "consent" in a complex and unstable world through its ability as a middle term to function "in training us without our being aware of it for an unending task of mediation and conciliation" (40). For a classic statement regarding the bildungsroman and the theme of social integration, see the discussion of Goethe's *Wilhelm Meister* in Lukács, *Theory of the Novel*, esp. pt. 2, ch. 3.

3. With his typical blend of the laconic and aphoristic, Forster writes in *Howards End*, "We are not concerned with the very poor. They are unthinkable, and only to be approached by the statistician or the poet" (43).

4. Moretti, *Way of the World*, 233.

5. Bakhtin, *Speech Genres*, 19.

6. Esty, *Unseasonable Youth*, esp. 202–14.

7. See Schwarz, *Misplaced Ideas*.

8. Bakhtin, *Speech Genres*, 23.

9. Esty, *Unseasonable Youth*, Introduction and chaps. 2 and 3.

10. Schwarz, *Ao Vencedor as Batatas*; and Schwarz, *Um Mestre na Periferia*.

11. Candido, *Literatura e Sociedade*, 15, 18–19, 25.

12. Faoro, *Machado de Assis*.

13. G. Franco, *Economia*.

14. Chalhoub, *Machado de Assis*.

15. For Alencar's fascination with Scott, see Vasconcelos, "Figurações do passado," 21–22.

16. The pairing of Lusophone writers Alencar and Azevedo with their Francophone masters, Balzac and Zola, will raise no eyebrows. These can be taken as given. Machado and Flaubert? Not so obvious. Machado, after *Memórias Póstumas*, really defies characterization. The search for literary antecedents in Machado can easily slip into a rather pointless game of hide-and-seek, where the Brazilian author dashes first behind one and then another European master until we become completely disoriented. Reading Helen Caldwell's otherwise fine study *Machado de Assis* generates a bit of this sensation—we

get Dickens, Sterne, and Le Sage all in a few pages and throw in *Tom Jones* for good mea-sure (75–77). In likening Machado to Flaubert, I am not suggesting that they are similar in style or that Machado was consciously copying the French master. Rather, I am at-tempting to place them in a common frame of literary history, a frame in which the sequence and temperament rather than the direct literary borrowings are what matter.

17. James, *Notes on Novelists*, 113.

18. Alencar's near contemporary Alberto Blest Gana worked along similar lines, albeit from a liberal rather than conservative political standpoint. Blest Gana's master-piece, *Martín Rivas* (1862), tells a similar story of a young man from the provinces find-ing his way in the metropolis, falling in love with and winning the heart of the daughter of a rich man, and melding the virtue of the country to the dynamic but morally un-settled city. As with Alencar, Blest Gana's Chilean version of the bildungsroman suggests that the problem lies not in the emerging bourgeois capitalist order but in the character of the people at its commanding heights.

19. Lukács, *Theory of the Novel*, 124–25.

20. Vargas Llosa, *Perpetual Orgy*, 123. For examples of characters whose dreams are crushed by reality, consider in particular Rubião in Machado's *Quincas Borba* and Capitu in his *Dom Casmurro*.

21. Zola, "The Experimental Novel," in Weber, *Movements*, 187.

22. For this controversy, see Pardal Mallet, *Gazeta de Notícias*, May 22, 24, and 26, 1890 (reprinted in Azevedo, *Ficção completa*, 1: 83–89); countering the claim that Azevedo copied Zola, Araripe insists that he had his own distinctive style (*Obra Crítica*, 2: 90).

23. In one of the few works concerning Azevedo's *O Coruja*, Maria Aparecida Viana Schtine Pereira classifies it explicitly in the category of the bildungsroman ("'O Coruja' de Aluísio Azevedo"). Her reading of Brazilian literary history diverges from my own inasmuch as she argues that the novel of growth is otherwise generally lacking in Brazil. This disagreement is a matter of definition. I choose to define the bildungsroman broadly along the lines marked out by Moretti. In other respects, I have found her study of *O Coruja* extremely illuminating.

24. Sommer, *Foundational Fictions*, 15–16, 30.

25. Alencar's *Sonhos d'Ouro* remains in print in a variety of formats. Azevedo's *O Coruja* is out of print; the last stand-alone edition I was able to track down was pub-lished in 1973. However, *O Coruja* is available in the recently published *Ficção Completa de Aluísio Azevedo* (2005). In the case of all three novels I discuss, references are to the de-finitive complete works of each author published by Aguilar. Readers who wish to access these works free of charge will find them at the following websites (as of December 2014):

Alencar: www.dominiopublico.gov.br/

Azevedo: www.dominiopublico.gov.br/

Machado de Assis: machado.mec.gov.br/

26. Berlin, *Many Thousands Gone*, 8.

27. For the events leading to the suppression of the Atlantic slave trade, see Bethell, *Abolition of the Brazilian Slave Trade*. Of particular importance, as Bethell shows, was

British policy toward Brazil, beginning with negotiations regarding recognition of the newly independent nation in the 1820s and continuing through the final, definitive suppression of the trade in 1851. Bethell also shows, quite clearly, that internal Brazilian politics was an equally important factor in the final abolition of the trade, British pressures notwithstanding (363).

28. A good overview of the process can be found in Emília Viotti da Costa's general survey, *Brazilian Empire*, chaps. 6 and 8. The literature on the subject in Portuguese is immense. Viotti da Costa's *Da Senzala à Colonia* remains a classic.

29. A major character of this type is Cotrim in Machado's *Memórias Póstumas*.

30. For a discussion of the Law of the Free Womb and the debates surrounding its passage, see Chalhoub, *Machado de Assis*. A different perspective is found in Needell, *Party of Order*.

31. A convenient summary of the major censuses for Rio de Janeiro city can be found in Holloway, *Policing Rio de Janeiro*, App. 1, p. 295. The total number of slaves in the city in the three years mentioned was 36,182 (1821), 78,855 (1849), and 37,567 (1872). The profound influence of the illegal Atlantic trade stands out in the 1849 figure.

32. In this regard, it is well to remember that Machado's narrative strategy in *Memórias Póstumas* encompasses tales of an earlier period, when slavery was far more salient. It is no accident that this novel grapples more directly and consistently with slaves and their place in society, including, critically, in the lives of the elite who would later seek to disengage their concern for, if not ever their reliance on, the institutions and people involved.

33. In mainstream economics the institutional critique of neoclassical economics is best developed in the work of Douglass North and his followers in the field of the new economic history. For a classic overview of his position, emphasizing the importance of institutions governing property rights and the role of ideology, see North, *Structure and Change in Economic History*.

34. Brenner, "Origins of Capitalist Development."

35. For analysis of partnerships and joint-stock companies in the 1870s–1890s, see Abramitzky et al., "Risk, Incentives and Contracts."

36. Viotti da Costa, *Brazilian Empire*, 183.

37. Viotti da Costa, *Brazilian Empire*, 190.

38. For an extended discussion of the use of estate inventories, including their limitations and degree of representativeness, see Frank, *Dutra's World*, 171–85.

39. Note that similar trends can be seen at the national level. In the case of bonds, Brazilian issues of *apólices* bearing 6% interest were issued at a value of 54,253 contos over the period 1828–1848; in the 1860s, driven in part by the Paraguayan War, the value issued was 170,355 contos; in the 1870s, as financialization continued apace, the value issued was 109,240 contos. In other words, 82.4% of all such bonds issued between the 1820s and 1882 were dated in the decades of the 1860s and 1870s. The rise in paid-in capital devoted to joint-stock companies was even more vertiginous. From a low base of 6,134 contos in 1851, the year after the new Commercial Code was promulgated, the capital invested in these firms rose to 78,454 contos by 1860 and to 250,202 contos by 1885, after a second burst of

activity, owing to liberalized incorporation terms after a reform in 1882. Figures cited in Summerhill, "Sovereign Credibility," esp. Table 5. It is well to acknowledge that Summerhill, who focuses on longer run comparative economic performance and financial development, reads these figures as evidence of underdevelopment—they are too small to initiate robust industrial growth.

40. Data derived from samples of registered partnerships, 1869–1870 and 1888, "Registros, Junta Comercial," Arquivo Nacional, Rio de Janeiro.

41. The validity of this estimate, at least for incomes among free skilled workers, professionals, government employees, and businessmen, is bolstered by data from the partnership records discussed previously. A sample of 678 partner payouts (annual draw on the capital account, hence income) for 1870 yields a Gini coefficient of 0.53. Thus we have independent confirmation of the rough level of inequality in income among the sectors of society contemplated in the novels under review. Needless to say, a calculation that includes all incomes across Rio society would result in a much higher value for the Gini coefficient.

42. For a good biography of Mauá, see Caldeira, *Mauá, Empresário do Império*. Souto, for his part, was head of one of the biggest private banking houses ever to go broke in imperial Brazil.

43. See Pang, *Pursuit of Honor*.

44. For a study of foreigners and particularly the Portuguese in business partnerships, see Abramitzky et al., "Risk, Incentives, and Contracts."

45. *Recenseamento Geral*, 1872, p. 8.

46. On architecture, see Underwood, "'Civilizing' Rio de Janeiro." For fine art and the particular role of the French in nineteenth-century Rio de Janeiro, see Bruand, "Fondation de l'Enseignement académique." The influence of European political ideologies, modulated through Brazilian political thought, is addressed in detail in Needell, *Party of Order*. For legal reforms pertaining to financial institutions based on European ideas and forms, see Musacchio, *Experiments in Financial Democracy*. For legal debates concerning slavery and Brazil's place in the international (European-dominated) order, see Chalhoub, *A Força da Escravidão*. Finally, a good introduction to the penetration of European consumption patterns in Rio de Janeiro can be found in Needell, *Tropical Belle Époque*.

Chapter 1

1. For a good brief biographical sketch regarding this period in Alencar's life, see Proença, "José de Alencar"; for a longer treatment, see Magalhães, *José de Alencar*, ch. 21.

2. Law 2040, September 28, 1871; for a trenchant analysis of the law and Alencar's thinking regarding slavery, see Chalhoub, *Machado de Assis*, 171–72.

3. For a detailed discussion of the conservative party, see Needell, *Party of Order*.

4. I will return to Alencar's opinion on this topic in the followup volume of this study in a discussion of Alencar's play *O Demônio Familiar*. For an overview of Alencar's positions in relation to the 1871 law and slavery more generally, see Chalhoub, *Machado de Assis*, 192–96.

5. Magalhães, *José de Alencar*, 150–57.

6. Alencar, *Sonhos d'Ouro*, 707 (ch. 1). This soliloquy calls to mind Lucien in Balzac's *Ilusões perdidas* [*Illusions perdues*]: "O ouro é o unico poder diante do qual o mundo se ajoelha" (213); or, for that matter, Balzac himself, as narrator, in *Eugénie Grandet*: "The modern god,—the only god in whom faith is preserved,—money, is here in all its power, manifested in a single countenance" (37). It is worth noting that Ricardo is later shown translating *Eugénia Grandet*, suggesting that Alencar himself was deeply affected by its tale of greed and unrequited love.

7. The reference to paying for noble titles suggests Alencar's pique with the emperor and what he saw as a corrupt and money-dominated society. Mainly because of the costs and consequences of the Paraguayan War, the 1860s saw the ennoblement of an unprecedented number of new barons and counts—169 in 1865–1871 alone (about 15% of the total for the whole period of the empire, 1822–1889). For a detailed survey of the purchase of titles, see Pang, *Pursuit of Honor*, 162–65.

8. Alencar, *Sonhos d'Ouro*, ch. 1.

9. Alencar, *Sonhos d'Ouro*, ch. 2.

10. Alencar, *Sonhos d'Ouro*, ch. 4.

11. Alencar, *Sonhos d'Ouro*, 776 (ch. 10).

12. Alencar, *Sonhos d'Ouro*, 776.

13. Alencar, *Sonhos d'Ouro*, 827 (ch. 18).

14. Candido, *Formação*, 541.

15. Candido, *Formação*, 541.

16. Put in perspective of the earnings of a middling lawyer, however, it would have taken many years of careful saving for someone in Ricardo's position to amass such a sum from his earnings alone. A single young lawyer earning the average income of his professional group and saving half of it would have needed approximately eight years. For example, fourteen lawyers registered as voters in Glória and Candelária parishes, all single and under age 40, had a reported mean income of 5:200$ (i.e., 5 contos and 200 mil-réis). Figures from Eleitores, Arquivo Geral da Cidade, Rio de Janeiro. This level of income would have been significantly higher than Ricardo's to start with, because he lacked connections and because his office was located in an out-of-the-way place.

17. Schwarz, *Master on the Periphery*. As an aside, a case that both proves and complicates this rule can be found in Antonio Candido's wonderful little study of the middling success of Antônio Nicolau Tolentino: *Um Funcionário da Monarquia: ensaio sobre o Segundo Escalão* (2007). The case of Tolentino is striking because of his success as a bureaucrat despite his modest origins and because of the important role that powerful men played in sponsoring him along the way. Talent does matter, but it cannot triumph alone.

18. Alencar, *Sonhos d'Ouro*, 717–18.

19. "You were on the market; I bought you" ("O senhor estava no Mercado; comprei-o" (Alencar, *Senhora*, 1029 [pt. 1, ch. 13]). For a good critical overview, see Candido, *Literatura e Sociedade*; see also Schwarz, *Ao Vencedor as Batatas*.

20. Candido, "Os três Alencars," in *Formação*, 536–48.

21. Regarding the central theme of *Senhora* and its heroine, Schwarz writes: "Wealth

is reduced to a question of virtue versus corruption, which is inflated until it becomes the measure of everything. The result is a dense combination of revolt and conformity—the indignation of the bien pensante—which of course is not restricted to Alencar" ("A riqueza fica reduzida a um problema de virtude e corrupção, que é inflado, até tornar-se a medida de tudo. Resulta um andamento denso de revolta e de profundo conformismo—a indignação do bem pensante—que não é só de Alencar", Schwarz, *Ao Vencedor as Batatas*, 34).

22. Doris Sommer, drawing on Rene Girard, observes that in many Latin American novels from the nineteenth century it is an alternative social order that serves as a "fecund rather than frustrating" third drawing the lovers together (Sommer, *Foundational Fictions*, 18). This is a subtle and sound observation. Still, in Alencar's *Sonhos d'Ouro*, it does not quite fit.

23. Candido nominates Guida as one of Alencar's more complex creations, but with qualification (*Formação*, 546).

24. Ricardo notes wisely, "Se eu fosse algum dos muitos apaixonados que há de ter esta moça, dizia Ricardo consigo e continuando o seu passeio, havia de empregar os maiores esforços para preparar estes encontros casuais" ("If I were one of the many admirers that this girl must have, Ricardo said to himself as he continued his walk, I'd have to employ the greatest efforts to set up these casual encounters") (Alencar, *Sonhos d'Ouro*, 739 [ch. 5]).

25. Candido, *Formação*, 542.

26. Alencar, *Sonhos d'Ouro*, ch. 7.

27. Alencar, *Sonhos d'Ouro*, ch. 7.

28. Alencar, *Sonhos d'Ouro*, 748.

29. Alencar, *Sonhos d'Ouro*, ch. 21, and also chaps. 9 and 25. Goffman, *Presentation of Self*, 6–13.

30. Alencar, *Sonhos d'Ouro*, 709 (ch. 1).

31. Schwarz, *Master on the Periphery*, 70. Similar arguments about the role of protection from powerful older men can be found in other studies of Brazilian society. Needell, for instance, shows many examples of the sponsor-protégé relationship in his study of imperial politics (*Party of Order*).

32. Alencar, *Sonhos d'Ouro*, 722 (ch. 3).

33. Alencar, *Sonhos d'Ouro*, 753.

34. R. Graham, *Patronage*.

35. Balzac, *Illusions perdues*, 284.

36. Faoro, *Machado de Assis*, 14–16. Faoro contrasts entry into society by way of *cunhagem* (literally "stamping," as with a gold coin—meaning the right education and the right personal connections and protectors) with that of enrichment. The two go hand in hand, of course, and according to Faoro, enrichment is the faster and easier pathway to acceptance.

37. It is not certain that his uncle supported Ricardo during his studies. This information is provided by Guimarães, a rival for Guida's affection, who obviously has motives to exaggerate the degree of Ricardo's poverty.

38. Alencar, *Sonhos d'Ouro*, ch. 28.

39. I will pursue this question further in my discussion of Azevedo's *O Coruja* (Chapter 3 of this book).

40. The famous first line of *Pride and Prejudice* is, "It is a truth universally acknowledged that a single man in possession of a good fortune must be in want of a wife" (Austen, *Pride and Prejudice*, 5).

41. "By extending from poetry to everyday realism and from a heroic vision to the close observation of society, his work has the capaciousness it has, making him our little Balzac" ("Por estender-se da poesia ao realismo cotidiano, e da visão heróica à observação da sociedade, a sua obra tem a amplitude que tem, fazendo dele o nosso pequeno Balzac"; Candido, *Formação*, 546).

42. Alencar, *Sonhos d'Ouro*, ch. 3.

43. Moretti, *Way of the World*, 41.

44. Moretti, *Way of the World*, 4.

45. Alencar, *Sonhos d'Ouro*, 855 (ch. 21).

46. Alencar, *Sonhos d'Ouro*, 855.

47. Alencar, *Sonhos d'Ouro*, 765 (ch. 8).

48. Alencar, *Sonhos d'Ouro*, 887 (ch. 25).

49. Alencar, *Sonhos d'Ouro*, 886–87 (ch. 25).

50. Williams, *Country and City*, 53. Alencar signals his sensitivity to the conundrum of marriage and money as a general literary theme through his insertion of a reference to Balzac's *Eugénie Grandet*, which Ricardo is depicted translating in his office in lieu of doing proper legal work (Alencar, *Sonhos d'Ouro*, 857 [ch. 22]). In Balzac's novel, money is the modern god that corrupts the miser and lays traps for young lovers (*Eugénie Grandet*, 37 [English]). Ricardo is wary and self-conscious; Alencar references Balzac and draws a distinction between the inner state of Ricardo and his counterpart, the character of Charles, in *Eugénie Grandet*.

51. Moretti, *Way of the World*, 15.

52. Schwarz, *Ao Vencedor as Batatas*, 74.

53. Schwarz, *Ao Vencedor as Batatas*, 54.

54. Candido, referring to Alencar's more famous *Senhora*, notes how in that novel, "as próprias imagens do estilo manifestam a mineralização da personalidade, tocada pela desumanização capitalista" ("the very images of the style manifest the crystalization of a personality dehumanized by capitalism") (Candido, *Literatura e Sociedade*, 16).

55. Candido, *Formação*, 543.

56. Williams, *Country and City*, 174.

Chapter 2

1. Machado, *Epitaph*, 131–32; Machado, *Memórias Póstumas*, 583 (ch. 71).

2. The four novels are *Memórias Póstumas de Brás Cubas* (1881), *Quincas Borba* (1891), *Dom Casmurro* (1899), and *Esaú e Jacó* (1904). A fifth novel, *Memorial de Aires* (1908) was published in Machado's lifetime. It is excellent but not in the same class as the other four. John Gledson has argued that the long story *Casa Velha* should also be included in the list of Machado's mature novels (Gledson, *Machado de Assis*, 13).

3. Magalhães, *Vida e obra*, 1: 13–17.

4. The inauspicious start to Machado's literary career is described in Magalhães, *Vida e obra*, 1: 24–25. The biographer notes that it was in the same year, 1854, that José de Alencar emerged with his series "ao correr da pena," in the pages of the *Correio Mercantil*.

5. Machado's work in the ministry was frequently related to the great issue of the 1860s and 1870s—that is, the means by which the system of slavery might be gradually unwound in Brazil. On this subject, see Chalhoub's excellent *Machado de Assis*, esp. 203–65.

6. On Carolina's family background, see Magalhães, *Vida e obra*, v. 2, ch. 33. For a description of Carolina's contribution to the composition of *Memórias Póstumas*, see Magalhães, *Vida e obra*, v. 3.

7. Schorske, *Fin-de-Siècle Vienna*, 14. Schorske observes that "aspiring to tragedy, Schnitzler achieved only sadness" in his great novel *The Road into the Open*.

8. Schwarz, *Master on the Periphery*, passim.

9. Buarque de Holanda, *O Homem Cordial*, 59.

10. Machado, *Epitaph*, ch. 11; Machado, *Memórias Póstumas*, 528 (ch. 11).

11. Machado, *Epitaph*, ch. 10; Machado, *Memórias Póstumas*, 526 (ch. 10).

12. Machado, *Memórias Póstumas*, 527 (ch. 11).

13. Machado, *Memórias Póstumas*, 528–31 (ch. 12).

14. Machado, *Epitaph*, ch. 13.

15. Machado, *Epitaph*, ch. 13; Machado, *Memórias Póstumas*, 532 (ch. 13).

16. Machado, *Memórias Póstumas*, 534–36 (ch. 15).

17. Machado, *Epigraph*, ch. 20.

18. Machado, *Epitaph*, ch. 37. As Antonio Candido notes in his study of Antônio Nicolau Tolentino, a good marriage was taken as a necessary step toward a successful career in politics (*Um Funcionário da Monarquia*, 26–29).

19. Machado, *Epitaph*, ch. 35. There are no scales to fall from Brás's eyes. Dead, he is possessed of a terrible clarity of vision. See Meyer, *Machado de Assis*.

20. Machado, *Memórias Póstumas*, 556–68 (ch. 38).

21. Machado, *Memórias Póstumas*, 559–60 (ch. 41).

22. Machado, *Epitaph*, ch. 42; Machado, *Memórias Póstumas*, 560 (ch. 42).

23. Machado, *Epitaph*, ch. 43.

24. Meyer, *Machado de Assis*, 18.

25. Machado, *Epitaph*, ch. 70; Machado, *Memórias Póstumas*, 582–83 (ch. 70).

26. This calculation is based on the prevailing unskilled wage in 1845–1849 stated in slave rental advertisements in the *Jornal do Commercio*; data presented in Frank, *Dutra's World*, 100.

27. Machado, *Memórias Póstumas*, 585–86 (ch. 74).

28. Machado, *Epitaph*, 136–37 (ch. 75); Machado, *Memórias Póstumas*, 586 (ch. 75).

29. Machado, *Epitaph*, 137 (ch. 76).

30. Machado, *Epitaph*, 192–93 (ch. 123); Machado, *Memórias Póstumas*, 620 (ch. 123).

31. Machado, *Epitaph*, 193 (ch. 123).

32. Meyer, *Machado de Assis*, 15.

33. Candido, "Esquema de Machado de Assis," in *Vários Escritos*, 31.

34. Machado, *Epitaph*, 210 (ch. 144); Machado, *Memórias Póstumas*, 631 (ch. 144).

35. Goffman, *Encounters*, 110.

36. Machado, *Epitaph*, ch. 20, ch. 24.

37. Gomes, *Machado de Assis*, 52–62.

38. Data from "Recebedoria das sizas dos bens de raiz do ano financeiro de 1849/50" (Arquivo Nacional, Rio de Janeiro, livro 19), filtered on the term *casa* and limited to addresses in and around the city of Rio de Janeiro.

39. The average value of slaves over the age of 14, according to estate inventories sampled from the year 1849, was 425 mil-réis ($N = 59$); Arquivo Nacional, Rio de Janeiro. Wages calculated on the basis of newspaper advertisements for common laborers in the *Jornal do Commercio*, 1849.

40. Machado, *Memórias Póstumas*, ch. 46.

41. Machado, *Memórias Póstumas*, 542–43 (ch. 21). In Austen's *Sense and Sensibility*, it is Mrs. Dashwood who plants the seeds of doubt as to the correct amount to settle upon her poor in-laws (ch. 2).

42. "On the outside the episode I had witnessed was grim; but only on the outside. When I opened it up with the knife of rational analysis, I found a curious and profound kernel. It was Prudêncio's way of ridding himself of the blows he had received—passing them on to someone else. . . . He bought a slave and paid to him, in full and with interest, the amount he had received from me. See how clever the rascal was!" (Machado, *Epitaph*, 129 [ch. 68]).

43. In Machado, *Epitaph*, 166–67 (ch. 99), Bras goes on to describe the "exquisite voluptuousness" of being indifferent to a "sea of gestures and words" surrounding him. In other words, the theater as a place to be seen and to see, but also to blend in and disappear.

44. Machado, *Epitaph*, 128 (ch. 67).

45. Sidney Chalhoub, personal communication, 2011.

46. The front and back regions, as described by Goffman, *Presentation of Self*, esp. ch. 3.

47. Machado, *Epitaph*, 85 (ch. 33).

48. Machado, *Epitaph*, 77 (ch. 27), emphasis mine; Machado, *Memórias Póstumas*, 549 (ch. 27).

49. "Alencar sentiu muito bem a dura opção do homem de sensibilidade no limiar da competição burguesa. Não tinha, contudo, o senso stendhaliano e balzaquiano do drama da carreira, nem a ascensão, na sociedade em que vivia, demandava a luta áspera de Rastignac ou Julien Sorel. . . . Em *Sonhos d'Ouro*, por exemplo, faz Guida e o pai auxiliarem Ricardo sem que esta perceba" ("Alencar well understood the difficulties facing a sensitive man in the face of bourgeois competition. He lacked, nevertheless, the Stendhalian and Balzacian sense of the drama of career and social climbing, in the society in which he lived, that were demanded in the bitter struggles of a Rastignac or Julien Sorel") (Candido, *Formação*, 542). Here, I am afraid I must disagree with the master. Candido is too hard on Alencar; after all, both Sorel and Rastignac have protectors, sometimes unknown to them.

50. Machado, *Epitaph*, 65 (ch. 20).

51. "Guimarães was a young man of twenty six, son of an old red-faced attorney, who was destined to leave him an inheritance of some 600 contos. The father by dint of compulsion managed to educate the son in the laws; but only for show, in order to give the youth the title [doctor] that the father had so desired for himself. As it happened, no one took the case seriously, not even the youth" ("Guimarães era um moço de vinte e sete anos, filho de um antigo procurador muito ginja, que devia deixar-lhe uma legítima de uns seiscentos contos de réis. O pai à custa de empenhos conseguira formá-lo em Direito; mas só por luxo, para dar-lhe o título que tanto invejara. Sucedeu porém que ninguém tomou ao sério a coisa, nem mesmo o rapaz"; Alencar, *Sonhos d'Ouro*, 760 [ch. 8]).

Chapter 3

1. Mérian, *Aluísio Azevedo*, 32.

2. Mérian, *Aluísio Azevedo*, 41; the kind of things the boys read in the 1870s would have included articles such as this one on begging in Paris: Maxime du Camp, "La mendicité a Paris," *Revue des Deux Mondes* (May–June 1870), www.revuedesdeuxmondes.fr/archive/article.php?code=59024 (accessed June 29, 2015).

3. Mérian, *Aluísio Azevedo*, 45.

4. On the subject of Aluísio's father's failed business, see Mérian, *Aluísio Azevedo*, 39.

5. Published in 1881, *O Mulato* explores a different theme of *Bildung*: the incomplete integration of a racially mixed individual in provincial society. As the reader may have noticed, the Naturalist novel appeared in Brazil in the same year that Machado's *Memórias Póstumas* was published in book form. The pace of literary change in the 1880s was quickening.

6. "Ruy Vaz" appeared in *A Semana* between May 23 and June 13, 1885; *O Coruja* appeared in *O País* between June 2 and October 12, 1885.

7. Mérian, *Aluísio Azevedo*, 91–93. See also Mérian, *Un roman anachevé*.

8. Azevedo, "Ruy Vaz," *A Semana* 1.21 (May 23, 1885): 5.

9. *Estado de São Paulo*, February 22, 1912 (reprinted in Azevedo, *Ficção Completa*, 1: 105–12).

10. Mérian, *Aluísio Azevedo*, 494. Eugênio Gomes found traces of readings of Dostoyevsky and Hugo in *O Coruja*, which can be taken as further evidence of the seriousness and heterodoxy mixed together in the book (cited in Azevedo, *Ficção completa*, 1: 27).

11. In this opinion I follow in the path suggested by Oliveira Lima and Antonio Candido, just to name two critics who indicated that *O Coruja* is an important book. Having pointed it out is one thing; conducting a detailed analysis and placing the book in a broader social and literary context is another.

12. Moretti, *Way of the World*, passim.

13. Azevedo, *O Coruja*, 199.

14. By way of contrast, Alencar takes a sanguine view of the provinces in *Sonhos d'Ouro*. A similarly positive depiction is noted by Antonio Candido in *Tese e Antítese* (43) with regard to Eça de Queiróz's *Os Maias*. Azevedo, by demoting the country to the

same moral plane as the city, shifts the novel to a more thoroughgoing pessimism and critical stance in relation to rural plantation society.

15. Azevedo, *O Coruja*, 201.

16. Azevedo, *O Coruja*, 201; it is here that Sampaio, the businessman and associate of Teobaldo's father, says to Teobaldo that his definition of a "serious man" is "everyone who works."

17. Azevedo, *O Coruja*, 201–4.

18. Azevedo, *O Coruja*, 204.

19. The educated but idle heroes of Machado's *Memórias Póstumas* and *Dom Casmurro*; of Eça de Queiroz's *Os Maias*; of Gustave Flaubert's *L'Education Sentimentale*; and of Pérez Galdós's *Fortunata y Jacinta*, respectively.

20. Azevedo, *O Coruja*, 237.

21. Azevedo, *O Coruja*, 341.

22. Azevedo, *O Coruja*, 204. Note the contrast with Teobaldo's vacant days here.

23. Azevedo, *O Coruja*, 395 (loss of the *colégio*); 397 (loss of Inez).

24. André, having been shot accidentally in the foot, is bedridden for a time and rededicates himself to the history project (Azevedo, *O Coruja*, 397).

25. Azevedo, *O Coruja*, 400. The gourmand of the literary aside will have noted the reference to *alfarrábios*, meaning, literally, "old tomes" but also referring obliquely to a historical novel of the same title by José de Alencar.

26. Azevedo, *O Coruja*, 259.

27. Azevedo, *O Coruja*, 261.

28. Azevedo, *O Coruja*, 237.

29. Azevedo, *O Coruja*, 238.

30. Azevedo, *O Coruja*, 241. Note the non sequitur between determinative circumstances and physiological laws; as with many nineteenth-century determinists, Azevedo tended to mix the social and the biological in ad hoc fashion.

31. Azevedo, *O Coruja*, 241.

32. Azevedo, *O Coruja*, 243.

33. Azevedo, *O Coruja*, 252.

34. Azevedo, *O Coruja*, 253.

35. LeFebvre, *Production of Space*.

36. Certeau, *Practice of Everyday Life*, esp. 34–39, where Certeau outlines the difference between strategy and tactics.

37. Azevedo, *O Coruja*, 200.

38. Azevedo, *O Coruja*, 200.

39. Azevedo, *O Coruja*, 201.

40. Azevedo, *O Coruja*, 215.

41. Azevedo, *O Coruja*, 265.

42. Azevedo, *O Coruja*, 327.

43. Azevedo, *O Coruja*, 329–30.

44. Azevedo, *O Coruja*, 333.

45. Azevedo, *O Coruja*, 348.

46. Azevedo, *O Coruja*, 352.

47. Azevedo, *O Coruja*, 361.

48. Azevedo, *O Coruja*, esp. 340–41.

Interlude

1. The ultimate attempt to explore the social diversity and experience of these changes remains Balzac's monumental *Comédie humaine*, perhaps best expressed in his masterpiece, *Lost Illusions* (*Illusions perdues*). In the English novel, albeit in a provincial setting, the great example is George Eliot's *Middlemarch*.

2. Here, I paraphrase Lukács: "The contingent world and the problematic individual are realities which mutually determine one another" (*Theory of the Novel*, 78). For a more recent discussion of failed bids at integration in the later nineteenth-century European novel, see Esty, *Unseasonable Youth*.

3. Watt, *Rise of the Novel*, 27.

4. Watt, *Rise of the Novel*, 30.

5. Cohen, *Sentimental Education*, 40–46.

6. See Schwarz, *Ao Vencedor as Batatas*. Note, particularly, the contrast that Schwarz draws between Alencar and Machado with respect to their handling of this contradiction. For a recent perspective on Machado, the bourgeois, and capitalism, see Moretti, *The Bourgeois*, 145–49. By juxtaposing Balzac and Machado, Moretti underscores the argument originally set forth by Schwarz.

7. Schwarz, *Master on the Periphery*, passim.

8. See, for instance, M. Franco, "As ideias estão no lugar." More recently, the critique has been picked up by Abel Barros Baptista; see, for example, Baptista, "Ideia de Literatura Brasileira."

9. Borges, "Relevance of Machado."

Chapter 4

1. See, for example, Moretti, *Way of the World*.

2. The study of comportment in nineteenth-century Rio de Janeiro society will be complemented in a planned companion volume to this book addressed to the study of works of the theater. On the stage (or the pages of dramatic works) these stances and readings of character through attitude and positioning are, if anything, even more patent, although without the depth provided by the novel form.

3. Goffman, *Presentation of Self*, 4. Wilhelm Reich developed a similar argument in *Character Analysis*, where he attempted to extend the psychoanalytic tradition beyond the talking cure and into the realm of the body and its gestures.

4. Santayana, *Soliloquies*, 134. The language used by Santayana gestures more clearly toward the theater than the novel. It would be interesting to explore the reasons for our cultural tendency to see the everyday practice of life as theatrical rather than novelistic. Here, I limit myself to the observation that what goes with the stage also goes, in a different register, with the novel.

5. George Eliot offers a classic definition for provincial life: "Sane people did what

their neighbours did, so that if any lunatics were at large, one might know and avoid them" (*Middlemarch*, 4). Intelligibility is setting-dependent, and one cannot choose to wear monstrous masks and expect to operate in society, especially in small, closed communities. The city will offer greater range.

6. Burke, *Attitudes Toward History*, 43.

7. Bourdieu's concept of the habitus provides a similar framework in sociological terminology.

8. The foundational work of Émile Durkheim remains a useful starting point in any discussion of social integration. In *De la division du travail social* (1893), Durkheim develops the concept of organic solidarity, which hinges on functional interdependence and the regulation of social relations through legal and moral norms rather than simple force or family or clan relations. Larger, more economically complex societies will, according to this theory, develop mechanisms of organic solidarity and thereby internalize normative rules to handle the problem of inequality and social integration in a heterogeneous context.

9. By deprovincialization, I mean a refusal to see Brazilian novels of the era as growing apart from (or derivative of) the main trunk of the world history of the novel. Rather, these novels are fairly read as coproducing and participating in the development of the genre.

10. In this respect the normative content of female education depicted in the Brazilian novels under consideration follows a universal nineteenth-century bourgeois pattern. The superficiality (but also the earnestness) of this mode of education is parodied, to nice effect, by George Eliot when she refers to Rosamond's schooling: "Where the teaching included all that was demanded in the accomplished female—even to extras, such as getting in and out of a carriage" (*Middlemarch*, 97). The emphasis here is on the external, on comportment and bodily movement, whether at the piano or alighting from a carriage.

11. Pena, *O Diletante*, 367. Driving home the point, the mother goes on to say, "The more of them the worse, they can't all be judges." There are not enough good places for all these young lawyers, and this is something every mother must have known, as is implied by the confident and offhand way she delivers the lines. Pena takes artistic license in citing the figure of "hundreds" arriving every year. In the 1840s this would rather have been measured in the dozens.

12. The increase in the number of lawyers was calculated from lists of lawyers in the *Almanak Laemmert*. Lawyers numbered 63 in 1849 and 229 in 1870. Not all lawyers are necessarily listed in the directory. Actively practicing lawyers, however, almost assuredly were.

13. Moretti, *Way of the World*, 147.

14. Balzac, *Old Goriot*, 103; Balzac, *Père Goriot*, 139. Alencar may also have had in mind another of Balzac's novellas, *Z. Marcas*, in which two lawyers choose to forgo the struggle for position against the odds of "hundreds" of combatants chasing each place: "Il y a cent avocats, cent médecins por un" (Balzac, *La Comédie humaine*, 8: 831).

15. Candido, *Formação*, 542. Rastignac is explicit on this point: "for life in Paris is one continual battle" (Balzac, *Old Goriot*, 81).

16. Balzac, *Old Goriot*, 68; Balzac, *Père Goriot*, 109.

17. "J'aurai dès lors deux protectrices" (Balzac, *Père Goriot*, 110); Balzac, *Old Goriot*, 69.

18. Balzac, *Old Goriot*, 92.

19. Lucien comes from more humble provincial origins than does Rastignac, at least in terms of his initial financial resources. In a later volume in the *Comedie humaine*, Lucien's mother's distinguished ancestry, coupled with the patronage of the shady Vautrin, allows him to reappear in Paris as Lucien de Rubempré in *Splendeurs et misères des courtisanes*. Protection, again, proves essential, if potentially fatal.

20. Bourdieu, *Distinction*, 165.

21. Candido, *Formação*, 542.

22. Chalhoub, "Dependents Play Chess."

23. Almeida, *Memoirs of a Militia Sergeant*, 144.

24. More than one reader has pointed out Alencar's foot fetish, most fully on display in the novella *A Pata da Gazela*.

25. Watt, *Rise of the Novel*, 165, quoting the poet Brooke.

26. It is noteworthy that no such disqualification is attached to widows or, for that matter in a different key, to married women who entered into extramarital affairs. In either case the original position of sexual initiation within the bounds of marriage ensured a different reading of subsequent sexual relations.

27. As Schwarz points out, the manner in which Brás meets Marcela is nearly identical to the way Lúcia and Paulo meet in the earlier novel, *Lucíola* (Schwarz, *Um Mestre na Periferia*, 74–75). Meetings are one thing, but willingness another.

28. Machado, *Epitaph*, 89; Machado, *Memórias Póstumas*, 557.

29. Azevedo, *O Coruja*, 425.

30. Alencar, *Lucíola*, 457.

31. Azevedo, *O Coruja*, 427.

32. Azevedo, *O Coruja*, 434.

33. This third dimension was not, according to our authors, limited to women. Teobaldo, for instance, is repeatedly referred to as elegant and beautiful, whereas his friend André is ugly like an owl.

34. Branca is 15 years old and possesses a dowry worth perhaps 100 contos when Teobaldo kidnaps her and forces an elopement (dowry value given in Azevedo, *O Coruja*, 321). Guida is 18 with a future inheritance, as her father's sole heir, of 1,000 contos (Alencar, *Sonhos d'Ouro*, 759). Aurélia, in Alencar's *Senhora*, is 18 when first introduced and 19 at the time of her marriage. She possesses a fortune rumored to be close to 1,000 contos (Alencar, *Senhora*, 980). In all three cases the amount of money these young girls have or are bound to have is far in excess of what would be considered a substantial fortune by the standards of the era.

35. Machado, *Epitaph*, 91; Machado, *Memórias Póstumas*, 558.

36. Azevedo, *O Coruja*, 237 (ch. 9).

37. Machado, *Epitaph*, 55; Machado, *Memórias Póstumas*, 536.

38. Alencar, *Lucíola*, 131.

39. For a discussion of the popularity of *Camille* and other French plays on similar subjects in Brazil during the second half of the nineteenth century, see Silveira, *Fábrica de contos*, 246–51. As Silveira points out astutely, the discourse of the Camille complex often coincides with a medicalized discourse regarding the symptoms of female emotional and physical degeneration when unmoored from male authority.

40. Dijkstra, *Idols of Perversity*. Oddly, Dijkstra does not mention Camille in his discussion of the trope of the consumptive "fallen woman."

41. Alencar, *As Asas de um Anjo*. In the play the heroine, Carolina, spurns her virtuous cousin Luís for the flashy Ribeiro. This mistake in love leads to a moral collapse followed by redemption through innate goodness and the love of the cousin.

42. Alencar, *Lucíola*, 314 (ch. 2).

43. Alencar, *Lucíola*, 315.

44. This scoundrel reappears throughout the novel as a constant source of corruption and reminder of the way of the world outside Paulo and Lúcia's thin shell of private love.

45. Alencar, *Lucíola*, 435–37 (ch. 19).

46. Alencar, *Lucíola*, 403 (ch. 15).

47. "No Meio da Rua," *Semana Illustrada* 57 (January 12, 1862): 7.

48. Alencar, *Lucíola*, 324 (ch. 4).

49. Alencar, *Lucíola*, 350 (ch. 7).

50. Alencar, *Lucíola*, 328–30 (ch. 5).

51. Azevedo, *O Coruja*, 205 (pt. 2, ch. 2).

52. Azevedo, *O Coruja*, 205.

53. Azevedo, *O Coruja*, 205.

54. Azevedo, *O Coruja*, 208–11 (pt. 2, ch. 3).

55. Azevedo, *O Coruja*, 220–21 (pt. 2, ch. 5).

56. Azevedo, *O Coruja*, 223 (pt. 2, ch. 6).

57. Azevedo, *O Coruja*, 217 (pt. 2, ch. 5).

58. Azevedo, *O Coruja*, 243 (pt. 2, ch. 9).

59. Azevedo, *O Coruja*, 251 (pt. 2, ch. 11).

60. "Teme a obscuridade, Brás; foge do que é ínfimo," but "o mais seguro de todos é valer pela opinião dos outros homens" (Machado, *Memórias Póstumas*, 550). The parallel with the attitude displayed by Teobaldo in *O Coruja* should be obvious.

61. Simmel, *Individuality*, esp. ch. 20 ("The Metropolis and Mental Life").

62. Simmel, *Individuality*, 326.

63. Simmel, *Individuality*, 330.

64. Simmel, *Individuality*, 331.

65. The title of the chapter in which this passage appears could not be more ironic: "Disconsolation." The blasé is never disconsolate. Machado, *Epitaph*, 194; Machado, *Memórias Póstumas*, 621 (ch. 126).

66. Machado, *Memórias Póstumas*, 630–31. The chapter titles are "I Won't Go" and "A Limited Purpose" (Machado, *Epitaph*, 209).

67. Machado, *Quincas Borba*, 656–57 (ch. 18) (Portuguese); Machado, *Quincas Borba*, 27 (English).

68. Meyer, *Machado de Assis*, 18.

69. Simmel, *Individuality*, 329.

70. Benjamin, *One Way Street*, 49.

71. Machado, *Epitaph*, ch. 11, title and last line, respectively. Note that boys can be flowers too.

72. Meyer, *Machado de Assis*, 15.

73. In this sense, Alencar's mixing of internal character and external environmental influences is close to George Eliot's conception of the matter, as evinced in her editorializing on Dorothea's environmentally bounded subjectivity: "For there is no creature whose inward being is so strong that it is not greatly determined by what lies outside it" (*Middlemarch*, 888). The nature of this determination is not, in Eliot, the determination of natural selection. Rather, it is a social determination indicative of the received range of ways of being in the world. This view of social determination also fits with part of Azevedo's vision for Teobaldo, the other part being determined by blood.

74. The Darwinian theme and the mocking attitude toward "scientism" or Positivism is also present in many of Machado's short stories (*contos*). This subject is examined in depth in Silveira's *Fábrica de contos*. A key example of this, following Silveira, is the famous "Chapter of Hats" story, which is available in translation in Machado, *A Chapter of Hats*, 65–84. In that story, a dispute between husband and wife over fashion (the husband's lack thereof in his choice of a hat) spills over into a comical mock-scientific discussion.

75. Magalhães, *Vida e obra*, 3: 14–16.

76. Magalhães, *Vida e obra*, 3: 14–16. Chapter 7 of *Memórias Póstumas* can be used as an example: "Egoísmo, dizes tu? Sim, egoísmo, não tenho outra lei; Egoísmo, conservação. A onça mata o novilho porque o raciocínio da onça é que ela deve viver, e se o novilho é tenro, tanto melhor; eis o estatuto universal" (Machado, *Memórias Póstumas*, 522) ("Egoism, you say? Yes, egoism, I have no other law; Egoism, self-preservation. The tiger kills the lamb because the tiger's philosophy is that, above all, it must live, and if the lamb is tender so much the better; this is the universal law," Machado, *Epitaph*, 34).

77. Azevedo, *O Coruja*, 168–69 (ch. 5). The expert reader will detect the contrast here with Alencar's first indigenista novel, *Iracema*, where the theme of mixing Portuguese and indigenous blood is presented as a "foundational fiction" rather than as a source of emotional instability.

Chapter 5

1. It is crucial to note that children born to unwed mothers in Brazil were not, by definition, considered "bastards" or otherwise shunned and dispossessed. Rather, they were "natural" and could be recognized and legitimated at a later date. There was relatively little stigma against such children, and they could attain positions of social prominence. The definitive study of the status of natural children is found in Lewin, *Surprise Heirs*.

2. Nazzari, *Disappearance of the Dowry*, 163–68.

3. See, for example, Metcalf, *Family and Frontier*; and Nazzari, *Disappearance of the Dowry*.

4. "População considerada em relação às profissões," Recenseamento Geral do Brasil 1872, Municipio Neutro, Parochia do Santissimo Sacramento.

5. The emphasis on money as a problem relating to marriage was not limited in imaginative literature to novels. It was also common in the dramatic works of the era, where the marriage plot served as the most popular motivating theme. In a planned companion volume to the present study, I will analyze this theme in nineteenth-century dramatic works. Good examples of plays that emphasize the issue of money and the agency and maneuverings of men and women in the marriage market include Martins Pena's *O caixeiro da taverna*, Joaquim Macedo's *Luxo e Vaidade*, and França's *Maldita Parentela*. In a different register from novels, these plays and many others like them explore the challenge of finding a marriage partner against a backdrop of false suitors, dowry chasers, meddling parents, and social pressures. Money always plays a significant role in the plot, although the sentimental outcome usually entails the victory of love over money, or at least the cleansing of money with love.

6. Schwarz, *Um Mestre na Periferia*, esp. chaps. 4 and 5. Schwarz, it must be noted, does not simply equate volubility with Brás and the elite. His analysis extends to other levels of the social universe. The point I wish to make is simply that the focus on Brás has led to a tendency to equate volubility with elite men.

7. Eliot, *Middlemarch*, 3–4.

8. The trope of women as flowers is ubiquitous in nineteenth-century literature. Alencar refers to Amália as belonging to the "gênero rosa." For a discussion of this theme in literature, see Dijkstra, *Idols of Perversity*.

9. *Memórias Póstumas de Brás Cubas, Quincas Borba, Dom Casmurro*, and *Esaú e Jacó*. Some would place *Memorial de Aires* in this list simply because it was written last and thus falls in the period of the author's great works, but that book, as interesting as it is, simply is not in the same category as the four great novels in Machado's oeuvre.

10. Tolstoy formulated this maxim differently, as the subject was happiness rather than boredom.

11. For an extended discussion of this theme, especially in the realm of business, see Zimmerman, "Women of Independent Means."

12. Candido, *Formação*, 543.

13. The 1960 edition of *Filomena Borges* has an introduction by Antonio Candido.

14. Azevedo, *Filomena Borges*, 1001.

15. Azevedo, *A Condessa Vesper*, 1144.

16. An entire shelf of books and articles is devoted to answering this rather misguided question, which, to be fair, has beguiled readers of the novel ever since its publication. On early reception, see Guimarães, *Os leitores de Machado de Assis*, 235–38. The ambiguity in *Dom Casmurro* regarding the question of Capitu's culpability is the point of the book. Machado is still laughing. In staking out this position, I am following the lead of John Gledson in *The Deceptive Realism of Machado de Assis*. Notwithstanding Gledson's revisionist arguments, I still find Eugenio Gomes's reading in *O Enigma de Capitu*—which is really about much more than Capitu's innocence or guilt—to be quite instructive. One can learn many things from Gomes. On the "undertow eyes," for instance,

he points out how this aspect of the novel draws heavily on a tradition from Balzac and Dickens, which characterizes the eyes as the "windows to the soul." The distinctive Machadean move, according to Gomes, is to use a frightening and ambiguous metaphor, *olhos de ressaca*, to introduce this element. See Gomes, *O Enigma de Capitu*, 98–103.

17. Girard, *Deceit, Desire, and the Novel*, 14. See also Watt, *Rise of the Novel*, 167. Jealousy is not the only emotion, of course, that can play this role in structuring novels of this type. Boredom and solipsism can do the trick, as in Eça de Queiróz's *O Primo Basílio*. In other words, Bovaryism.

18. See Chalhoub, "Dependents Play Chess"; see also Schwarz, *Master on the Periphery*. Throughout this study I use the terms *strategy* and *tactics* in keeping with the concepts developed in Certeau, *Practice of Everyday Life*.

19. Machado, *Dom Casmurro*, 908–9.

20. Machado, *Dom Casmurro*, 910.

21. Machado, *Dom Casmurro*, 912.

22. Machado, *Dom Casmurro*, 912.

23. Machado, *Dom Casmurro*, 934–35.

24. Machado, *Dom Casmurro*, 939.

25. Literary examples often involve a bigamy plot. Indirect evidence, which must be read with caution, because the reason behind a husband's absence from the household cannot be inferred with precision, is also available in nominal lists from other parts of Brazil. Granting that some men were absent for reasons of business, it is nonetheless striking that married women were found living without their spouses at a much higher rate than the other way around. In São José del Rei, Minas Gerais, 103 married women (average age 44) were listed alone as the head of household versus just 31 men (average age 54) in a similar situation in a total sample of 2,330 households. See "Listas nominativas da década de 1830, organizadas em banco de dados pelo Núcleo de Pesquisa em História Econômica e Demográfica do Cedeplar/UFMG," Arquivo Público Mineiro, Seção Provincial.

26. Alencar, *Sonhos d'Ouro*, 940.

27. Azevedo, *O Coruja*, 371–72 (pt. 3, ch. 11).

28. Azevedo, *O Coruja*, 372.

29. Eliot, *Middlemarch*, 883.

30. Recall Brás's family history recounted in the chapter "Genealogia." Machado, *Memórias Póstumas*, 515.

31. Azevedo, *O Coruja*, 247 (ch. 9).

32. Machado, *Memórias Póstumas*, 536 (ch. 17), 583 (ch. 70).

33. Alencar, *A Viúvinha*, 232–33, 242.

34. Azevedo, *A Condessa Vesper*, 1141. From the "letter" of a condemned man presented as an introduction to his manuscript at the start of the novel.

35. Recall that in Machado's *Quincas Borba*, as Rubião arrives in Rio de Janeiro, the scoundrel Palha warns him not to share confidences with strangers. Later on, the major adds: "I can vouch that he's your very good friend." The novel in this sense is a meditation on betrayal and friendship.

36. Machado, *Quincas Borba*, 713–14 (ch. 82) (Portuguese).

37. Candido, *Formação*, 541.

38. "Inventários," Arquivo Nacional, Rio de Janeiro, JO 3823–853–1816c.

39. In this regard, João Fragoso's study of wealthy merchants in Rio during the first half of the nineteenth century is telling. The aim of many a rich trader was to invest in land, buildings, and slaves and to exit the commercial class and enter the landed elite. See Fragoso, *Homens de grossa aventura*, 13, 352.

40. Azevedo, *O Coruja*, ch. 7.

41. Fragoso, *Homens de grossa aventura*, esp. 241–52, on credit networks. See also Sweigart, "Financing and Marketing."

42. For the classic study of this crisis, see Stein, *Vassouras*. See also Viotti da Costa, *Da Senzala à Colonia*.

43. Lobo, *História do Rio de Janeiro*; Triner, *Banking*; Dean, *Industrialization of São Paulo*; and Hanley, *Native Capital*.

44. *Relatório da Commissão Encargada pelo Governo Imperial . . . inquerito sobre as causes principaes e accidentaes da crise do mez de Setembro de 1864* (Rio de Janeiro: Typ. Nacional, 1865), 42.

45. *Relatório da Commissão Encargada*, 39–41, 45.

46. *Relatório da Commissão Encargada*, 87.

47. Candido, *Formação*, 541. *Comendador* refers to an honorary title of high status. It is sometimes translated as "knight," but the connotation in nineteenth-century Brazil would have been slightly different.

Chapter 6

1. For a good social and cultural history of this theme, see Graham, *House and Street*, esp. ch. 1.

2. For example, Bourdieu writes in *Distinction*, "Bringing together in simultaneity, in the scope of a single glance—this is its heuristic value—positions which the agents can never apprehend in their totality and in their multiple relationships, social space is to the practical space of everyday life, with its distances which are kept or signaled, and neighbors who may be more remote than strangers, what geometrical space is to the 'traveling space' (*espace hodologique*) of ordinary experience, with its gaps and discontinuities" (169). Typically gnomic in his delivery, Bourdieu is writing here of social space in the context of an intervention in sociological theory in which the classifying operations objectively given to subjects can be seen as *producing* practice. Hence habitus is a "system of schemes generating classifiable practices and works" and a "system of schemes of perception and appreciation ('taste')" (171).

3. Da Matta, *Carnivals*, 21.

4. Auerbach, *Mimesis*, 468–70 and 473 for the concept of "atmospheric realism," wherein "every milieu becomes a moral and physical atmosphere which impregnates the landscape" in the novels of Balzac. Alencar was faithful to the master.

5. Alencar, *Senhora*, 976 (ch. 5).

6. Alencar, *Senhora*, 977.

7. Alencar, *Senhora*, 978.

8. I take from Bourdieu the idea of complex simultaneity and apply it idiosyncratically to social space and practice in Rio de Janeiro. The classic example of Bourdieu's method along these lines is found in the chapters on habitus in *Distinction*, for example, the multidimensional projection of economic and cultural capital in a simultaneous figure.

9. The nineteenth-century Brazilian novel shares this privileging of the space of the salon as the center of much social life with the classic European works of the genre. See Bakhtin, *Dialogic Imagination*. Bakhtin says, "From a narrative and compositional point of view, this is the place where encounters occur . . . in salons and parlors the webs of intrigue are spun, denouements occur and finally—this is where dialogues happen, something that acquires extraordinary importance in the novel, revealing the character, 'ideas' and 'passions' of the heroes" (246–47). True enough. But as we also see, cities provide semipublic spaces, such as the theater, where nonrandom but nonetheless unplanned encounters may also occur.

10. Machado, *Resurrection*, 160; Machado, *Ressurreição*, 194–95.

11. Note that all the movement and social interaction from the return to the city to the sherbet at Carceler's takes place in the course of five pages (Machado, *Resurrection*, 49–53).

12. Machado, *Resurrection*, 81.

13. Goffman, *Presentation of Self*, esp. ch. 3.

14. Goffman, *Presentation of Self*, 123–24.

15. Machado, *Memórias Póstumas*, 530–31; Machado, *Quincas Borba*, 671 (Portuguese); Machado, *Dom Casmurro*, 823 (Portuguese).

16. Goffman, *Presentation of Self*, 36.

17. Azevedo, *Filomena Borges*, 1003–4.

18. On the dangers of failed performances and false fronts and the techniques used to mitigate these risks, see Goffman, *Presentation of Self*, 58–60 and ch. 6 ("The Arts of Impression Management").

19. Azevedo suggests that Teobaldo followed a common pattern in maintaining this false front: "E assim se foi habituando a essa fictícia existencia, que no Rio de Janeiro levam muitos rapazes" ("Thus he became habituated to the fictitious existence carried on in Rio de Janeiro by many a young man") (Azevedo, *O Coruja*, 237). For more on the importance of avoiding scandal, see Azevedo, *O Coruja*, 313.

20. Machado, *Quincas Borba*, 121 (English); Machado, *Quincas Borba*, 715 (Portuguese).

21. Machado, *Quincas Borba*, 98–100 (English).

22. For a good overview of the lives of clerks in commercial establishments, see Popingis, *Proletários da casaca*.

23. Azevedo, *Casa de Pensão*, 753–55.

24. Azevedo, *Casa de Pensão*, 755.

25. Azevedo, *Casa de Pensão*, 947.

26. José Dias is overheard by Bento in conversation with his mother. The *agregado* is worried that the young boy is spending too much unsupervised time "hiding away in

corners with Turtleback's daughter" (Machado, *Dom Casmurro*, 8 [English]) ("metido nos cantos com a filha do Tartaruga," Machado, *Dom Casmurro*, 811 [Portuguese]).

27. Machado, *Dom Casmurro*, 5 (English); Machado, *Dom Casmurro*, 810 (Portuguese).

28. In a recent study, Franco Moretti analyzed the plot structure as revealed through networks of *Hamlet*, *Macbeth*, and other generally well-known works. Familiarity with the material helped Moretti see things in the graphs and also helped readers see what he was seeing. He was thus able to make strong interpretive moves on the basis of visual inspection of the graphs rather than strictly quantitative measures. Moretti, *Distant Reading*, 211–40 (the chapter "Network Theory, Plot Analysis").

29. Guida speaks 5,233 words, including soliloquies; Ricardo speaks 5,413 words.

30. For a good overview of network statistics, see Wasserman and Faust, *Social Network Analysis*.

31. Tijuca, as we have seen repeatedly from *Sonhos d'Ouro* onward, appears as a critical space for retreat and reflection for the city's wealthier residents. It serves a similar function in Machado's *Ressurreição*; for example, "The following day Félix departed for Tijuca, where he maintained a residence for relaxation and refuge" (Machado, *Resurrection*, 49).

32. Virgília, Brás's dominant love interest, has, for example, a degree of 12 and a betweenness score of 136. Brás's scores are 48 and 969, respectively. The drop-off is dramatic and is even more pronounced with the lesser characters in the novel.

33. The sample of novels is admittedly small, containing *Lucíola*, *Sonhos d'Ouro*, *Senhora*, *Memórias Póstumas*, and *O Coruja*.

34. See Schwarz, *Misplaced Ideas*, esp. 21–22 and 26–27.

Conclusion

1. Balzac, *Old Goriot*, 304 (1959 Penguin edition translated by M. A. Crawford).

2. If not the very last lines, these are the culminating lines, which I have edited slightly for aesthetic purposes, preserving the meaning, from the following novels: *Lucíola, Diva, A Pata da Gazela, Sonhos d'Ouro, Senhora, Encarnação*. Alencar, *Obra Completa*, v. 1.

3. These are the last lines of *Memórias Póstumas de Brás Cubas, Quincas Borba, Dom Casmurro, Memorial de Aires*, and *Esaú e Jacó*. I have not forgotten Aluísio Azevedo. His endings are akin to Machado's, without the enigmatic wit. André, at the end of *O Coruja*, says, "E manquejando, a limpar os olhos com a manga do casaco, lá se foi, rua abaixo, perguntando a si mesmo 'Onde diabo iria, aquelas horas, arranajar dinheiro para dar de comer ao seu povo?'" (Azevedo, *O Coruja*, 437) ("And limping, wiping his eyes with the sleeve of his jacket, off he went, down the street, asking himself where in the devil, at that late hour, he might find a bit of money to feed his folk?").

4. Moretti, *Signs Taken for Wonders*, 40.

5. Schwarz, *Master on the Periphery*, 140–41.

WORKS CONSULTED

Historical and Literary Studies

Abramitzky, Ran, Zephyr Frank, and Aprajit Mahajan. "Risk, Incentives, and Contracts: Partnerships in Rio de Janeiro, 1870–1891." *Journal of Economic History* 70.3 (2010): 686–715.

Almanak Laemmert. Rio de Janeiro: Typ. Laemmert, 1849 and 1878.

Araripe, Júnior. *Obra Crítica*, vol. 2. Rio de Janeiro: Casa de Rui Barbosa, 1960.

Auerbach, Erich. *Mimesis: The Representation of Reality in Western Literature*. Princeton, NJ: Princeton University Press, 2003.

Bakhtin, M. M. *The Dialogic Imagination*, trans. Caryl Emerson and Michael Holquist. Austin: University of Texas Press, 1981.

———. *Speech Genres and Other Late Essays*. Trans. Vern W. McGee. Austin: University of Texas Press, 1986.

Baptista, Abel Barros. "Ideia de Literartura Brasileira com propósito cosmopolita." *Revista Brasileira de Literatura Comparada* 15 (2009): 61–87.

Benjamin, Walter. *One Way Street*. London: Verso, 1979.

Berlin, Ira. *Many Thousands Gone: The First Two Centuries of Slavery in North America*. Cambridge, MA: Harvard University Press, 2009.

Bethell, Leslie. *The Abolition of the Brazilian Slave Trade: Britain, Brazil and the Slave Trade Question*. Cambridge, UK: Cambridge University Press, 1970.

Borges, Dain. "The Relevance of Machado de Assis." In *Imagining Brazil*, ed. Jesse Souza and Valter Sinder, 235–50. New York: Lexington, 2005.

Bourdieu, Pierre. *Distinction: A Social Critique of the Judgement of Taste*. Cambridge, MA: Harvard University Press, 1984.

———. *The Rules of Art: Genesis and Structure of the Literary Field*. Stanford, CA: Stanford University Press, 1996.

Brenner, Robert. "The Origins of Capitalist Development: A Critique of Neo-Smithian Marxism." *New Left Review* 104 (1977): 25–92.

Bruand, Yves. "Fondation de l'Enseignement académique et néo-classicisme au Brésil: Marc et Zéphirin Ferrez, sculpteurs français fixés à Rio de Janeiro." *Cahiers du monde hispanique et luso-brésilien* 23 (1974): 101–20.

Buarque de Holanda, Sergio. *O Homem Cordial*. São Paulo: Companhia das Letras, 2012.

Burke, Kenneth. *Attitudes Toward History*, 3rd ed. Berkeley: University of California Press, 1984.

Caldeira, Jorge. *Mauá, Empresário do Império*. São Paulo: Companhia das Letras, 1995.

Caldwell, Helen. *Machado de Assis: The Brazilian Master and His Novels*. Berkeley: University of California Press, 1970.

Candido, Antonio. *Formação da literatura brasileira, momentos decisivos*. São Paulo: Ouro sobre Azul, 1999.

———. *Um Funcionário da Monarquia: ensaio sobre o Segundo Escalão*. Rio de Janeiro: Ouro sobre Azul, 2007.

———. *Literatura e Sociedade*. Rio de Janeiro: Ouro sobre Azul, 2010.

———. *Tese e Antítese*. São Paulo: Companhia Editora Nacional, 1964.

———. *Vários Escritos*. Rio de Janeiro: Ouro sobre Azul, 2011.

Certeau, Michel de. *The Practice of Everyday Life*. Berkeley: University of California Press, 1984.

Chalhoub, Sidney. "Dependents Play Chess: Political Dialogues in Machado de Assis." In *Machado de Assis: Reflections on a Brazilian Master*, ed. Richard Graham, 51–84. Austin: University of Texas Press, 1999.

———. *A Força da Escravidão: Ilegalidade e costume no Brasil oitocentista*. São Paulo: Companhia das Letras, 2012.

———. *Machado de Assis: historiador*. São Paulo: Companhia das Letras, 2003.

Cohen, Margaret. *The Sentimental Education of the Novel*. Princeton, NJ: Princeton University Press, 2002.

Da Matta, Roberto. *Carnivals, Rogues, and Heroes: An Interpretation of the Brazilian Dilemma*. South Bend, IN: University of Notre Dame Press, 1991.

Davis, Natalie Zemon. *The Return of Martin Guerre*. Cambridge, MA: Harvard University Press, 1983.

Dean, Warren. *The Industrialization of São Paulo, 1880–1945*. Austin: University of Texas Press, 1969.

Dijkstra, Bram. *Idols of Perversity: Fantasies of Feminine Evil in Fin-de-Siècle Culture*. New York: Oxford University Press, 1986.

Durkheim, Émile. *De la division du travail social*. Paris: Les Presses universitaires de France, 1967. classiques.uqac.ca/classiques/Durkheim_emile/division_du_travail/division_travail_1.pdf (accessed June 7, 2015).

Esty, Joshua (Jed). *Unseasonable Youth: Modernism, Colonialism, and the Fiction of Development*. New York: Oxford University Press, 2012.

Faoro, Raymundo. *Machado de Assis: a piramide e o trapezio*. São Paulo: Companhia Editora Nacional, 1974.

Fragoso, João. *Homens de grossa Aventura: acumulação e hierarquia na praça mercantile do Rio de Janeiro (1790–1830)*. Rio de Janeiro: Arquivo Nacional, 1992.

Franco, Gustavo Henrique Barroso. *A Economia em Machado de Assis: o olhar oblique do acionista*. Rio de Janeiro: Zahar, 2008.

Franco, Maria Sylvia Carvalho. "As ideias estão no lugar." In *Cadernos de Debate 1*, 61–64. São Paulo: Brasiliense, 1976.

Frank, Zephyr. *Dutra's World: Wealth and Family in Nineteenth-Century Rio de Janeiro*. Albuquerque: University of New Mexico Press, 2004.

Girard, René. *Deceit, Desire, and the Novel: Self and Other in Literary Structure.* Baltimore: Johns Hopkins University Press, 1965.

Gledson, John. *The Deceptive Realism of Machado de Assis: A Dissenting Interpretation of Dom Casmurro.* Liverpool, UK: F. Cairns, 1984.

———. *Machado de Assis: ficção e história.* Rio de Janeiro: Paz e Terra, 1986.

Goffman, Erving. *Encounters: Two Studies in the Sociology of Interaction.* Indianapolis: Bobbs-Merrill, 1961.

———. *The Presentation of Self in Everyday Life.* New York: Anchor Books, 1959.

Gomes, Eugênio. *O Enigma de Capitu: ensaio de interpretação.* Rio de Janeiro: Livraria José Olympio, 1967.

———. *Machado de Assis.* Rio de Janeiro: Livraria São José, 1958.

Graham, Richard. *Patronage and Politics in Nineteenth-Century Brazil.* Stanford, CA: Stanford University Press, 1990.

Graham, Sandra Lauderdale. *House and Street: The Domestic World of Servants and Masters in Nineteenth-Century Rio de Janeiro.* Cambridge, UK: Cambridge University Press, 1988.

Guimarães, Hélio. *Os leitores de Machado de Assis: o romance machadiano e o public no século 19.* São Paulo: Nankin Editorial, 2004.

Hanley, Anne G. *Native Capital: Financial Institutions and Economic Development in São Paulo, Brazil, 1850–1920.* Stanford, CA: Stanford University Press, 2005.

Harvey, David. *Paris, Capital of Modernity.* London: Routledge, 2003.

Holloway, Thomas. *Policing Rio de Janeiro: Repression and Resistance in a Nineteenth-Century City.* Stanford, CA: Stanford University Press, 1993.

James, Henry. *Notes on Novelists.* New York: Scribners, 1914.

LeFebvre, Henri. *The Production of Space.* Oxford, UK: Blackwell, 1991.

Lewin, Linda. *Surprise Heirs*, vol. 2, *Illegitimacy, Inheritance Rights, and Public Power in the Formation of Imperial Brazil, 1822–1889.* Stanford, CA: Stanford University Press, 2003.

Lobo, Eulalia Maria Lahmeyer. *História do Rio de Janeiro: do capital comercial ao capital industrial e financeiro.* Rio de Janeiro: IBMEC, 1978.

Lukács, Georg. *The Theory of the Novel.* Cambridge, MA: MIT Press, 1974.

Magalhães, Raimundo, Jr. *José de Alencar e sua época.* São Paulo: Livros Irradiantes, 1971.

———. *Vida e obra de Machado de Assis*, 4 vols. Rio de Janeiro: Civilização Brasileira, 1981.

Mérian, Jean-Yves. *Aluísio Azevedo, vida e obra.* Rio de Janeiro: Editora Espaço e Tempo, 1988.

———. "Un roman anachevé." In *Manuel Bandeira, Aluísio Azevedo, Graciliano Ramos, Ariano Suassuna: Travaux présentés au séminaire de 1974 du Centre de Recherches Latino-Américaines de l'Université de Poitiers*, 97–116. Poitiers: Université de Poitiers, 1974.

Metcalf, Alida. *Family and Frontier in Colonial Brazil: Santana de Parnaíba, 1580–1822.* Berkeley: University of California Press, 1992.

Meyer, Augusto. *Machado de Assis (1935–1958).* Rio de Janeiro: José Olympio, 2008.

Moretti, Franco. *The Bourgeois: Between History and Literature*. London: Verso, 2013.

———. *Distant Reading*. London: Verso, 2013.

———. *Signs Taken for Wonders: Essays in the Sociology of Literary Forms*. London: Verso, 1983.

———. *The Way of the World: The Bildungsroman in European Culture*. London: Verso, 1987.

Musacchio, Aldo. *Experiments in Financial Democracy*. Cambridge, UK: Cambridge University Press, 2009.

Nazzari, Muriel. *Disappearance of the Dowry: Women, Families, and Social Change in São Paulo, Brazil (1600–1900)*. Stanford, CA: Stanford University Press, 1991.

Needell, Jeffrey D. *The Party of Order: The Conservatives, the State, and Slavery in the Brazilian Monarchy, 1831–1871*. Stanford, CA: Stanford University Press, 2006.

———. *A Tropical Belle Époque: Elite Culture and Society in Turn-of-the-Century Rio de Janeiro*. Cambridge, UK: Cambridge University Press, 1987.

North, Douglass C. *Structure and Change in Economic History*. (New York: Norton, 1981).

Pang, Eul-Soo. *In Pursuit of Honor and Power: Noblemen of the Southern Cross in Nineteenth-Century Brazil*. Tuscaloosa: University of Alabama Press, 1988.

Pereira, Maria Aparecida Viana Schtine. "'O Coruja' de Aluísio Azevedo: romance de formação sob o prisma do grotesco." MA thesis, University of São Paulo, 2013.

Popingis, Fabiane. *Proletários da casaca: trabalhadores do comércio carioca (1850–1911)*. Campinas: Editora da Unicamp, 2007.

Praxedes, Vanda Lúcia. "A teia e a trama da "fragilidade humana": os filhos ilegítimos em Minas Gerais (1770–1840). In *Anais do XI Seminário sobre a Economia Mineira* (2004). www.cedeplar.ufmg.br/diamantina2004/textos/D04A018.PDF (accessed June 8, 2015).

Proença, Cavalcanti. "José de Alencar." In José de Alencar, *Obra Completa*, 1: 34–36. Rio de Janeiro: Editora Nova Aguilar, 1958.

Reich, Wilhelm. *Character Analysis*, trans. Mary Boyd Higgins. New York: Farrar, Straus & Giroux, 1990.

Santayana, George. *Soliloquies in England, and Later Soliloquies*. New York: C. Scribner's Sons, 1923.

Schorske, Carl. *Fin-de-Siècle Vienna*. New York: Vintage Books, 1981.

Schwarz, Roberto. *A Master on the Periphery of Capitalism: Machado de Assis*. Durham, NC: Duke University Press, 2001.

———. *Um Mestre na Periferia do Capitalismo*. São Paulo: Duas Cidades, 1990.

———. *Misplaced Ideas: Essays on Brazilian Culture*. London: Verso, 1992.

———. *Ao Vencedor as Batatas: forma literaria e processo social nos inicios do romance brasileiro*. São Paulo: Livraria Duas Cidades, 1977.

Silveira, Daniela Magalhaes da. *Fábrica de contos: Ciencia e Literatura em Machado de Assis*. Campinas: Editora Unicamp, 2010.

Simmel, Georg. *On Individuality and Social Forms: Selected Writings*. Chicago: University of Chicago Press, 1971.

Sommer, Doris. *Foundational Fictions: The National Romances of Latin America*. Berkeley: University of California Press, 1991.

Stein, Stanley J. *Vassouras, a Brazilian Coffee County, 1850–1900*. Cambridge, MA: Harvard University Press, 1957.

Summerhill, William. "Sovereign Credibility With Financial Underdevelopment: The Case of Nineteenth-Century Brazil." Working draft prepared for the Hoover Seminar on Collective Choice, March 6, 2007. www.hoover.org/sites/default/files/uploads/documents/Sovereign_Credibility.pdf (accessed June 7, 2015).

Sweigart, Joseph Earl. "Financing and Marketing Brazilian Export Agriculture: The Coffee Factors of Rio de Janeiro, 1850–1888." Ph.D. diss., University of Texas, Austin, 1980.

Triner, Gail D. *Banking and Economic Development: Brazil, 1889–1930*. New York: Palgrave, 2000.

Underwood, David. "'Civilizing' Rio de Janeiro: Four Centuries of Conquest Through Architecture." *Art Journal* 51.4 (1992): 48–56.

Vargas Llosa, Mario. *The Perpetual Orgy: Flaubert and Madame Bovary*. New York: Farrar, Straus & Giroux, 1986.

Vasconcelos, Sandra G. T. "Figurações do passado: o romance histórico em Walter Scott e José de Alencar." *Terceira Margem: Revista da Pós-Graduação em Ciência da Literatura* 12.18 (2008): 15–37.

———. "A Formação do Romance Brasileiro: 1808–1860 (vertentes inglesas)." www.unicamp.br/iel/memoria/Ensaios/Sandra/sandra.htm (accessed June 8, 2015).

Viotti da Costa, Emília. *The Brazilian Empire: Myths and Histories*. Chapel Hill: University of North Carolina Press, 2000.

———. *Da Senzala à Colonia*. São Paulo: Difusão Europeia do Livro, 1966.

Wasserman, Stanley, and Katherine Faust. *Social Network Analysis: Methods and Applications*. Cambridge, UK: Cambridge University Press, 1994.

Watt, Ian. *The Rise of the Novel: Studies in Defoe, Richardson, and Fielding*. Berkeley: University of California Press, 2001.

Weber, Eugen. *Movements, Currents, Trends: Aspects of European Thought in the Nineteenth and Twentieth Centuries*. Lexington, MA: D. C. Heath, 1992.

Williams, Raymond. *The Country and the City*. New York: Oxford University Press, 1973.

Zimmerman, Kari Elaine. *Women of Independent Means: Female Entrepreneurs and Property Owners in Rio de Janeiro, Brazil, 1869–1904*. Ph.D. diss., Stanford University, 2010.

Novels and Short Fiction

Alencar, José de. *Encarnação*. In *Obra Completa*, 1: 1215–1324.

———. *O Guarani*. In *Obra Completa*, 2: 5–406.

———. *Iracema*. In *Obra Completa*, 3: 223–406.

———. *Lucíola*. In *Obra Completa*, 1: 293–458.

———. *As Minas de Prata*. In *Obra Completa*, 2: 407–1258.

———. *Obra Completa*, 3 vols. Rio de Janeiro: Editora José Aguilar, 1959.

———. *A Pata da Gazela*. In *Obra Completa*, 1: 571–688.

———. *Senhora*. In *Obra Completa*, 1: 941–1214.

———. *Sonhos d'Ouro*. In *Obra Completa*, 1: 689–940.

———. *A Viúvinha*. In *Obra Completa*, 1: 229–92.

Almeida, Manuel Antônio de. *Memoirs of a Militia Sergeant*, trans. Ronald Sousa. New York: Oxford University Press, 1999.

Austen, Jane. *Pride and Prejudice*, 2 vols. New York: Frank S. Holby, 1906.

———. *Sense and Sensibility*, 2 vols. New York: Frank S. Holby, 1906.

Azevedo, Aluísio. *Casa de Pensão*. In *Ficção Completa*, 1: 751–996.

———. *A Condessa Vesper*. In *Ficção Completa*, 1: 1137–1415.

———. *O Cortiço*. In *Ficção Completa*, 2: 439–634.

———. *O Coruja*. In *Ficção Completa*, 2: 143–438.

———. *Ficção Completa de Aluisio Azevedo*, 2 vols. Rio de Janeiro: Editora Nova Aguilar, 2005.

———. *Filomena Borges*. In *Ficção Completa*, 1: 997–1136.

———. *O Mulato*. In *Ficção Completa*, 1: 261–504.

Balzac, Honoré de. *César Birotteau*. In *La Comédie humaine* 6: 37–312.

———. *La Comédie humaine*, 12 vols. Paris: Gallimard, 1976–1981.

———. *Eugénie Grandet*. In *La Comédie humaine*, 3: 989–1199.

———. *Eugénie Grandet*, trans. Katherine Wormeley. London: Vintage, 2011.

———. *A Harlot of High and Low*, trans. Rainer Heppenstall. New York: Penguin, 1970.

———. *Illusions perdues*. In *La Comédie humaine*, 5: 123–732.

———. *Old Goriot*, no trans. given. New York: Current Literature, n.d.

———. *Père Goriot*. In *La Comédie humaine*, 3: 49–290.

———. *Splendeurs et misères des courtisanes*. In *La Comédie humaine*, 6: 425–935.

Blest Gana, Alberto. *Martín Rivas*. Santiago: Origo, 2013.

Eliot, George. *Middlemarch*. New York: Modern Library, 1994.

Flaubert, Gustave. *Bouvard and Pécuchet*, trans. A. J. Kraischeimer. New York: Penguin, 1976.

———. *Bouvard et Pécuchet*. In *Oeuvres*, 2: 711–987. Paris: Gallimard, 1952.

———. *L'Education Sentimentale*. In *Oeuvres*, 2: 31–457. Paris: Gallimard, 1952.

———. *A Sentimental Education*, trans. Douglas Parmée. New York: Oxford University Press, 1989.

Forster, E. M. *Howards End*. New York: Barnes & Noble Classics, 2003 [1910].

Goethe, Johann Wolfgang von. *Wilhelm Meister's Apprenticeship*. Princeton, NJ: Princeton University Press, 1989.

Hardy, Thomas. *Jude the Obscure*. New York: Norton, 1999.

Machado de Assis, Joaquim Maria. *A Chapter of Hats*, ed. and trans. John Gledson. London: Bloomsbury, 2008.

———. *Counselor Aires' Memorial*, trans. Helen Caldwell. Berkeley: University of California Press, 1972.

———. *Dom Casmurro*. In *Obra Completa*, 1: 807–944.

———. *Dom Casmurro*, trans. John Gledson. New York: Oxford University Press, 1997.

———. *Epitaph of a Small Winner* [*Memórias Póstumas*], trans. William Grossman. New York: Noonday Press, 1952.

———. *Esau and Jacob*, trans. Elizabeth Lowe. New York: Oxford University Press, 2000.

———. *Esaú e Jacó*. In *Obra Completa*, 1: 945–1094.

———. *Memorial de Aires*. In *Obra Completa*, 1: 1095–1200.

———. *Memórias Póstumas de Brás Cubas*. In *Obra Completa*, 1: 511–639.

———. *Obra Completa*, 3 vols. Rio de Janeiro: Editora Nova Aguilar, 1979.

———. *Quincas Borba*. In *Obra Completa*, 1: 641–806.

———. *Quincas Borba*, trans. Gregory Rabassa. New York: Oxford University Press, 1998.

———. *Ressurreição*. In *Obra Completa*, 1: 115–95.

———. *Resurrection*, trans. Karen Sotelino. Pittsburgh: Latin American Literary Review Press, 2013.

Pérez Galdós, Benito. *Fortunata y Jacinta*. In *Obras Completas*, 5: 9–548. Madrid: Aguilar, 1967.

Queiroz, Eça de. *Obras de Eça de Queiroz*, 4 vols. Lisbon: Lello Editores, 2007.

———. *Os Maias*. In *Obras de Eça de Queiroz*, 2: 5–496.

———. *O Primo Basílio*. In *Obras de Eça de Queiroz*, 1: 865–1173.

Richardson, Samuel. *Pamela, or Virtue Rewarded*. Boston: Houghton Mifflin, 1971.

Schnitzler, Arthur. *The Road into the Open*, trans. Horace Samuel. Evanston, IL: Northwestern University Press, 1991.

Stendhal. *The Red and the Black*, trans. Horace B. Samuel. New York: Dover, 2004.

Zola, *L'Assommoir*, trans. Margaret Mauldon. New York: Oxford University Press, 1995.

Drama

Alencar, José de. *As Asas de um Anjo*. In *Teatro Completo*, 2: 175–252. Rio de Janeiro: Serviço Nacional de Teatro, 1977.

———. *A Expiação*. In *Teatro Completo*, 2: 375–438. Rio de Janeiro: Serviço Nacional de Teatro, 1977.

Dumas, Alexandre. *Camille*. In *Camille and Other Plays*, trans. Edith Reynolds and Nigel Playfair; ed. Stephen S. Stanton, 105–64. New York: Hill & Wang, 1957.

França, Joaquim José de, Jr. *Maldita Parentela*. In *Teatro Completo*, 1: 157–80. Rio de Janeiro: Serviço Nacional de Teatro, 1980.

Macedo, Joaquim Manuel de. *Luxo e Vaidade*. In *Teatro Completo*, 1: 27–95. Rio de Janeiro: Serviço Nacional de Teatro, 1979.

Pena, Martins. *O caixeiro da taverna*. In *Comédias (1844–45)*, 265–326. São Paulo: Martins Fontes, 2007.

———. *O diletante*. In *Comédias (1833–44)*, 347–410. São Paulo: Martins Fontes, 2007.

INDEX

Note: page numbers followed by *t* refer to tables; those followed by *f*, to figures or illustrations; those followed by *n* refer to notes, with note number.

Lightning Source UK Ltd.
Milton Keynes UK
UKHW011040160322
400138UK00003B/170